Essentials
of
Labor Relations

David H. Rosenbloom
Syracuse University

Jay M. Shafritz
University of Colorado at Denver

Reston Publishing Company, Inc.
A Prentice-Hall Company
Reston, Virginia

Library of Congress Cataloging in Publication Data

Rosenbloom, David H.
    Essentials of labor relations.

    Includes bibliographies.
    1. Industrial relations.   I. Shafritz, Jay M.
II. Title
HD6961.R615   1985   331   84-15019
ISBN 0-8359-1765-7

© 1985 by Reston Publishing Company, Inc.
A Prentice-Hall Company
Reston, Virginia 22090

10   9   8   7   6   5   4   3   2   1

Interior design and production: Meridee Mucciarone

Printed in the United States of America

Contents

Chapter 9   The Future   241

Index   259

Preface

Essentials of Labor Relations is an examination of collective bargaining and unionization in the United States. Our goal has been to review the evolution of the labor movement and explain the contemporary practices of labor relations in both the private and public sectors. We have sought to present all of the information that is critical to an understanding of labor relations in a way that makes it intelligible to students and practitioners with little or no prior knowledge of, or experience in, collective bargaining.

Note that all of the **boldfaced** words in the text are defined at the bottom of the page on which they appear. Most of these definitions are adapted from *The MBA's Dictionary* by Daniel Oran and Jay M. Shafritz (Reston, VA: Reston Publishing Company, 1983), and the *Dictionary of Personnel Management and Labor Relations* by Jay M. Shafritz (Oak Park, IL: Moore Publishing, 1980).

We wish to thank those who made valuable contributions to the development and writing of this book: Bernalee LoSasso, Marshall Kaplan, Dan Oran, Albert C. Hyde, John Moore, Steve Rockwell. Michael Haberberger read the manuscript and made a number of valuable suggestions for improving it. Deborah D. Goldman and Louise Alexander engaged in extended discussions of the book's contents and provided invaluable aid in its conceptualization. Leah, Sarah, and Joshua Rosenbloom and Noah and Todd Shafritz all provided assistance of one kind or another.

David H. Rosenbloom

Jay M. Shafritz

1 The American Labor Movement

Prologue
The Birth of the U.S. Department of Labor

The United States Department of Labor was born on March 4, 1913. But as early as 1864 bills and resolutions calling for it were introduced in Congress. During 1867 the House created a standing committee on labor. Nevertheless, all nineteenth century efforts to create a Department of Labor failed. Too many influential politicos felt that it would be illegitimate for a "voice of labor" to speak in the President's cabinet.

Because of slight prospects of success at the national level, the early labor movement concentrated on creating state bureaus of labor statistics. The first of these was established in Massachusetts in 1869. But, its tactic of presenting the commonwealth's legislature with reports designed to arouse "surprise, shame, and indignation" discredited the bureau by giving it a partisan taint. By 1873 the governor was denouncing the reports of the bureau and calling for a more objective approach. He then appointed Carroll D. Wright to head the bureau and gave him a mandate to "make it or bust it." Wright's approach marked the beginning of modern labor statistics. His bureau began to turn out the kind of dull—but accurate—reports that earned the confidence of all parties. As the Massachusetts bureau grew in stature, other states created bureaus as well. By 1883 thirteen states had bureaus of labor statistics.

The impetus for such a bureau was felt at the national level, too. In 1884 President Chester A. Arthur signed a bill which established the U.S. Bureau of Labor in the Department of the Interior. Arthur initially nominated John Jarrett, president of the steelworkers' union, to head the bureau. But Jarrett was heard to injudiciously assert that Arthur was unfit even to be a dishwasher at Delmonico's, a New York restaurant. When this was reported to Arthur, he promptly withdrew Jarrett's nomination. Later, as a lame duck president, Arthur nominated the same Carroll Wright who for almost two decades had been creating the reputation of the Massachusetts bureau and inventing the field of labor statistics. (Wright was also the statistical wit who first observed that "figures won't lie, but liars will figure.") When the new President, Grover Cleveland, also asked him to head the national bureau, Wright began twenty years (1885–1905) of impartial analyses of labor problems. Wright's nonpartisan tone and his philosophy— that supplying facts and not advocating particular solutions was the proper function of a labor bureau—went far to create the climate that allowed for the eventual creation of the present Department of Labor.

In 1888 the bureau was upgraded to a department, but without cabinet status. President Theodore Roosevelt in 1901 called for a cabinet level Department of Commerce and Industries which would subsume the noncabinet Department of Labor. This proposal became law in 1903 with the creation of the Department of Commerce and Labor. President Roosevelt's appointment of Oscar Straus as secretary led to one of Roosevelt's more embarrassing public moments. Because Straus was the nation's first Jewish cabinet member, a testimonial dinner was held in Roosevelt's honor. There he told the largely Jewish audience: "I did not name him [Straus] because he was a Jew. I would despise myself if I considered the race or religion of a man named for high political office." After warm applause the President sat down and Jacob Schiff, one of the most influential of Jewish business leaders rose to speak. Because Schiff was almost totally deaf (but did his best to hide it), he had not heard a word of what Roosevelt had said. So he innocently told the crowd that Roosevelt had earlier "sent for me and informed me that he wished to appoint a Jew as a member of his cabinet and asked me to recommend the ablest Jew ... I recommended Oscar Straus." Roosevelt, it was reported, simply stared into space.

But Straus aside, organized labor was totally opposed to this new entity, holding that the functions of a Secretary of Commerce and a Secretary of Labor were inherently contradictory; combining the two was, according to the American Federation of Labor, creating a "Dr. Jekyll and Mr. Hyde."

It would not be until 1912 that labor had enough support in Congress to pass a bill calling for a separate Department of Labor. President William Howard Taft was opposed to the bill and did not sign it until his very last day in office, March 4, 1913. President-elect Woodrow Wilson had already named William B. Wilson (no relation) as the proposed new secretary. To have vetoed the bill would have been futile as the Congress would have quickly reenacted it for Wilson to sign. So a reluctant presidential signature gave labor the "voice" in the president's cabinet for which it had fought since the Civil War.

THE GOALS OF THE LABOR MOVEMENT

The American **labor movement** has been embroiled in controversy and conflict for the better part of the two centuries since its beginning. The word "union" continues to evoke emotional responses from workers, managers, citizens, and politicians alike. The term **strike** conjures up images of disruption, strife, violence; even chaos and anarchy. It is hard to be dispassionate about the labor movement not just because it has been so important in American economic, social, and political life, but also because it has been engaged in a protracted struggle over some very fundamental matters.

Unionization in the United States has been overwhelmingly concerned with control and influence in the workplace. The labor movement has sought to organize individual employees into collective groups as a means of increasing their power to determine the conditions that will prevail at work and to advance their general interests. The following are among these conditions.

TERMS   **Labor Movement**   An inclusive term for the progressive history of American unionism. Sometimes it is used in a broader sense to encompass the fate of "the workers."

Strike   A mutual agreement among workers, whether members of a union or not, to a temporary work stoppage in order to obtain (or resist) a change in their working conditions. The term is thought to have nautical origins because sailors would stop work by striking or taking down their sails. A strike or potential strike is considered an essential element of the collective bargaining process. Many labor leaders claim that collective bargaining can never be more than a charade without the right to strike.

Compensation   Those who are not self-employed neither control nor consume the fruits of their labor. Hence, they must be compensated—paid for their work. While labor adds to the value of a product, commodity, or service, it is often but one of many factors that must be rewarded. For instance, in capitalist economies, ownership of the means of production, such as tools and factories, must be compensated. So must those who own and sell the natural resources that are the basic elements of manufactured products. Management, too, must be compensated for its efforts. However, the mix of compensation to ownership, management, and labor can vary with the ability of labor to bargain for or demand a larger share. At the root of the American labor movement is the belief that whereas the individual worker is virtually powerless to increase his or her share of compensation (as compared to ownership and management), organized employees, speaking as a group with one voice, can effectively win more for themselves.

Employment   The effort to control conditions in the workplace necessarily requires that organized labor seek to control the recruitment and retention of workers by private firms and public agencies. The **bargaining strength** of unions is enhanced tremendously where they can control employment. Labor is a commodity. Where it can be sold by individuals, some workers will always sell their labor for less than others. In times of high unemployment, this will tend to depress wage rates for all workers. Unions seek to counteract this tendency by gaining control of the labor market. Ideally, unions may prefer a **closed shop,** that is, a workplace in which membership in the union is an absolute prerequisite to employment. By regulating the supply of labor, unions can drive up the price paid for the worker's labor. By speaking on behalf and *contracting* on behalf of all employees in a given workplace, labor organizations can prevent individual workers from competing to sell their labor for *less* than one another. Similarly, unions seek to control dismissals from employment in order to protect their members and to assure

TERMS   **Bargaining Strength**   The relative power that each of the parties holds during the negotiating process. The final settlement often reflects the bargaining power of each side.

Closed Shop   A union security provision that would require an employer to only hire and retain union members in good standing. The Labor-Management Relations (Taft-Hartley) Act of 1947 made closed shops illegal.

that management will not try to "break" the union by firing its members or threatening to do so to those who join it.

Hours of Work   Unions are concerned with the economic position of workers, their social lives, and their health. A long working day, such as the twelve-hour workday that prevailed in the early days of the **industrial revolution** in the United States, takes a heavy toll on the worker. It is physically damaging and harmful to the worker's family life. Throughout the nineteenth century, American labor organizations fought first for the ten-hour day, and then for the eight-hour day. Again the effort was to control the hours of work as a collectivity in order to prevent individual workers from having to bid against one another in order to get jobs.

Occupational Health and Safety   Work can be dangerous. Work environments can be unhealthful. In the past, conditions in some factories were abominable. Workers routinely lost fingers and limbs due to unsafe and overcrowded conditions. Fires were a constant threat. Even today, some workers are routinely exposed to harmful substances, such as asbestos. Unorganized workers, in particular, may face hellish conditions, as is frequently true of migrant farm workers. Unions have sought to force owners and managers to create better health and safety conditions in the workplace, even though this may increase operating costs and reduce profit levels. Concomitantly, organized labor's demands for better health and safety in the workplace seek to force owners and managers to recognize the humanity of laborers, and not treat them as simply one more **factor of production.**

The Organization of Work   Occupational diseases are generally considered to be physical manifestations of unhealthful conditions at work. But the organization of work can also have psychological effects on workers and

---

TERMS   **Industrial Revolution**   A very general term that refers to a society's change from an agrarian to an industrial economy. The industrial revolution of the western world is considered to have begun in England in the eighteenth century.

Factors of Production   The resources used to produce goods and services. There are three traditional factors: land, labor, and capital. Recently, management or entrepreneurship has come to be considered a factor as well.

can even lead to mental illness. For instance, assembly line production is efficient in many respects, but it may also make jobs boring, repetitive, tedious, and unsatisfying. The worker may be denied the satisfaction often associated with the completion of a product or an understanding of his or her contribution to it. On-the-job boredom may promote alcoholism, drug abuse, and antisocial behavior. The nature of managerial supervision can aggravate these problems by demeaning the worker and reducing his or her self-esteem. In consequence, labor unions have sought a role in determining how work will be structured. They have been even more forceful in attempting to limit managerial discretion in the treatment, assignment, and disciplining of employees.

"Fringe" Benefits   So called "fringe" benefits are really a form of nonwage compensation. Unions have bargained hard for a number of benefits of this kind that make the worker's life more satisfying. Among common fringe benefits are health and life insurance programs, paid vacations, and pensions.

Diffuse Social and Political Objectives   It would be a mistake to consider the labor movement's objectives as being limited to relatively specific conditions in the workplace. Organized labor has also sought to use change in the workplace as a means of reforming society as a whole. For example, American labor organizations were in the forefront in the struggle against **child labor.** Some have strongly supported equal opportunity in the workplace as well.

While the labor movement is about all of these elements, it is also about the workers' welfare in general. Unions have long been concerned with the overall quality of life of working men and women. Indeed, one reason workers join unions is to gain a sense of social belonging and a feeling of group solidarity. Many unions engage in elaborate social functions. Some provide retirement homes and vacation places for their members. A general interest in workers' lives necessarily requires that unions be concerned with the overall nature of society. Consequently, many American unions have been politically active in supporting candidates for public office and lobbying on behalf of legislation and public

TERMS   **Child Labor**   Originally this meant employing children in a manner that was detrimental to their health and social development; but now that the law contains strong child labor prohibitions, the term refers to the employment of children below the legal age limit.

policies. It is no wonder that the American labor movement has
been controversial.

GENERAL BARRIERS
TO DEVELOPMENT

Despite the labor movement's active role in the workplace and in
political and social life, unionization in the United States has not
been as comprehensive as in some other industrialized democracies. In fact, only about 25 percent of all nonagricultural employees currently hold union membership—a proportion that is
considerably down from the post–World War II high point of about
33 percent. Nor was the American labor movement able to develop
rapidly. Indeed, it took almost a century and a half for it to win its
major struggle—the legal *right* to engage in **collective bargaining**
and to promote its demands through the use of strikes, if necessary.
Why did collective bargaining take so long to win protection by
federal law? Why is union membership relatively small in comparison with the industrialized nations of western Europe? A variety of factors acted as barriers to the development of a strong labor
movement prior to the 1930s.

Capitalism

The American economic system is largely capitalist. The means of
production are privately owned, as are natural resources to a large
extent. Decisions concerning production, sales, and consumption
are made by private individuals. The "market," rather than government or a body of central planners, is relied upon to coordinate
relationships among owners, producers, and consumers. Prices are
set through **supply** and **demand**. Government intervention, according to capitalist theory, should be kept to a minimum. Competition is fundamental to capitalism. There must be many producers and many consumers, each in competition with one another. Producers compete for consumers' money by developing and
manufacturing products with the desired quality and price levels.

TERMS

Collective Bargaining A comprehensive term that encompasses the negotiating process that leads to a contract between labor and management on
wages, hours, and other conditions of employment as well as the subsequent
administration and interpretation of the signed contract.

Supply In economics, this is the quantity of goods and services available for
purchase if income and other factors are held constant. Increases in price
either induce increases in supply or serve to ration the supply.

Demand The strength of buyer desire for and willingness to pay for a product or service.

Consumers compete with one another by offering money for these products. The greater the demand among consumers for a scarce product, the higher the price is likely to be. And vice versa.

Labor can be conceptualized as a product (or commodity) for which the owners of the means of production (capitalists) compete. Unions, by seeking to regulate the price of labor through collective action, were long considered conspiracies against the public interest. This was because they sought to limit competition by preventing one firm from bidding against another for laborers and, more importantly, by preventing individual workers from competing with one another to sell their labor. Unionization was long opposed because it would "artificially" raise wages which, in consequence, would increase prices. This could be seen as damaging the public interest. Indeed, nowadays, some argue that higher prices would make the United States uncompetitive with other nations and, eventually, restrain increases in the standard of living.

It is important to understand that capitalism stands for inequality. Inequality is necessary to enable some to become very rich and invest their wealth in additional means of production, such as factories. This creates new jobs and new products and, as a result, the society as a whole benefits. Labor organizations, on the other hand, seek to promote economic equality. They want a larger share of the returns from the selling prices of commodities, finished products, and services to go to the worker. This necessarily spreads the wealth of a society out to more people. Unions believe that this is in the public interest. They argue that by increasing the income of the mass of individuals in the society, consumer demand will rise, and new products and jobs will be created in response. As a matter of fact, the National Labor Relations Act of 1935, which provides federal protection for collective bargaining, was premised in part on the belief that the lack of effective collective bargaining was responsible for depressing wage rates and reducing the demand for commodities, manufactured products, and services. In other words, the lack of consumer demand which was thought to result in part from inadequate wages (disposable income) was considered an important contributing factor to the Great Depression of the 1930s.

The Frontier   The United States had a western frontier until the 1890s. It has often been argued that this had an inhibiting impact on the labor movement because it meant that free land was available to laborers and others who were dissatisfied with their lot in life.

Moreover, laborers who left for the frontier obviously showed initiative and may very well have been the segment of the labor force that would have been most likely to lead a labor movement. Of course the "closing" of the frontier after 1890 had the opposite effect; there being less opportunity to move on, working men and women felt that they had few choices but to stay and organize.

Slavery   The existence of slavery until 1865 inhibited the labor movement for at least two reasons. First, it removed a large number of workers (those who were slaves) from any possibility of joining labor organizations or engaging in collective bargaining. Second, it inhibited free (nonslave) labor by constantly holding open the threat that their jobs might be reallocated to slaves. High wage rates in free states could have spurred the movement of industries to slave states.

Economic Growth   The United States economy had its ups and down during the nineteenth and early twentieth centuries, but the overall pattern was one of rapid economic growth. Although the distribution of the benefits of this growth was not equal among all segments of the population, for the most part the standard of living was on the rise. The majority of people were probably better off economically at the end of each decade than at the beginning. Consequently, despite the drastic dislocations associated with the Civil War and the rapid industrialization and urbanization that followed it, the capitalist system seemed to work in promoting economic growth. Because capitalism depends upon inequality to generate **investment** there was little call for a redistribution of wealth through government intervention. Indeed, it was not until the Great Depression in the 1930s that the assumption of continued economic growth was widely questioned and economic redistribution became a major public policy issue. This was inherent in the social security programs and collective bargaining legislation of the **New Deal**, which were considered a means for workers to attain a larger share of the national income.

TERMS   **Investment**   Using money to make money by, for example, lending it for interest, buying property for gain in value, leasing property, buying an ownership share in a business, etc.

New Deal   The domestic programs and policies of the administration of President Franklin D. Roosevelt (1933–1945).

The Business Cycle   Although the overall pattern of the nineteenth century was one of economic growth, it was characterized by the boom and bust periods of the **business cycle.** There were "panics" (that is, depressions or severe recessions in modern parlance) in 1819, 1837, 1857, 1873, and 1893. The bust of 1929 was part of the same phenomenon. Unemployment during these panics was substantial in terms of numbers and length. Real income per capita also declined substantially. Bankruptcies reached alarming levels. In short, there was good reason to "panic" because it looked like the economy had fallen to pieces. Under such circumstances, it was virtually impossible to organize labor unions or to sustain many of those already in existence. Workers needed protection, but the competition among the unemployed for jobs virtually precluded employer **recognition** of unions as the contracting agent for laborers. Moreover, some employers were hard-pressed enough without having to cope with unions, which, they thought, might push them over the brink into bankruptcy. In boom periods, by contrast, workers often failed to see the potential advantages and benefits offered by unions and did not want to risk their jobs when things were functioning smoothly.

The Socio-Legal   Since the earliest days of colonization of New England by British
Concept of Work as   subjects work has been viewed as a virtue in which an *individual* has
"Liberty"   both a right and an obligation to engage. This is sometimes referred to in shorthand form as the **Protestant ethic,** although Protestants are hardly the only people who manifest it. Since work was viewed as a good and as a matter of individual responsibility, any organization or law limiting an individual's ability to personally contract out his or her labor was viewed as inherently undesirable. As a result, labor unions were considered threats to one's individual

---

TERMS   **Business Cycles**   The recurrent phases of expansion and contraction in overall business activity. Although no two business cycles are alike, they are all thought to follow a pattern of prosperity, recession (or depression), and recovery.

Recognition   An employer's acceptance of a union as the bargaining agent for all of the employees in a particular bargaining unit.

Protestant Ethic   Max Weber's term from *The Protestant Ethic and the Spirit of Capitalism* (1904) which refers to his theory that modern capitalism has its origins in the Calvinistic concern for moral obligation and economic success. While some dispute Weber's historical analysis, any society whose members have a strong drive for work and the accumulation of wealth is colloquially said to have a "Protestant" or work ethic.

liberty and right to work, as were wage and hour laws. No wonder that in *Lochner v. New York* (1905) the U. S. Supreme Court declared unconstitutional a New York State statute limiting employment in bakeries to no more than ten hours per day and sixty hours per week on the basis that "there is no reasonable ground for interfering with the liberty of a person or the right of free contract, by determining the hours of labor, in the occupation of a baker." For many years, child labor laws ran up against the same logic and set of values.

THE ORIGINS OF AMERICAN LABOR UNIONS

The United States never had **serfdom** as was commonly practiced in Europe. Still, in the seventeenth and eighteenth centuries there were relatively few "free" workers. Most people were engaged in largely subsistence agriculture. People who worked outside their families tended to be slaves or indentured servants. Eventually, the rise of commerce led to a greater demand for "free" labor among craftsmen, small shops, and small manufacturing establishments. The great advantage of the wage worker is that he or she can be fired in times of economic downturn. Moreover, since the employer makes a comparatively small investment in the free worker, the employer does not need to be particularly concerned with an employee's health, diet, or general welfare. Eventually, enough skilled craftsmen emigrated from Great Britain and Europe to provide the basis for the organization of free laborers into unions.

There were a great many efforts at labor organization and regulation during America's colonial period. For example the shoemakers of Boston formed an organization in 1648, and the printers in New York combined to demand a wage increase in 1778. But the first labor organization created specifically for collective bargaining was the Philadelphia Cordwainers (shoemakers), who formed a union in 1792. While their union lasted only about a year, it was part of a more general trend. Other skilled craftsmen, including tailors, masons, cabinet makers, and printers, soon organized as well. The cordwainers themselves later established the Federal Society of Journeymen Cordwainers which lasted from 1794 to 1806. For the most part these early unions were interested in the basics of labor relations: control of entry into the trade (the closed shop), higher wages, and shorter hours. They also wanted to

---

TERMS   **Serfdom**   The condition of living in feudal servitude, bound to work a master's land and a subsequent master if the land changes ownership.

make sure that apprenticeship conditions were adhered to, which reflected an interest in training and what would now be called "contract enforcement."

The unions of this period made two lasting contributions to the American labor movement. First, they were organized on the basis of *crafts*. The cordwainers were in their union, the printers were in another, and so on. There was no general union of workers in different crafts. Craft unionism remains the basis of much of the organization of the American labor force today; although nowadays it is complemented by industrial unionization, which includes workers in different crafts within one union. Second, the early unions were locals. The cordwainers of Philadelphia did not combine with those of Boston and Baltimore, for example. And the "local," which may be confined to a single firm or plant, remains a vital part of collective bargaining today.

During the 1820s and 1830s, there were some important exceptions to "craftism" and local organization. The Philadelphia Mechanics Union of Trade Associations, organized in 1827, included workers in fifteen trades. It sought a ten-hour day among other objectives and served as a brief example of what a general labor union might look like; but it soon dissolved into a local political party. While similar workingmen's parties appeared in other cities, this was not to be a successful or even meaningful direction for the American labor movement.

In the early 1830s, some efforts were made to organize national unions, as opposed to locals. But such efforts were temporarily wiped out by the panic of 1837 and the economic turmoil of the business cycle in the 1840s. For example, the National Trades' Union was formed in New York in 1834; but this first attempt toward a national labor federation failed to survive the panic of 1837.

One of the major problems unions faced throughout this period was their dubious legal status. Here, again, the Philadelphia cordwainers were at the forefront, but at the forefront of a major setback. In the case of *Commonwealth v. Pullis* (1806), the Philadelphia Mayor's Court found them guilty of engaging in a criminal conspiracy when they went out on strike. The court upheld an indictment charging eight of the cordwainers with (1) conspiring that "none would work in the shoemaking trade except for higher wages than had customarily been paid," (2) conspiring to use "threats, menaces, and other unlawful means" to prevent other craftsmen from working at lower rates, and (3) seeking to control entry into the trade through a strictly enforced apprenticeship program. The cordwainers were each fined a week's pay (eight dollars) plus court costs—and that was the end of their union.

Strikes in the 1850s

These strikes did not follow negotiations as we know them. Instead unions would decide on their objectives and then issue notices such as the following: "On Wednesday evening September 4 the Bricklayers and Plasterers by an unanimous vote declared that they would not work after Wednesday the 11th ... for a sum less that $2 per day, on and after that day." If the employer accepted these terms, a "trade agreement" would be concluded. Such agreements were increasingly sought not from individual employers but from employers' associations, in order to establish uniform wages and other conditions in the craft as a whole. Strikes were often directed against recalcitrant or non-association employers.

Source: Edward Pessen, "Labor from the Revolution to the Civil War," *Monthly Labor Review*, Vol. 99, No. 6 (June 1976).

Until 1842, the criminal conspiracy doctrine served as a very important barrier to development of labor organizations. Cases were not always brought and juries did not always convict, but the law itself seemed clearly against unionization. This changed with the Massachusetts case of *Commonwealth v. Hunt* (1842) in which a confusing opinion held that unionization itself was not illegal; that is, as long as the labor organization did not use illegal means or pursue illegal ends, it would not be condemned by law. This decision made it harder, in general, to apply the criminal conspiracy doctrine. However, it hardly put the law on the side of unionization and collective bargaining activities because employers still had several legal devices available to deal with combinations of workers and strikes.

The decade of the 1850s rounded out the early period of efforts to organize viable unions. The first national union to last to the present day, the National Typographical Union, was founded in 1852. Other nationals were established as well, and some even persisted through the panic of 1857. However, the onset of the Civil War and the period of rapid industrialization that followed it would fundamentally change the nature of the American labor movement.

THE WARS OF ORGANIZATION

In the years following the Civil War, the American economy was transformed from one that was primarily agrarian to one based on industrialism. Manufacturing output grew at a tremendous rate, production was shifted from the home to the factory, and machine tools were introduced on a widespread basis. In 1830 there were about 1.2 million nonagricultural workers in the labor force; fifty years later, in 1880, there were almost 10 million. Such a massive change in the nature of work could not help but have a considerable impact on the labor movement.

Although the economy was generally strong from the close of the Civil War to the panic of 1873, workers were increasingly threatened with insecurities. Because work itself was becoming more specialized with the widespread introduction of machinery, workers were correspondingly becoming more vulnerable to technological change. **Mass production**, coupled with the use of machines, reduced the skill level necessary to manufacture many products. Under these conditions, the workplace also became increasingly impersonal. Eventually, rapid industrialization would transform the concept of the worker; no longer regarded as human beings, workers were viewed as a factor of production. Like any other nonhuman resource, the laborer was but a specialized "cog" in the manufacturing process. Workers also felt threatened by massive immigration from abroad, which assured a ready supply of "hands" to take their place. Finally, increasing urbanization made workers almost completely dependent upon their wages—

TERMS   **Mass Production**   Generally, a high volume of output; but more specifically, mass production also assumes product simplification, standardization of parts, continuous production lines, and the maximum possible use of automatic equipment.

the proportion of factory workers who could "retreat" to a family farm continued to dwindle.

One result of these changes was that the labor movement was unsettled. Large unions formed almost overnight and collapsed just as rapidly. For example, the Knights of St. Crispin, a union of shoemakers, was formed in 1867; it quickly grew to 50,000 members in 600 chapters, but it disappeared with the panic of 1873. Some unions adhered to the craft basis for organization. Others, such as the Knights of Labor, sought to organize virtually everybody except, of course, for "economic parasites" such as doctors, lawyers, bankers, and saloonkeepers. Some unions retained a local focus; others tried to develop on a nationwide basis. Some sought widespread social and economic reforms as a means of promoting the workers' welfare; others concentrated on conditions prevailing in the workplace. Still others, such as the **Molly Maguires**, sought to promote change through terror tactics. It was a time for the labor movement to sort things out.

In retrospect, it is possible to understand the period between the Civil War and World War I as largely a struggle between two types of unionism. The first can be called "welfare unionism." It concerned itself with the general welfare of the workers and sought to promote its objectives through politics as well as through collective bargaining. Welfare unionism was best represented by the Noble Order of the **Knights of Labor**. The second type was "business unionism," which was most closely associated with the emergence of the American Federation of Labor. Business unionism assumes that the worker is interested primarily in conditions prevailing on the job, not in creating a new society or economic order. It is pragmatic in philosophy and has as its primary end the promotion of the economic well-being, health, and safety of the working

TERMS **Molly Maguires** Originally members of an Irish secret society (the Ancient Order of Hibernians) founded in 1843 to prevent the eviction of tenant farmers by process servers of the English landlords, the Molly Maguires got their name because of a tendency to disguise themselves as women while engaging in terrorist activities. After the Civil War, they established themselves as secret worker societies in the coal fields of Pennsylvania and West Virginia. Their terror tactics ceased and their organization disappeared in 1876 when ten of their leaders were executed and fourteen others jailed.

Knights of Labor The first significant national labor organization in the United States. It was founded in 1869 as a secret society in order to protect its members from employer reprisals, but its sundry rituals gained it the opposition of the Catholic Church. It lifted its veil of secrecy in 1881, removed the religious connotations from its rituals, saw the Catholic Church withdraw its condemnation, and grew to over 100,000 members within three years.

union member. It is also exceedingly practical in nature and therefore willing to compromise and treat each case of bargaining on its own terms. Being nonideological, business unionism does not place a heavy emphasis on political action or seek to promote its objectives through legislation. However, even business unionism can incorporate a broad vision of how society could be improved.

The Knights of Labor epitomized the approach of welfare unionism. Membership was open to almost anyone who produced something. Organized on a nationwide basis, it engaged in political action as well as collective bargaining. Some of its goals seemed far-fetched. For instance, it proposed workers' cooperatives to replace capitalism and wanted to do away with the wage system. But other goals eventually came to fruition; among them were the eight-hour day, the abolition of child labor, the creation of a national bureau of labor statistics, and a weekly payday.

The Knights started out relatively slowly. Founded in 1869, it could claim only 60,000 members by 1884. Yet, unlike many other labor organizations, it survived the depression of 1873–1878. By the mid-1880s, the Knights had become the wonder of the American labor movement. It staged successful strikes against the powerful railroads, encouraged the Congress to create a U.S. Bureau of Labor, and saw its membership soar to 700,000. But in May of 1886, the beginning of the end for the Knights of Labor came in Chicago's Haymarket Square.

What history has called the "Haymarket Riot" was a critical event in the development of the American labor movement; it was also the nineteenth century's most famous confrontation between police and labor demonstrators. It started when workers struck for an eight-hour day at the McCormick Harvesting Machine Company. When strife between strikers and strikebreakers occurred, the police, firmly on the side of the strikebreakers, fired at the strikers. Four were killed and many others were wounded. (Incidents like this only confirmed railroad magnate Jay Gould's boast of the time that he could "hire one half of the **working class** to kill the other half.") In protest, the strikers called a mass rally for the night of May 4 in Haymarket Square. Police arrived toward the end of the meeting and ordered the crowd to disperse. Suddenly, a bomb exploded among the approximately 180 police. Sixty-three officers were wounded; seven would die. The uninjured police opened fire on the crowd. Estimates of the killed vary from several to ten; of

TERMS   **Working Class**   All who work. When the term is used politically, it tends to exclude managers, professionals, and anyone who is not at the lower end of the educational and economic scales.

Biracial Unionism

Because the weakest links in the chain of labor solidarity were found at the points where the white, black, and yellow races met, the numerous episodes of cooperation between white and black workers during the 1880s provided a noteworthy feature of the labor upsurge . . . It was in the eighties that large numbers of blacks first unionized, especially among dockworkers, coal miners, and construction workers in the South. The Knights alone had some 60,000 black members by 1886. More than a fifth of the early members of United Mine Workers . . . were black.

The New Orleans waterfront was a stronghold of biracial unionism. When the white scalemen and packers there allied with the black teamsters to strike for a 10-hour day in October 1892, the city's Board of Trade offered concessions to the whites but refused to negotiate with blacks. In response, 49 unions shut down the entire city and kept it shut, despite venomous attacks on the blacks in the local press. In the end, the Board of Trade capitulated entirely, giving labor one of its greatest victories of the century.

Source: David Montgomery, "American Labor, 1865–1902: the Early Industrial Era," *Monthly Labor Review,* Vol. 99, No. 7 (July 1976).

the wounded from 50 to 200. The identity of the bomb thrower was never determined. In the midst of an hysterical atmosphere, eight labor leaders were tried and convicted of murder on the grounds that they had conspired with or aided an unknown murderer. Four were hanged, one committed suicide, and three remained in prison until pardoned in 1893.

Although hardly responsible for the Haymarket carnage, the Knights were widely blamed. After all, they advocated the eight-hour day, they supported strikes, and they were the largest and most visible union. The net result was a temporary setback for the entire union movement.

Riots aside, welfare unionism as represented by the Knights was vulnerable to a number of pitfalls. Its ideological bent could be seen as utopian, but also as anarchic. Its diverse membership made internal dissension likely. In seeking to achieve nationwide goals, it inevitably diminished the importance of collective bargaining at the local level. Skilled workers believed that they had little in common with the unskilled masses or with a leadership preaching social gospel instead of fighting for bread-and-butter issues. The size and importance of the Knights declined precipitously. By 1900, it had only 100,000 members; it was disbanded in 1917.

THE TRIUMPH OF THE AMERICAN FEDERATION OF LABOR

The rise of business unionism was one response to the failure of the Knights of Labor and the welfare unionism for which it stood. The basics of business unionism had long existed, but were given powerful restatement by Adolph Strasser and Samuel Gompers. As leaders of the Cigar Makers' International Union, which was founded in the 1860s and which was the first to make use of the union label, these two presented a stark contrast to the ideological approach of the Knights. This is shown by Strasser's famous testimony to a congressional committee. In discussing his union's objectives, he stated that: "We have no ultimate ends. We are going on from day to day. We are fighting only for immediate objects— objects that can be realized in a few years. . . .We are all practical men." In 1886, Strasser and Gompers were the leaders who transformed a more or less dormant Federation of Organized Trades and Labor Unions into the American Federation of Labor (AFL).

The AFL sought to organize only skilled workers. The unskilled industrial worker was not viewed as a solid basis for union organization and collective bargaining. According to the AFL philosophy, the basis for bargaining should be a union organized among workers of a specific craft. Only they would have the solidarity of interests to eliminate problems of internal dissension. Only they would have the skills upon which employers depend, skills which could not be readily replaced by untrained workers or strikebreakers. These craft unions would be federated into the national organization, the AFL. This union of unions would enhance their strength, resolve disputes among them, provide technical assistance, and furnish financial aid to strikers.

The AFL was not immediately noted for its size. But it endured. It rode out the political and economic turmoil of the 1890s. When major strikes of industrially organized workers, such as the **Homestead Strike** and the **Pullman Strike**, failed so badly that they cast doubt on the viability of industrial unionism itself, the AFL and its craft workers remained relatively secure. When more radical unions such as the **Industrial Workers of the World** failed to achieve the overthrow of the capitalistic system, the AFL was content in its conservatism. In 1898 it had 275,000 members. By 1904, in the wake of the Spanish-American War, it had 1.7 million members. During World War I, its membership increased to 4.1 million. Wartime demand for skilled labor was an important factor in the AFL's growth. But the AFL also endured because of its emphasis on collective bargaining by skilled employees. While its achievements were not spectacular, it negotiated enough agreements and displayed enough conservatism to convince many in the business community that the collective bargaining process could not be avoided. The AFL would remain the most comprehensive American labor organization until the 1930s, when the rise of industrial (as opposed to craft) unionism posed a serious threat to its structure and organizational pattern.

It was during this period that public sector unions were first organized. While collective bargaining by public employees would not be common until the 1960s, many workers' associations and

---

TERMS   **Homestead Strike**   A strike by 4,000 of the workers at the Homestead (Pennsylvania) plant of the Carnegie Steel Company (forerunner of the United States Steel Corporation) in 1892. When the company hired 300 Pinkerton detectives to enable it to import strikebreakers, the strikers met them as they were arriving. After a twelve-hour "battle," the Pinkertons, with three dead and dozens wounded, literally ran up a white flag, laid down their weapons, and were allowed to return to Pittsburgh. A week later 8,000 state militia opened the plant to strikebreakers. In the end only 800 of the 4,000 strikers were ever rehired. The industrial unionism of the steel industry suffered a setback that would last for decades.

Pullman Strike   A strike by workers at the Pullman Palace Car Company in response to an arbitrary wage cut by the company. The strike was so effective—no member of the American Railway Union would handle trains with Pullman (sleeper) cars—that it spread to twenty-seven states. The federal government used federal troops to break the strike.

Industrial Workers of the World   A radical union founded in the belief that "it is the historic mission of the working class to do away with capitalism." Organized in 1905, it had its greatest strength before World War I. Most of its waning membership joined the American Communist Party when it was organized in 1919.

fraternal orders were formed earlier. The first national organization of federal employees, the National Association of Letter Carriers, was organized in 1890.

The infamous Boston Police Strike of 1919 was the nation's first taste of municipal labor problems. While the patrolmen struck for a variety of reasons, including the right to form a union and affiliate with the AFL, the strike brought chaos to the city. Samuel Gompers protested the police commissioner's refusal to allow the union to affiliate with the AFL. Calvin Coolidge, then Governor of Massachusetts, responded with his famous assertion that "there is no right to strike against the public safety by anybody, anywhere, anytime." These words so captured the public's imagination that a tidal wave of support gained him the Republican vice-presidential nomination in 1920. The failure of the Boston Police Strike (state troops restored order and the strikers were dismissed) was a lesson that would inhibit municipal unionization for many decades.

THE LABOR MOVEMENT PRIOR TO THE 1930S

The 1930s marked a dual turning point in the history of the American labor movement. The rise of the industrial union was one facet. Another was the AFL's willingness to turn to politics and legislation as a means of advancing the working person's quality of life. Until this time, the AFL rarely viewed federal legislation as pertinent to its cause, preferring instead the "voluntarism" associated with negotiating labor contracts among private parties (the union and the employer). Nevertheless, the labor movement was able to have a marked impact on working conditions *in general* prior to its emphasis on political action.

Remember that the labor movement coincided with some very fundamental changes in the workplace. Throughout the nineteenth century work continued to shift from the home and small shop to the factory. Hand production was replaced by mechanization, greater specialization of labor, and the use of early forms of the assembly line. The worker, originally treated as a human being, eventually was conceived of as a "cog" who sold a commodity. Management was somewhat deferential to workers' skills in the early part of the last century. But by the second decade of the twentieth century, **scientific management** beseeched managers to take more of a role in instructing the worker on how to do the job, as well as when to rest, what tools to use, etc.

TERMS   **Scientific Management**   A systematic approach to managing that seeks the "one best way" of accomplishing any given task by discovering the fastest, most effective, and least fatiguing production methods.

Such changes clearly made the workplace of 1930 radically different from that of 1800. From the workers' perspective not all the change was good. He or she was eventually so far removed from legal and psychological ownership of the tools of production and, often, the finished product, that work itself could be intrinsically unsatisfying—which is one reason why workers turned to unions and had an early flirtation with welfare unionism. But these changes also brought greater productivity and, with it, substantial benefits. Three changes were of outstanding importance.

First, greater productivity meant that the hours of work could be reduced *without* reducing wages. In 1840 President Martin Van Buren authorized a ten-hour day for most federal employees; this when the average workweek was seventy-two hours. By 1890, the ten-hour day had more or less been achieved. The typical worker was on the job for sixty hours a week. Holidays, sick leave, and paid vacations were still very rare. By 1929, about half of all manufacturing employees worked less than forty-eight hours a week. Since then the "standard" workweek has been reduced to forty hours. Even today there is a good deal of variation from occupation to occupation and season to season. The big difference, however, is that nowadays overtime pay is the rule rather than the exception. Although these gains have been made possible by increases in productivity, they were also the result of organized labor's efforts to gain better contracts and favorable federal legislation.

A second major change in the workplace was the reduction of child labor. In the nineteenth century, the United States was a land of vast resources and an inadequate supply of labor. In part, this limitation on economic development was overcome through the continual introduction of new and improved technologies. And in part, it was alleviated through the widespread use of child labor. In the early decades of this century, technology and child labor combined to create an extremely abusive situation. As machines did more and more labor, less and less physical strength was necessary for the worker to be productive. And as jobs became more specialized, they often became simpler to conceptualize and perform. In fact, they became "childlike"; consequently, it was no surprise that employers sought to hire children to perform them.

Children could be paid less than adults, they were easier to control through physical force and psychological manipulation, and they were less likely to organize and strike. In 1831, about 7 percent of all workers were under the age of twelve. By the early decades of this century, about 20 percent of all children between the ages of ten and fifteen were employed. Efforts by the labor movement and social reformers to prevent the exploitation of

Solidarity Forever

The union movement encouraged the singing of stirring "message" songs as a way of building morale and gaining membership. Some unions even issued official songbooks designed to fit into an overall pocket. Perhaps the most famous of all union songs (many of which were parodies of well known hymns) is *Solidarity Forever,* which should be sung to the tune of *The Battle Hymn of the Republic.*

It is we who plowed the prairies, built the cities
  where they trade,
Dug the mines and built the workshops, endless
  miles of railroad laid;
Now we stand outcast and starving mid the wonders
  we have made
But the union makes us strong!

Solidarity forever!
Solidarity forever!
Solidarity forever!
For the union makes us strong!

children in the workplace date back well into the nineteenth century. As early as 1842, some states (Connecticut and Massachusetts), legislated a maximum ten-hour workday for children. In 1848, Pennsylvania established a minimum working age of twelve for factory jobs. But it would be twenty years more before any state had inspectors to enforce child labor laws. And it would not be until the late 1930s that federal laws would outlaw child labor (mainly through the **Fair Labor Standards Act**). The practice was

TERMS   **Fair Labor Standards Act (FLSA)**   The 1938 law providing a minimum age of sixteen for general work and eighteen for hazardous jobs. It contained similar minimum age requirements as the National Industrial Recovery Act (NIRA) of 1935, and was enacted partly in response to the NIRA being declared unconstitutional by the Supreme Court. The FLSA also set the forty-hour standard workweek and provided for the establishment of a minimum wage.

so entrenched that earlier federal attempts to outlaw child labor were construed by the Supreme Court as being unconstitutional infringements on the power of the states to regulate conditions in the workplace.

The third major change in the workplace associated with the rise of the labor movement was a very marked increase in **real wages.** Between 1820 and 1930, real wages just about tripled. Thus, the average worker was working fewer hours and making substantially more money.

These fundamental changes coincided with a host of others. The reduction of the workweek gave labor more leisure time. The rise in real wages provided laborers with enough money to go beyond the necessities of food, housing, and clothing; recreation became a possibility for the typical worker. The abolition of child labor encouraged children to stay in school longer, so the population became better educated. Eventually, labor in the United States became "middle-class." It sought home ownership, greater education for its young, and security against economic downturns, unhealthful or dangerous conditions at work, and economic hardship upon retirement. Far from being at the forefront of radical political change, organized labor became part of the political establishment. But the change did not come easily or without pain and violence. It took about a century and a half to go from the Philadelphia Cordwainers' rudimentary organization to the dominance of the AFL in the early 1930s. Then the Great Depression threatened the labor movement with a new crisis.

THE TRADE UNION VERSUS THE INDUSTRIAL UNION

Historically, the AFL stood on three legs: pragmatism, the organization of skilled and semiskilled workers by craft, and voluntarism—the achievement of gains for workers primarily through collective bargaining, rather than by legislation. During the 1930s each of these legs would be subjected to severe stress, two to outright fracture.

The United States has always had a number of radical unions or organizations within the general labor movement. These groups, often taking the form of political parties, have tended to be more ideological than the mainstream unions. While the latter have tended to be interested in "business unionism" and gains on a piecemeal basis, the radical unions have had a vision of society

TERMS   **Real Wages**   Wages after they have been adjusted for changes in the level of prices.

that required vast economic, political, and social change. These radical unions, such as the Industrial Workers of the World, charged the AFL with being part of the "capitalist" class and with being imbued with capitalist economics. And worse, they viewed the AFL as creating a barrier to solidarity among workers by refusing to organize and serve the needs of industrial workers. As the 1930s unfolded, the AFL became vulnerable to those in the labor movement who sought fundamental change in the economic organization of the United States. The threat became all the greater as unemployment went from 3 percent to ten times that amount.

The boom and bust cycle had always been with us, but the crash of 1929 and its aftermath seemed to many to require a radical reorganization of the society. It appeared as though the capitalist system had failed. The Socialist, American Labor, and Communist Parties began to attract many who had previously supported the pragmatic, and consequently status quo, outlook of the AFL. But while the AFL made some concessions in the direction of supporting government intervention in the economy, on the whole it remained so steadfast in its adherence to pragmatism and nonintervention by government that initially it even opposed some **public works** programs.

Naturally, the AFL's continued conservatism offered little appeal to the radicals; but its rejection of the concept of industrial unionism led even moderates to question the sagacity of its leadership. It is important to recognize the difference between craft and industrial workers in order to appreciate what was at issue in the AFL's insistence on organization by craft alone. The craft worker has a skill that he or she sells to an employer, who, in turn, organizes at least part of the work itself around the worker. The skill itself may even have to be learned in the workplace through apprenticeship. Assuming the skill is scarce, the employer would have difficulty replacing it. Learning and practicing the skill may also provide the workers with a social basis for organization.

The industrial worker, in contrast, has no particular skill in the sense of the craft worker. He or she may specialize in a facet of production, but the bane of the industrial worker is replaceability. He or she is viewed as but a factor of production, one that can be bought when necessary and laid-off or fired when no longer needed. It is assumed that another worker can do the same work

---

TERMS   **Public Works**   A generic term for government-sponsored construction projects.

with comparatively little training or replacement cost. Moreover, the industrial worker typically works on an assembly line; he or she is fitted into the production process where a machine, robot, or animal cannot be used. The industrial worker is seen as an appendage to a mechanized form of production. The work is not organized around the worker; the worker is organized around the work. The plant, or industry, becomes the basis for unionization as in the automobile and steel industries. Here, assembly line workers, secretaries, cafeteria workers, and others may all be in the same union. Under these conditions, what the worker does can hardly be the basis for economic or social organization. Instead that basis must be found in the industry or plant in which he or she works.

These differences give the craft and industrial workers different outlooks. The craft worker is particularly interested in maintaining the saleability of his or her skills. Consequently, they may oppose new technologies—even though they may be labor saving. The industrial worker is more likely to be accepting of new technologies if they do not endanger health, make the job more unpleasant, or threaten displacement. In addition, craft workers, such as electricians or plumbers, do not always work for the same employer. This gives them greater autonomy. It also means that the union rather than the employer is the constant in the workplace. This requires the union to more or less assure the temporary employer that the employees are qualified to do the work at hand. Membership in the union, therefore, may be taken as an indicator of competence. The union is also the appropriate organization for the administration of some fringe benefit programs, such as health insurance. Furthermore, the craft union often faces a different bargaining situation than the industrial union. It may deal with a large number of relatively small employers in a limited geographic area, rather than with a few nationwide employers, such as the automobile companies. The threat of a strike may be a more potent weapon in the hands of a craft union. Consequently, they may be able to engage in more forceful collective bargaining. Finally, craft workers may feel ill at ease with members of an industrial union, feeling that being organized by industry, rather than trade, tends to diminish their status and fails to allow them to adequately bargain for the worth of their contribution to the finished product.

So it is not surprising that the AFL, being based on craft unions, was reluctant to seek to organize industrial workers. There were a few exceptions to this general rule, such as the United Mine Workers, who were AFL members. But even in the depths of the depression, the AFL approached the issue of industrial unionization gingerly. In 1935, a group of labor leaders within the AFL

Mr. Dooley on the Open Shop

" 'What's all this that's in the papers about the open shop?' asked Mr. Hennessey.

" 'Why, don't ye know?' said Mr. Dooley. 'Really, I'm surprized at yer ignorance, Hinnissey. What is th' open shop? Sure, 'tis where they kape the door open to accommodate th' constant stream av' min comin' in t' take jobs cheaper than th' min what has th' jobs. 'Tis like this, Hinnissey: Suppose wan av these free-born citizens is workin' in an open shop f'r th' princely wage av wan large iron dollar a day av tin hour. Along comes anither son-av-gun and he sez t' th' boss, "Oi think Oi could handle th' job nicely f'r ninety cints." "Sure," sez th' boss, and th' wan dollar man gets out into th' crool woruld t' exercise hiz inalienable roights as a free-born American citizen an' scab on some other poor devil. An' so it goes on, Hinnissey. An' who gits th' benefit? Thrue, it saves th' boss money, but he don't care no more f'r money thin he does his right eye.

" 'It's all principle wid him. He hates t' see men robbed av their indipindence. They must have their indipindence, regardless av anything else.'

" 'But,' said Mr. Hennessey, 'these open-shop min ye menshun say they are f'r unions if properly conducted.'

" 'Shure,' said Mr. Dooley, 'if properly conducted. An there we are: an' how would they have them conducted? No strikes, no rules, no contracts, no scales, hardly iny wages, an' dam' few mimbers.' "

Source: Finley Peter Dunne, "Mr. Dooley on the Open Shop," *Literary Digest*, November 27, 1920.

organized the Committee for Industrial Organization (CIO). This precipitated a split in the AFL because many older union leaders refused to depart from the craft union concept. In 1937, those unions associated with the CIO were formally expelled from the AFL. One year later, they formed their own **international** federation, the Congress of Industrial Organizations, with **John L. Lewis** as president.

The American labor movement has seen the rapid rise of many unions that fill a particular void in the representation of workers. The CIO was part of this pattern, but with a difference— it demonstrated staying power. The CIO was able to organize workers at General Motors and Unites States Steel, among other major corporations. By 1941, it had about five million members. And this at a time when unemployment was still high.

The AFL felt appropriately apprehensive. The CIO had been so successful that it threatened to eclipse the AFL, which once so stodgily refused to deal with the plight of the industrial worker. So the AFL, feeling threatened, abandoned its strict adherence to craft organization and sought to outdo the CIO. Eventually, the AFL gained more members. But the big winner was the labor movement itself because record numbers of workers joined unions.

Eventually, the AFL and the CIO took to raiding each other's ranks for new members, a practice that was wasteful of both organizations' resources. But in the 1950s they began to cooperate. First, they signed pledges not to raid one another's members. Then, in 1955, they formally merged into the massive AFL-CIO. **George Meany**, former head of the AFL, became the leader of the new organization, which had some sixteen million members.

The depression not only threatened the AFL's pragmatism and forced it to embrace the industrial union, it also compelled the AFL to move away from strict adherence to voluntarism. The 1930s were a decade of vast economic turmoil and reform. Labor could not escape the net of federal legislation. But oddly, in retrospect, even though the overwhelming direction of federal labor

---

TERMS   **International**   A union with locals in more than one country. Most American unions are "international" solely because of locals in Canada.

John L. Lewis   (1880–1969) President of the United Mine Workers from 1920 to 1960, a founder of the Congress of Industrial Organizations, and probably the most controversial, most hated, and most revered labor leader of his time.

George Meany   (1894–1979) A labor leader who started out as a plumber in a Bronx local and became the president of the AFL-CIO from its creation to 1979.

legislation was to protect labor and the right to collectively bargain and strike, the AFL was reluctant to see the federal government intervene in the workplace. Its rationale was that in the long run government intervention would reduce the freedom or "voluntarism" associated with a labor contract negotiated between two private parties. Some in the AFL were also suspicious of government intervention on the grounds that it would tend to benefit the rich and powerful corporate chieftains more than the worker. This, after all, had been the case in the past with some federal efforts affecting worklife. Indeed, at first the AFL even opposed the federal government's social security plan. But by the end of the decade, the AFL's leadership recognized the widespread support of workers for federal labor legislation and consequently abandoned its earlier outlook.

Along with its support of the labor policies emanating from the Democratic Party, the AFL was drawn into electoral politics as never before. It began to support candidates and became staunchly supportive of the Democrats. In the future much of the success of the labor movement would be connected to partisan politics and much of its effort would be devoted to lobbying for favored legislation and public policies. In a sense the AFL had come almost full circle. By the end of World War II it supported industrial unionism. By becoming politically involved and seeking improvements in working conditions through legislation it had moved closer to the welfare unionism which it had so vehemently rejected at its birth. As a result, the labor movement today is far more comprehensive, in concept if not in numbers, than at any time in the past.

THE LABOR MOVEMENT TODAY

Today the American labor movement faces complex challenges associated with the need to adapt to a rapidly changing economy and an increasingly professionalized workforce. In particular, the "deindustrialization" of the economy has eroded labor's strength in terms of the proportion of the workforce it represents. In 1945, about one-third of the labor force was represented by unions. By 1983, this figure dropped to less than 25 percent. This decline reflects the movement of jobs out of heavy industries, such as steel, rubber, mining, and automotive, where the drive to organize workers had been particularly effective in the past. At present, by contrast, a larger proportion of the nation's jobs are in the service and professional sectors—areas that historically have resisted unionization. Equally threatening from labor's perspective is that the great northern cities that constituted the core of labor's organizational and political strength have rapidly declined. The "union towns" such as Detroit, Pittsburgh, and Chicago are still important in national elections, but nowadays they are balanced against cities in the "sun belt," where unionization has lagged.

Defections from the ranks of the AFL-CIO have also posed a problem for labor solidarity. The Teamsters were expelled from the AFL-CIO in 1957 for corruption within its leadership. Although presently affiliated, in 1968 the United Auto Workers withdrew partly because of philosophical differences concerning the direction of the labor movement; at the time the United Auto Workers considered the AFL-CIO too politically conservative on various foreign policy and domestic matters.

The charge of being too conservative is frequently levied against the AFL-CIO and other large American unions. Sometimes this view is called "corporativism," meaning that there has grown to be a harmony of interest between capital and labor. Unions, it is alleged, are themselves beginning to look like corporations. Because they manage huge pension and investment funds, high ranking union officials, just like any other investors, become more concerned with the rates of return and less interested in considerations of ideology. They, it is alleged, even begin to look and think like corporate executives. In consequence, they seek stable climates for their investments. They no longer take the lead in pressing for social reforms to help the working class. They are certainly not at the forefront of any movement for radical change. Indeed, unions and their members have even been divided over efforts to achieve equal employment opportunity for women, blacks, and other minorities through the use of **affirmative action.** In particular, unions continue to adhere to reliance on seniority as the determinant of which workers will be laid-off last and recalled first. This cannot help but have a detrimental effect on equal opportunity because it tends to perpetuate the "last hired, first fired," syndrome that has been so damaging to the employment interests of women and minorities.

The political challenges to organized labor today are formidable, not the least of which is the defection of traditional **blue collar** support from the New Deal coalition in the Democratic Party.

TERMS **Affirmative Action** When the term first gained currency in the 1960s, it meant the removal of "artificial barriers" to the employment of women and minority group members. Toward the end of that decade, however, it got lost in a fog of semantics and came out meaning the provision of compensatory opportunities for hitherto disadvantaged groups.

Blue Collar Workers, both skilled and unskilled, engaged primarily in physical labor.

Many in this group have become so middle-class that they can afford to turn their backs on many of the fundamental concepts of the New Deal. They look at welfare and other government programs for the disadvantaged as oppressive tax burdens.

This lessening of political support directly translates into less support in Congress for new legislation, and less of a voice in the management of programs and agencies already in existence. The U.S. Department of Labor is a prime example of this phenomenon. When it was created in 1913, its main function was control of immigration, a responsibility it later passed on to the Department of Justice. Aside from its statistical functions, the Department pretty much lay dormant until it was revitalized by the New Deal. For several decades it truly was the voice and advocate of organized labor. But in the early 1980s, under a conservative Republican administration, it considered itself the voice of "all" the workers— from a migrant farm worker "all the way up to the chairman of the board of General Motors." This change in representational philosophy also manifests itself in numbers. The workers of the Department have been reduced from 23,000 in 1979 to 18,600 in 1983. Its budget during this period was cut by $8 billion. Its main initiative has been increased attention to attacking corruption within unions, a noble goal whose nobility would have been all the more apparent if it had been balanced by other major initiatives.

Despite these indications of organized labor's decline and stagnation, there are also some areas of great encouragement for the future of the labor movement. Unions have been able to organize categories of employees who were previously unrepresented and whose jobs suggest that labor may be able to respond to the shift from an industrial to a service and technological economy. Especially important in this regard are public employees, whose ranks have helped stem the tide of labor union decline. Indeed, a much higher proportion of public employees (more than half of all government workers) are now represented by unions than are private sector employees. Unions have also made very strong inroads in some professions, including education and medicine. In one of the more visible developments, they have been able to organize professional athletes. This has provided one indicator of the continued legitimacy of unions in the public's mind in spite of their being in a period of relative decline. After all, people are reminded when the baseball or football players go on strike: What is more American than the "union"?

Of course the future is a challenge. Unions, as always, will have to adapt and adjust to new economic, political, and social conditions. However, ever since the Philadelphia Cordwainers got together they have always done that. Individual unions and federations have come and gone, but the movement itself has continually progressed. There is no reason to believe that this long-term trend will not continue into the future.

REVIEW QUESTIONS

1. One of the questions long debated by social scientists is why the United States never developed a strong socialist political party. How is the absence of such a party related to the directions taken by the American labor movement?

2. How did the heterogeneous character of the population and the economic diversity of the United States affect the development of "welfare unionism"?

3. The "voluntarism" associated with "business unionism" once served to distinguish the AFL from "welfare unions," such as the Knights of Labor. Now that the AFL-CIO is so heavily involved in lobbying and other political action, is the distinction between "business" and "welfare" unionism still valid?

4. In the 1930s the distinction between craft workers and industrial workers bitterly divided the labor movement. What kinds of distinctions remain between the two types of workers today? How might these affect collective bargaining?

5. Prior to the 1930s, cyclical panics, recessions, and depressions tended to weaken the labor movement severely. What was different about the Great Crash of 1929?

6. In what ways is the relationship between capital and labor adversarial? In what ways is it harmonious?

FOR ADDITIONAL READING

Auerbach, Jerold S., ed. *American Labor in the 20th Century.* Indianapolis: Bobbs-Merrill, 1969.

Dulles, Foster Rhea. *Labor in America: A History,* Third Edition. New York: Crowell, 1966.

Freeman, Richard B. and James L. Medoff. *What Do Unions Do?* New York: Basic Books, 1984.

Grossman, Jonathan. "The Origin of the U. S. Department of Labor," *Monthly Labor Review,* Vol. 96, No. 3 (March 1973).

Lens, Sidney. *The Labor Wars: From the Molly Maguires to the Sitdowns.* Garden City, NY: Doubleday, 1974.

MacLaury, Judson. "The Selection of the First U. S. Commissioner of Labor," *Monthly Labor Review,* Vol. 98, No. 4 (April 1975).

Morris, Richard B., ed. *The American Worker.* Washington, DC: U.S. Government Printing Office, 1976.

Raybeck, Joseph G. *A History of American Labor.* New York: The Free Press, 1966.

Taft, Philip. *Organized Labor in American History.* New York: Harper & Row, 1964.

Ulman, Lloyd. *The Rise of the American Trade Union.* Cambridge, MA: Harvard University Press, 1955.

2   The Growth and Influence of Unions

Prologue
The AFL-CIO Selects its Candidate

In October of 1983, more than a year before the presidential election of 1984, the General Board of the AFL-CIO met to endorse Walter Mondale for President of the United States. The AFL-CIO had never before endorsed a presidential candidate until after the nominating conventions of both major parties. But the desire to defeat Ronald Reagan in 1984 gave birth to new tactics.

When Lane Kirkland succeeded George Meany as President of the AFL-CIO in 1979, he inherited an organization that had lost much of its former political muscle. No longer did presidents seek to "clear it with **Sidney**." Indeed, Reagan still got about 40 percent of the labor vote in 1980 even after the AFL-CIO had formally endorsed then-President Carter for reelection.

In an effort to revitalize labor's sagging political influence,

TERMS   **Sidney**   "Sidney" was   Sidney Hillman (1887–1946), President of the Amalgamated Clothing Workers from its creation in 1913 until his death. Because he was a close political advisor to President Franklin D. Roosevelt, the president was reported to have said "clear everything with Sidney" in connection with the selection of his vice-presidential running mate in 1944. Because "clear it with Sidney" was widely publicized and criticized, it became symbolic of the labor movement's "pervasive" influence in government.

Kirkland developed a strategy. In 1981 he started floating the idea of a preprimary endorsement. After Senator Edward Kennedy announced his noncandidacy, former Vice-President Mondale became the obvious choice. Kirkland reasoned that with the unions' combined financial and organizational strength, their candidate for the Democratic Party's presidential nomination would win. The trick was for labor to stick together. In years past individual unions have endorsed and financially supported a variety of candidates. Some unions have even supported the Republican candidate in the general election. Labor's faltering political clout had to be mended. The only question was how. As Kirkland told one AFL-CIO Executive Council session: "We've tried everything else, why don't we try unity?"

The key to the strategy was the commitment of the heads of the individual unions to unite behind one candidate in advance of the primaries. This would mean that they would have to give up the usual courting by candidates and concomitant media attention—attention that significantly contributed to their own job security by making them appear to be influential in the eyes of their membership. Kirkland was able to form the needed consensus and the AFL-CIO became more actively involved in Democratic Party politics than it had ever been before.

In a sense the policy of preprimary endorsement is a sure winner for labor. If their candidate wins the nomination, his debt to labor will be obvious. If the convention contest is close, a unified group of labor delegates can have a great influence on the outcome. But what if labor's candidate loses and there is no opportunity to play kingmaker at the convention? Then labor is graciously prepared to support the winner who, no doubt, would be delighted to have the enthusiastic support of labor in the general election. In possible anticipation of this, AFL-CIO political operatives have been told not to openly criticize the other Democratic candidates. In the end, there must be unity. The goal in defeating **Ronald Reagan,** the former union leader who has turned out to be the most antilabor president of modern times, must be paramount. But what if the Democrats lose the presidential election in 1984? Labor still wins because it would have emerged as the most influential and unified force within the party—and the group that is the most experienced, most determined, and most ready for 1988.

As Kirkland explained his strategy to the AFL-CIO conven-

TERMS   **Ronald Reagan** (1911–   )   The only American president who was previously an elected union official; he was President of the Screen Actors Guild from 1947 to 1952 and again from 1959 to 1960.

tion in 1983: "If we do not do what we propose to do, we shall be reviled as toothless and irrelevant. If we succeed, we shall be condemned for daring to aspire to a share of power in our society. Given that choice of slurs, I assure you that I much prefer the latter."

THE GROWTH OF UNIONIZATION

As the history of the labor movement shows, unionization has been the product of a number of complex and varied forces. Like virtually any other major economic, political, or social development, it cannot be attributed to a single factor. Rather, unionization has been related to practically all of the forces of change in American life, as well as to the social and psychological responses of workers to those changes.

The evolution of unionization amply demonstrates the adaptability of labor organizations to these changes. The labor movement began with an emphasis on local craft unions and eventually grew to accommodate very large national industrial unions as well. Along with these changes has come a shift in the nature of union influence. Many aspects of collective bargaining have been shifted upward from the local level to the union's national level. And, to some extent, unions have placed increasing emphasis on **political action** as opposed to collective bargaining alone. These developments are complex and their various aspects will be fully explored as the chapters unfold. This chapter will concentrate on the major forces contributing to the growth of unionization; the factors currently fostering a challenge to unionization and contributing to a decline in the proportion of the workforce that belongs to unions; and the scope and nature of unions' political action and influence.

In discussing the growth of unionization it is important to bear in mind that large scale, *stable* unionization is a relatively recent phenomenon that only dates back to the 1930s. Consider the tumultuous period from 1900 to 1937. This witnessed such developments as the rise of the American Federation of Labor, **business unionism,** and the development of national collective bargaining legislation. But during this period union membership only grew

TERMS   **Political Action**   Any attempt to influence the political process from lobbying legislators to seeking the election (or defeat) of particular candidates.

Business Unionism   The labor union philosophy of concentrating on getting better wages and working conditions for their members rather than devoting significant efforts to political action.

from about one million to five million. Yet, between 1937 and 1950, total membership in unions tripled to some 15 million. After a period of temporary decline, growth picked up again in the 1960s and unions recorded a peak of some 23.4 million members in 1974. Since that time, membership has declined somewhat to 22.8 million in the early 1980s. Table 2-1 shows the trends in union membership by state.

The growth of union membership in absolute numbers tends to mask the fact that unionization has been subject to a longer-term decline in terms of the proportion of the nonagricultural workforce that belong to such organizations. In 1958, about one-third of all nonagricultural employees belonged to unions. By 1980 this figure was down to 25 percent. Yet, if the total workforce is considered, rather than just the nonagricultural workforce, unionization has remained reasonably stable from 1944 to 1980 at about 20 to 25 percent of the labor force. If one were to add employee associations, which account for about 3.3 percent of the nonagricultural workforce and have been growing rapidly, the extent of organization among members of the workforce is somewhat greater. In general, however, employee associations do not engage in collective bargaining, but rather provide a variety of professional, insurance, and group benefits to their members.

However one looks at the **statistics,** it is clear that union growth was spectacular from the 1930s to the 1950s and has had some impressive spurts since then. What accounts for growth? Sadly, one of the main factors is war. Note that the main periods of union growth were:

1897–1904 (a net gain of 1.6 million members);

1915–1920 (2.5 million net gain);

1933–1939 (3.6 million net gain);

1940–1944 (5.3 million net gain);

1949–1953 (2.6 million net gain); and

1964–1968 (2.3 million net gain).

TERMS   **Statistics** Benjamin Disraeli (1804–1881), the nineteenth-century British prime minister, once asserted that "there are three kinds of lies: lies, damned lies, and statistics." One is wise to always be suspicious of statistics. Most statistics for union membership are either estimates by the Bureau of Labor Statistics or self-reports by unions. While many analysts are rightly cautious about using such data, the gross numbers used in this chapter are fully adequate for their purpose—to give the reader a sense of the size and direction of the union movement.

TABLE 2-1.
UNION MEMBERSHIP BY STATE

State	Total (1,000)				Percent of Employment	
	1970	1974	1978	1980	1970	1980
U.S.	**21,852**	**23,408**	**23,306**	**22,811**	**30.8**	**25.2**
Ala.[1]	228	278	329	296	22.6	21.8
Alaska	32	45	53	57	34.4	33.6
Ariz.[1]	117	156	159	160	21.4	15.8
Ark.[1]	104	116	128	119	19.4	16.0
Calif.	2,477	2,607	2,659	2,661	35.7	27.0
Colo.	186	220	205	227	25.0	18.1
Conn.	329	382	356	327	27.5	22.9
Del.	55	55	59	65	25.8	25.1
Fla.[1]	348	416	415	420	16.2	11.7
Ga.[1]	273	287	314	323	17.5	15.0
Hawaii	89	129	134	113	30.3	27.9
Idaho	46	54	63	61	22.1	18.5
Ill.	1,613	1,684	1,590	1,487	37.3	30.6
Ind.[1]	694	729	700	649	37.5	30.4
Iowa[1]	216	251	250	244	24.5	22.0
Kans.[1]	143	137	144	146	21.1	15.5
Ky.	293	309	311	290	32.2	24.0
La.	201	211	240	257	19.4	16.4
Maine	73	83	100	101	22.0	24.1
Md.[2]	499	545	546	527	24.5	22.6
Mass.	616	632	692	660	27.2	24.9
Mich.	1,307	1,388	1,362	1,289	43.5	37.4
Minn.	420	421	464	463	31.9	26.2
Miss.[1]	86	93	122	135	14.9	16.3
Mo.	624	595	598	544	37.5	27.6
Mont.	69	73	83	82	34.3	29.2
Nebr.[1]	101	99	116	114	21.0	18.2
Nev.[1]	74	81	95	95	36.5	23.8
N.H.	55	58	61	61	21.2	15.8
N.J.	815	898	810	784	31.2	25.6
N. Mex.	55	63	66	88	18.8	18.9
N.Y.	2,876	3,215	2,877	2,792	40.2	38.7
N.C.[1]	167	201	242	228	9.4	9.6
N. Dak.[1]	35	38	45	42	21.4	17.1
Ohio	1,509	1,522	1,472	1,376	38.9	31.5
Okla.	143	148	177	174	18.8	15.3
Oreg.	260	270	296	272	36.7	26.0
Pa.	1,741	1,849	1,741	1,644	40.0	34.6
R.I.	96	111	119	113	27.9	28.4
S.C.[1]	98	105	101	93	11.6	7.8
S. Dak.[1]	26	31	34	35	14.9	14.7
Tenn.[1]	312	328	358	334	23.5	19.1
Tex.[1]	572	620	698	669	15.8	11.4

TABLE 2-1. (continued)

State	Total (1,000)				Percent of Employment	
	1970	1974	1978	1980	1970	1980
U.S.	**21,852**	**23,408**	**23,306**	**22,811**	**30.8**	**25.2**
Utah[1]	94	94	103	98	26.2	17.8
Vt.	31	37	43	36	21.0	18.0
Va.[1]	277	288	311	318	18.2	14.7
Wash.	489	485	547	553	45.3	34.4
W. Va.	242	239	248	222	46.8	34.4
Wis.	510	548	573	554	33.3	28.6
Wyo.[1]	27	33	37	39	24.8	18.6
Unallocated	108	149	61	376	(x)	(x)

X Not available. [1] State has a right-to-work law. [2] Includes District of Columbia.

Source: Adapted from U.S. Department of Commerce, Bureau of the Census, *Statistical Abstract of the United States, 1984* (Washington, D.C.: U.S. Government Printing Office, December 1983), p. 440.

The first of these periods was characterized by the Spanish-American War and recovery from a major depression. The second involved World War I. Growth during 1940–1944 was clearly due to World War II. The Korean War accounts for much of the growth between 1949 and 1953. The Vietnam War was associated with the growth in the 1964–1968 period. Growth during the 1930s was in response to the depression and federal legislation encouraging collective bargaining.

Why does war contribute to unionization? What lessons can be learned from the connection? War requires the manufacture of a wide variety of products, ranging from ships, trucks, tanks, and weapons systems of all kinds, to supplying the troops with clothing. This kind of manufacturing, in turn, requires the production of steel and other metals. Ore, coal, and energy are often at peak demand during wartime, as are a wide variety of other natural resources. Under these conditions there is generally a great demand for labor itself. All the more so, of course, if a large proportion of the potential workforce is serving in the military.

Historically, unionization has made its greatest strides when demand for labor is greatest. Workers have more economic power with which to bargain when they are in relatively scarce supply. In contrast, during panics, recessions, or depressions—when there is a surplus of labor—unions have often faltered. The major exception to this rule was during the Great Depression of the 1930s, when the federal government took positive steps to protect and encourage unionization. But the relative scarcity of labor during wartime is only part of the reason for rapid union growth during such periods. Another reason is that the demand for labor is largely in the mining and manufacturing sectors of the economy. And this poses a problem for unionization in today's rapidly changing, **postindustrial** economy.

During different economic periods, different kinds of unions tend to flourish. For example, by the end of the first quarter of this century (1925), about half of all union members were found working for railroads and in building trades. The United Mine Workers was also among the nation's largest unions at this time—indeed, the single largest union throughout much of the period from 1898 to 1933. By 1939, however, railroad unions could no longer be counted among the ten largest. Between 1951 and 1980 the Mine Workers suffered a precipitous decline from about 600,000 to 245,000 members—a loss of truly devastating proportions.

In sharp contrast, while the railroad unions and Mine Workers were declining, the Teamsters' union was undergoing very rapid growth. From fewer than 100,000 members in 1933, it increased to some 1.9 million by 1980. At the same time, the United Auto Workers emerged as a giant among industrial unions reaching 1.4 million members in 1980. These patterns indicate the shift from railroad transportation and coal energy to today's automotive society with its heavy reliance on truck transportation and the attendant need for petroleum products.

Among the other large unions at the beginning of the final two decades of this century are the United Steelworkers (1.2 million), the Electrical Workers (1.1 million), the International Association of Machinists (.75 million members), the International Ladies' Garment Workers (.32 million) and the Amalgamated Clothing and Textile Workers (.5 million). The size of these unions also stands as testimony to the importance of the **manufacturing sector** of the economy. And, it is this close association between

TERMS   **Postindustrial**   A term coined by Daniel Bell (1919–   ) to describe the new social structures evolving in modern society in the second half of the twentieth century. Bell holds that the "axial principle" of postindustrial society is the centrality of theoretical knowledge as the source of innovation and of policy formulation. Hallmarks of postindustrial society include a change from a goods-producing to a service economy, the preeminence of a professional and technical class of workers, and the creation of a new "intellectual" technology.

Manufacturing Sector   The segment of the national economy that produces things such as furniture and machines, as opposed to those segments that sell or repair them.

unionism and manufacturing that poses a major challenge to the labor movement today.

It has been said that as the United States moves further away from industrialism to a postindustrial, technological, and service-based economy, unionization will inevitably undergo considerable change. Manufacturing was central to the economy and unionization—and it will always have widespread ramifications for the nation's economic health. The problem for unions, though, is that manufacturing is declining as a proportion of all employment. A few statistics tell this story with great clarity: In 1947 some 40.5 percent of all people employed in the private sector were in manufacturing, but by 1980 the number of people employed in manufacturing dropped to less than 30 percent of the workforce. This is a loss of millions of union jobs that will never return— jobs that have been lost to foreign competition and **robotics.**

Obviously, the core of union strength, manufacturing, is being eroded by transformations in the economy that create far more jobs in other sectors. As a result, several of the nation's unions associated with industrialism—such as the United Mine Workers and the Steelworkers—have witnessed declining membership. Clearly, if unionization is to resume its growth after a period of decline, it will have to organize workers in the more rapidly growing sectors of the economy.

PUBLIC SECTOR GROWTH   The public sector has been one of the most rapidly growing segments of the economy during the past three decades. Public civilian employment at all levels of government doubled from about 6 million in 1951 to more than 12 million in 1981. Until the early 1960s, unionization in the public sector was the exception, rather than the rule. Public employees now have a recognized constitutional right to join organizations such as labor unions and employee associations. However, there is no constitutional right to engage in collective bargaining per se, and some jurisdictions still prohibit it.

After mounting a political campaign back in the late 1940s to win collective bargaining rights for federal employees, labor achieved a major success in 1962 when President John F. Kennedy

TERMS   **Robotics**   Robot is a general term for any machine that can do the work that a human being would otherwise have to do. Robotics is the use of robots.

issued an **executive order** authorizing formal labor relations in the federal government. The President declared that the recognition of employee organizations and negotiation with them would enhance both efficiency and democracy. This was an extremely important step. Previously, collective bargaining in the public sector had been opposed on the grounds that it violated governmental "sovereignty." Some even viewed it as contrary to virtually every constitutional principle upon which governments in the United States are based. But once the federal government lent such legitimacy to organized labor relations in the public sector, much of this traditional resistance crumbled. Nowadays, collective bargaining in the public sector is the rule rather than the exception.

Yet, even as collective bargaining became widely authorized in the public sector, a serious question remained. Would unions be able to organize public employees? After all, there were some important barriers. A great number of public sector jobs are **white collar** or **professional.** Some governmental positions are industrial, such as operations in the Government Printing Office and the Bureau of the Mint, but most are not. If unionization was to take place another kind of worker—one having greater education and higher socioeconomic status on average—would have to be convinced that collective bargaining was desirable. Moreover, many governments employ large numbers of women and members of minority groups, who traditionally have been resistant to unionization. In addition, many public employees have a good deal of job security as a result of civil service laws and procedures designed to

---

TERMS   **Executive Order**   Any rule or regulation issued by a chief administrative authority that, because of precedent and existing legislation, has the effect of law. Executive orders are the principle mode of administrative action on the part of the President of the United States. It was President Kennedy's Executive Order 10988 of January 17, 1962 that first established the right of federal employees to bargain with management over certain limited issues. This was superseded by President Nixon's Executive Order 11491 of October 29, 1969 which, in turn, was superseded by the Civil Service Reform Act of 1978.

White Collar   Employees whose jobs require slight physical effort and allow them to wear ordinary clothes.

Professional   A member of an occupation requiring specialized knowledge that can only be gained after intensive preparation. Professional occupations tend to possess three features: a body of academic and practical knowledge which is applied to the service of society, a standard of success theoretically measured by serving the needs of society rather than purely personal gain, and a system of control over the professional practice which regulates the education of new members and maintains both a code of ethics and appropriate sanctions.

TABLE 2-2.
FEDERAL EMPLOYEES COVERED BY UNION CONTRACTS*

Year	Number	Percent
1964	110,573	6
1965	241,850	12
1966	291,532	14
1967	423,052	20
1968	556,962	28
1969	559,415	28
1970	601,505	31
1971	707,067	36
1972	753,247	39
1973	837,410	43
1974	984,553	49
1975	1,083,017	53
1976	1,059,663	52
1977	1,059,635	51
1978	1,120,326	55
1979	1,148,822	56
1980	1,167,265	57
1981	1,152,509	57

*Excludes Postal Workers.
Source: Federal Labor Relations Authority.

protect them from politically motivated, arbitrary, or capricious treatment. Equal employment opportunity regulations have also afforded public employees greater protections against discriminatory treatment than many of their counterparts in the private sector. Finally, since the format of collective bargaining in the public sector differs considerably from that used in the private sector it has not always been clear either with whom or over what public employees might collectively bargain.

These barriers to unionization notwithstanding, the organization of public employees has been extremely rapid. From 1962 to 1980, the number of public employees belonging to unions increased from about 1.2 million to more than 6 million. Put differently, public employees constituted about 7 percent of all union members in 1962; but about 25 percent by 1980. Moreover, the three unions that have grown most during the last two decades were in the public sector: the American Federation of Teachers; the American Federation of State, County, and Municipal Employees; and the American Federation of Government Employees. To what can the success of unionization in the public sector be attributed?

The process of unionization is complex and involves so many economic, political, legal, social, and psychologial factors that it is very difficult to pin down. However, the following factors are often cited as the major contributors to unionization of the public sector:

1. The bureaucratic nature of much of government that makes it all but impossible for individual workers to be heard by their employer unless they speak with a collective voice.

2. A new-found appreciation by public employees of the gains that could be won by collective bargaining.

3. The lessons that less-skilled and minority employees learned from the civil rights movement of the early 1960s; namely, that concerted organized action can protect their rights—and even increase their wages.

4. An awareness on the part of union leadership that while private sector union membership was leveling off, the public sector was an almost untapped opportunity for organizing.

5. The willingness of national unions to offer their financial resources and expertise to assist public employees to get organized and recognized.

6. The **spillover effect** of the federal government's acceptance of limited collective bargaining, which gave an impetus to public employee organization in general.

7. The hostile attitudes of many public employers which made the question of union recognition the second most frequent cause of public sector strikes in the 1960s.

8. The growing danger of some public sector jobs. This encouraged employees to join together to bargain and lobby for safer conditions. This has been especially true of teachers in urban areas, firefighters, and police.

9. The growing recognition that collective bargaining and professionalism were not mutually incompatible. Indeed, teachers, nurses, social workers, and other professional and "quasi-professional" employees have recognized that collective bargaining can be used to support professional goals and to achieve greater professional freedom in the workplace.

TERMS   **Spillover Effect**   Benefits or costs to persons other than those directly involved in a transaction.

Despite a variety of changes in the nature of public sector employment in recent years, including widespread civil service reforms and budget cutbacks, there is every indication that unionization will remain a strong force in the public sector. Unions representing public employees will obtain an even stronger voice than they presently have in the labor movement as a whole.

WHITE COLLAR   White collar employees in the private sector offer another chal-
EMPLOYEES   lenge to unionization. Historically, they were resistant to unionization, but this stance appears to have changed with the massive unionization of white collar employees in the public sector. For the most part, the earlier resistance appears to have been associated with social factors. White collar employees are often acutely aware of the status difference between themselves and blue collar, industrial, or craft workers. Sometimes, this status is bolstered by accoutrements in the workplace: cafeterias, restrooms, and general work environments are often much more pleasant for white collar employees. Moreover, white collar employees are often not required to punch in and out, which implies that greater trust is placed in them by their employer. Outside of work, white collar employees may also seek to avoid association with blue collar workers in order not to risk a reduction in their social prestige. In the past, at least, unionization was seen as a threat to many of the white collar employee's prerogatives at work and to his or her social prestige generally.

This traditional attitude appears to have changed considerably during the 1960s. In a decade of political, social, and economic upheaval, white collar employees often sensed that they were falling behind economically compared to blue collar workers represented by strong unions such as the Teamsters and the United Auto Workers. Social distinctions also became more blurred as blue collar workers moved to suburban areas previously associated with middle-class and white collar employees. Americans also turned to more casual dress, which tended to place both the blue collar worker and the white collar employee in the same clothing style off the job. Blue jeans, informal shirts, and sneakers or boots became the standard leisure uniform for a very broad band of society.

As white collar employees became more relaxed about their social status, they were more willing to join unions. Once teachers, nurses, and other professionals in the public sector unionized, there appeared to be little social threat to white collar employees to do so as well. In 1956, about 2.5 million white collar employees belonged to unions. By 1980, the figure had almost doubled. Although about three-fourths of this gain was comprised of public employees, the total change is still impressive. Back in 1956 white collar employees constituted about 13 percent of all union members. But by 1980 their percentage had increased to about 25 percent (including membership in employee associations).

Despite these impressive gains, it is generally true that unions have made only limited inroads among white collar employees in the manufacturing sector of the economy. One reason for this appears to be very considerable efforts on the part of management to "buy out" white collar employees by automatically extending to them many of the benefits gained by blue collar unions. Whether this situation changes in the future may depend upon rather vast changes in the nature of status and authority relationships in the workplace—a subject that will be examined in the concluding chapter.

WOMEN   The growing number and proportion of women in the workforce represents another potential area of substantial unionization. Whatever their attitudes toward women and civil rights in times past, many unions now take strong stances in favor of civil rights and equal employment opportunity. Women now constitute at least one-sixth of all members of unions and employee associations. They tend to be heavily concentrated in such organizations as the National Education Association, the International Ladies' Garment Workers, the International Brotherhood of Electrical Workers, the Food and Commercial Workers, the Communications Workers, and some public sector unions.

During the 1970s, the labor movement sought to respond to the challenge of organizing women workers in several ways. In 1974, a Coalition of Labor Union Women was formed. It hoped to advance the interests of and representation for the 4.5 million women who were already union members. In addition, it sought to make unionization more appealing to the remaining 35 million unorganized women who work outside of the home. For example, it lobbied for federally funded "day care" facilities and the **Equal Rights Amendment.**

TERMS   **Equal Rights Amendment** In 1972 Congress passed the Equal Rights Amendment (ERA), but it never became law because not enough of the states ratified it. The proposed Twenty-Seventh Amendment held that: "Equality of rights under the law shall not be denied or abridged by the United States or any state on account of sex."

As in the case of white collar employees, unions have not yet tapped the full potential for organizing women. One of the most notable difficulties seems to be union leadership structures that do not yet show sufficient representation of (or interest in) women. Although women account for one-sixth of all union members, this fact is not yet reflected in union or association leadership, where women are grossly underrepresented. Even in the predominantly female (80 percent) International Ladies' Garment Workers' Union most of the leadership is male.

Though this situation will undoubtedly change as women gain greater seniority in their unions, some "women's issues" may not be readily amenable to resolution through collective bargaining. Perhaps the most important of these are sex-segregated occupations, such as nursing and secretarial work, and the attendant pay structures in them. Many now argue that although pay rates in such occupations are set by market forces, they do not reflect the actual value, or "comparable worth," of such employees to the employer (see Chapter 3 for a further discussion of this issue). In other words, it is thought that social discrimination and sex-role stereotyping in society generally act to depress wage rates in **pink collar jobs.** So far, this issue seems to have had greater exposure in the courts than on the bargaining table. Women may also tend to favor a number of changes in the workplace, such as flexitime, of which unions have traditionally been skeptical.

Eventually, however, given the pragmatic character of American unions and their long experience in accommodating the needs of different ethnic and social groups, there is every reason to expect that as women gain a stronger voice in the governance of unions, means of accommodating their particular concerns will be found.

BLACKS   Black workers are another group that present a challenge to unionization. Despite two decades of forceful federal civil rights and equal opportunity legislation, blacks continue to earn less than whites and to face a number of barriers to equality in the workplace. In 1980, for instance, black entrants to the workforce could

---

TERMS   **Pink Collar Jobs**   Those jobs in which noncollege women form the bulk of the labor force, in which the pay is usually low in comparison to men of the same or lower educational levels, in which unionization is nil or weak, and where "equal-pay-for-equal-work" provisions are of little effect because women tend to compete only with other women.

expect, on average, to earn less than white entrants. Thus, black men earned 88 percent of their white counterparts; black women earned 79 percent. While unionization has helped to combat discriminatory or unequal treatment, the black perspective on the labor movement is quite complex.

On the one hand, it is probably true, as **Bayard Rustin** has claimed, that "the labor movement is the most integrated major institution in American society, certainly more integrated than the corporations, the churches, or the universities." Certainly, many blacks do belong to unions. In the early 1970s, Rustin claimed that there were over 2.5 million black unionists in the United States, which meant "the percentage of blacks in the unions is a good deal higher than the percentage of blacks in the total population—15 percent as compared with 11 percent, to be precise." Indeed, since there were about 8.7 million blacks in the labor force at that time, the rate of black participation in the labor movement was roughly 30 percent—a rate that was probably somewhat higher than that for whites at the time.

However, since blacks were disproportionately concentrated in blue collar, industrial, and low-paying jobs, it might be expected that unionization would be more appealing to them than to white workers generally. This brings us to "on the other hand." The history of the American labor movement's treatment of blacks has been equivocal. So equivocal, in fact, that some blacks believe that, generally speaking, trade unions have made employer discrimination against black workers worse than what it would have been otherwise. The true extent to which such skepticism toward unions inhibits blacks from joining them is unknown. However, there can be no doubt that it does present a barrier to the growth of unionism among black workers. Nor can there be any real doubt as to the origins of this skepticism.

Historically, the labor movement's attitude toward blacks has been split. The industrial unions, which stressed organizing unskilled workers, have tended to be hospitable toward black workers. But at the same time, the craft unions, which were limited to skilled workers, tended to be highly discriminatory; they often excluded blacks or organized them into impotent **Jim Crow** locals. Consequently, the industrial unions and those imbued with "social

TERMS **Bayard Rustin** (1910–   ) Civil rights activist who helped organize the 1963 March on Washington.

Jim Crow A name given to any law requiring the segregation of the races. All such statutes are now unconstitutional.

welfare unionism," such as the Knights of Labor and the Industrial Workers of the World, had greater appeal to blacks.

Eventually, it was the CIO rather than the AFL that sought to organize black workers on a mass basis. In fact, during the late nineteenth and early twentieth century, although the attitudes of its leadership may have been nondiscriminatory, the AFL was willing to admit unions to its federation that clearly discriminated or excluded blacks. Apparently, white craft workers did not want competition from blacks and tried to use unions as a barrier to their entrance into a variety of skilled jobs. Where it was feared that blacks might be used as strikebreakers, white unionists sometimes facilitated the establishment of segregated (and relatively powerless) black unions. The railroad brotherhoods were a prime example of rampant discrimination against blacks. One response to such prejudice was the creation, in 1925, of the Brotherhood of Sleeping Car Porters, an all black union with a national base. It was organized and led for many years by **A. Philip Randolph.** Eventually, Randolph became a major force for the adoption of nondiscriminatory policies by the AFL-CIO—and, indeed, by the federal government as well.

A major change in the relationship between the labor movement and the black worker occurred with the establishment of the CIO. Industrial unions, such as the Longshoremen and the United Mine Workers, although not without prejudice, were very anxious to organize black workers. The CIO was created with a certain political fervor stressing the need for legislative action to protect the mass-production worker. It also expressed a commitment to civil rights and equal treatment of blacks, although its practices sometimes fell short of its stated objectives. It quickly forged a political alliance with black groups seeking greater equality. By organizing black workers, it also put pressure on the AFL to do likewise. Despite the CIO's capitulation to some racist elements which led it to organize workers on a segregated basis in the South, the CIO was of immense value to urban blacks and made a considerable contribution to improved race relations in the 1930s and 1940s. Its interracial unions gave black and white workers a sense of common interest and solidarity that transcended racial lines.

TERMS   **A. Philip Randolph** (1889–1979)   Perhaps the most prominent of the black labor leaders of his generation. He persuaded President Franklin D. Roosevelt (by threatening a march on Washington) to issue Executive Order 8802 of June 23, 1941, which required defense contractors not to discriminate against workers on account of race, creed, or national origin. He was later the prime organizer of the 1963 March on Washington.

Today, the AFL-CIO (and the American labor movement generally) is formally committed to civil rights and equal opportunity. It has been among the most potent political forces in support of programs and policies in these areas. Indeed, its leadership has sometimes taken pro–civil rights stands that have been unpopular with local unions and rank-and-file members. Nevertheless, some feel that before the labor movement will be able to attract black workers in greater numbers, it will have to overcome their skepticism by accomplishing two objectives. First, its leadership will have to meet the special needs of black workers by eliminating policies and contractual arrangements that adversely affect them. Various preferences based on seniority are one example. Black workers still suffer from the "last hired, first fired" syndrome and sometimes find their access to apprenticeships, training programs, and promotions limited by low seniority. Second, the racist attitudes of some rank-and-file union members must be addressed. In order to be more attractive to the black worker, the labor movement will have to convince them that they are welcome. Union leadership will have to convince the white membership, as the CIO attempted to do in the 1930s, that there is a solidarity of interest among workers that requires their unity and cooperation. Such solidarity can only be damaged by conflict along racial, ethnic, or social lines.

IMMIGRANTS

President Franklin D. Roosevelt once annoyed the Daughters of the American Revolution when he reminded them in a formal speech that they "are descended from immigrants." It is strange that a nation of immigrants should have so much trouble absorbing each new wave of immigration. Historically, American labor unions and workers have feared that immigrant workers would depress wage scales and lead to overall reductions in the working class's standard of living. The union approach, however, involved a two-fold strategy. First, labor usually sought to exclude immigrants and aligned itself with other groups seeking to maintain restrictive quotas on immigration. Second, though, once immigrants were admitted to the United States and joined the labor force, unions often sought to organize them and aid them in a variety of ways.

At present, due to the demographics of the United States population—especially the aging of the post–World War II "baby boom" generation—it appears that immigration may be further encouraged in the future. This would enable the nation to "smooth out" some of the bumps in the age distribution of its labor force. If more immigrants do join the workforce between now and the turn of the century, they will present labor with additional opportunities for growth. Actually a tremendous pool of new immigrants is already here or on the way. Great numbers of **undocumented workers** are continuously coming over our virtually unguarded border with Mexico. Legal issues notwithstanding, it is only a matter of time before unions stop viewing this spontaneous immigration as a failure of the U.S. Immigration and Naturalization Service and start seeing it as a great organizing opportunity. As has been true in the past, the challenge for the labor movement will be to meet the needs of immigrant workers without jeopardizing the interests of native unionists.

FACTORS ENCOURAGING UNION DECLINE

While there is potential for union growth in the future, there are also some strong forces that are likely to cause declines in membership. The shift of jobs from the industrial sector to white collar, service and "high-tech" sectors of the economy is the strongest force promoting a decline in union membership. Unions will have to respond to this by organizing in new sectors of the economy and by strengthening their appeal among various categories of workers, such as women and blacks.

Another factor encouraging decline in unionism is the movement of manufacturing and other jobs to areas of the nation that traditionally have been more resistant to labor organizations. The shift of industry and population from the Northeast and Midwest to the South and West has been an extremely important phenomenon in American social, political, and economic life. Indeed, the sunbelt/snowbelt dichotomy has come to stand for a whole range of differences in life styles and politics. A company cannot legally move its operations to the sunbelt solely and candidly to break a union. However, such a move can occur for a number of legitimate business motives, including the possibilities that labor and energy for any given kind of production are cheaper there. And, at least to date, the movement of jobs to the sunbelt seems certain to lead to declines in the proportion of workers who are members of labor

TERMS   **Undocumented Workers**   The name given by the Department of Labor to illegal aliens—individuals from other countries who are unlawfully working in the United States.

unions. Remember, if the South had the same kind of union orientation as the Northeast or Midwest, there would be at least another million union members today.

A major and unanswered question is whether unionization will eventually become more attractive to sunbelt workers. Some believe increasing industrialization, urbanization, affluence, and an influx of workers who have more favorable attitudes toward unions are forces that will eventually lead to further growth among labor organizations. Others maintain, however, that sunbelt hostility to unionization is written into "right-to-work" laws (see Chapter 3) that tend to discourage unionization. Between 1956 and 1980 the ten states with the lowest proportion of union members had an almost 70 percent increase in their manufacturing employment, while at the same time the nation's manufacturing employment as a whole grew by only 16 percent. Each of these states had a union membership that ranged from only 8 to 19 percent of the nonagricultural workforce. Except for New Mexico, each had a right-to-work law. The other states were the Carolinas, South Dakota, Mississippi, Florida, Texas, Virginia, Kansas, and Georgia. Union success in certification elections in the South also appears to run well below the national average of 39 percent. Consequently, the shift of jobs from the snowbelt to the sunbelt has also represented a shift of jobs from union to nonunion.

Another factor that may lead to a decline in unionization is the growth in employment in foreign-owned firms operating in the United States. Although relatively small in comparison to the amount of business done by United States firms abroad, the size of foreign investment in the United States has been growing in recent years. Today foreign-owned enterprises employ well over a million workers in the United States, 95 percent of whom are U.S. citizens. For the most part, foreign owners are from the United Kingdom, Canada, the Netherlands, Switzerland, France, Belgium, West Germany, and Japan. Although the labor relations practices of foreign-owned companies vary considerably, there have been enough instances of resistance to unionization and collective bargaining to raise concern among unionists. For instance, in 1975 at its convention, the AFL-CIO condemned the "unregulated takeover of the United States firms by foreign interests." Japanese management practices, in particular, do not seem to fit the U.S. model of labor relations and consequently Japanese firms have been viewed as particularly resistant to unionization. It is evident that in a complex and interdependent world economy, multinational corporations will offer new challenges to the American labor movement.

THE INDIVIDUAL
DYNAMICS OF
JOINING UNIONS

We have been discussing the major **macroeconomic** and other forces that encourage growth or decline in union membership. Although considerably less is known about the subject, some attention should also be paid to the reasons individuals elect to join or avoid unions. One analyst, Mark van de Vall, has classified individual decisions to join unions into three categories of motives. First, "egocentric" motives deal with such concerns as avoiding personal problems at work (including friction with other workers who are union members), being eligible for benefits offered by the union that are not directly job related, and obtaining personal information and advice. "Sociocentric" motives include solidarity with other workers (both in a specific workplace and in general), a desire to have greater influence, and a means of expressing idealism. Third, workers joined unions as a result of patterns of "social control"; that is, the influence of relatives and fellow workers. Of course, individuals also join unions as a result of legal compulsion or inducement, as in the case of the closed shop, the union shop, or the agency shop. Many unionists believe that a sense of social solidarity is the single most important element in encouraging workers to join together in unions.

The individual motives for declining to join a union or deciding to quit one are also threefold. First, there are "structural" motives which include the feeling that the union is useless or that membership is too expensive. Some women and younger members of the workforce have frequently adopted this approach. Joining a union may seem particularly pointless to one who views his or her employment situation as temporary. Second, "policy" motives such as objections to the union's leadership, policies, or principles can be an important reason for refusing to join or quitting. As noted above, black workers in particular may be motivated by policy considerations in their orientation toward unions. Finally, there are "functional" motives which include the feeling that the union did not afford the individual appropriate treatment or provide desired assistance.

There is a lesson for organized labor in the dynamics of the individual's decision to join or refrain from joining unions. The American labor movement is faced with a number of challenges and economic shifts that seem to foster decline. There are some economic changes that it probably cannot do much about, such as

TERMS   **Macroeconomics**   The relationships among broad economic trends such as national income, consumer savings, employment, money supply, etc., as well as the government's role in affecting these trends.

TABLE 2-3.
AMERICAN WORKERS' BELIEFS ABOUT TRADE UNIONS[1]
(In Percent)

Belief	Strongly agree	Agree	Neither agree nor disagree	Disagree	Strongly disagree
Big-labor-image beliefs:					
Influence who gets elected to public office	37.5	46.0	1.8	12.7	1.1
Influence laws passed	24.0	56.6	3.8	14.4	1.2
Are more powerful than employers	24.8	41.6	6.2	25.4	2.0
Influence how the country is run	18.1	53.4	4.8	21.7	1.9
Require members to go along with decisions	18.5	56.0	3.9	20.1	1.6
Have leaders who do what's best for themselves	22.8	44.7	6.4	24.0	2.1
Instrumental beliefs:					
Protect workers against unfair practice	20.5	63.0	3.4	11.2	2.0
Improve job security	19.2	61.0	2.8	14.5	2.5
Improve wages	18.9	67.6	3.2	8.7	1.7
Give members their money's (dues) worth	6.9	38.5	6.3	36.9	11.3

[1]In the survey, 1515 workers were polled.
Source: Thomas A. Kochan, "How American Workers View Labor Unions," *Monthly Labor Review*, Vol. 102 No. 4 (April 1979), pp. 23–31.

the decline in its traditional bastion of strength, the manufacturing sector of the economy. However, unions can make themselves more appealing to workers by changing their images and policies somewhat. For instance, many would probably agree that as the AFL-CIO and its constituent unions have matured, the labor movement has been continuously hampered by its socially conservative attitudes. Others believe that unionism has been seriously damaged by corruption and even more so by the image of rampant corruption. Such criticisms suggest that the labor movement is no longer as widely considered the progressive force in society that it once was. This in turn suggests that despite its past commitment to "voluntarism," the labor movement will have to continue to play a progressive role in American politics and to develop new ways of promoting its ideals of justice for the individual worker.

POLITICAL INFLUENCE

As discussed in the previous chapter, the American labor movement eventually became well-grounded on the principle of voluntarism. The AFL, in particular, represented the triumph of "business unionism" and the belief that labor's success depended upon its economic power and its legal right to negotiate contracts with employers. Prior to the 1930s, with few exceptions (the abolition of child labor being the major one) the AFL shunned efforts to attain labor's objectives through federal legislation that would mandate substantive conditions in the workplace.

But it should be remembered that voluntarism was always intended to be the beginning, not the end, of labor's influence on society. In Samuel Gompers' words: "economic power is the basis upon which may be developed power in other fields." Eventually, he thought, "when the economic movement has sufficiently developed so as to produce a unity of thought on all essentials . . . a political labor movement will be the result." Gompers' idea of voluntarism as the bedrock of labor's influence was challenged and eventually modified by the emergence of industrial unionism, as led by the CIO, during the 1930s.

Eventually, the merger of the AFL and the CIO in 1955 represented a joining of the two strands of labor's thought on political involvement and political influence. The AFL, already involved in politics, had become keenly aware that the economic power of unions had reached the point where it could be translated into political influence generally. The CIO had long perceived that the industrial worker could not rely upon collective bargaining alone, but needed to exercise political influence as well to obtain the kind of legislation that would improve the lot of the working class in general. Together, at the time of the merger, the AFL and CIO formed the **Committee on Political Education,** which over the years has become labor's major vehicle for exercising influence in electoral politics. But to exercise influence, one needs a theory, ideology, or set of values to guide one's action.

It is customary to view the American labor movement as non-ideological, especially in comparison with labor movements and labor political parties in some other industrialized democracies. However, this does not mean that American labor has no general political orientation. It does. Perhaps the broadest terms of this orientation were laid out by Gompers himself when he said: "I do not value the labor movement only for its ability to give higher wages, better clothes, and better homes. Its ultimate goal is to be found in the progressively evolving life possibilities for those who work and in its devotion to advancing the basic idea of freedom for all people everywhere." Using this broad orientation, we can subdivide labor's general political outlook into at least three categories.

First, labor favors the specific economic advancement of workers through substantive legislation and collective bargaining. In legislative terms, this means that labor is likely to be in favor of such legislation as minimum wage laws and measures to reduce unemployment and the hardship caused by it. It is no surprise, therefore, that during the early 1980s, the AFL-CIO supported such measures as a thirteen-week extension of unemployment benefits in states with high unemployment, a program to encourage the Department of Defense to award contracts to firms in areas with high unemployment, a public works program to reduce unemployment, various cost of living adjustments for retired workers, and retention of the **Davis-Bacon** prevailing wage policy which helps bolster the pay of workers in highway construction and repair programs. In addition, during the late 1970s, labor strongly supported two legislative measures aimed at strengthening its position in collective bargaining. One was the "common situs" bill (1977), which would have allowed greater picketing rights at

TERMS   **Committee on Political Education**   This formally nonpartisan organization is led by members of the AFL-CIO's Executive Council and has the responsibility, as spelled out in the AFL-CIO Constitution, of "encouraging workers to register and vote, to exercise their full rights and responsibilities of citizenship, and to perform their rightful part in the political life of the city, state and national communities."

Davis-Bacon Act   A federal law which requires contractors on federal construction projects to pay the rates of pay and fringe benefits that prevail in their geographic area.

construction sites (see Chapter 4). The other was a broader effort at labor law reform which would have made it easier for labor to organize workers by allowing union organizers to engage in organizing activity on the employer's property. It also included provisions to strengthen the authority of the National Labor Relations Board to levy sanctions upon employers who engaged in unfair delaying tactics to prevent unionization. Labor's defeat on both of these **bills** was a severe blow to its political influence and agenda.

Second, Gompers' statement indicates that labor is committed to broad social welfare concerns. Thus, among the measures strongly suported by the AFL-CIO over the past decades have been civil rights legislation, child nutrition legislation, the creation of a consumer protection agency, legal services for the poor, and a variety of expansions in the food stamp program. In the early 1980s, it continued to support social welfare legislation of this type, concentrating specifically on increased **Medicare** and **Medicaid** funding, subsidies for home mortgage interest rates, higher funding for educational programs, and targeting tax cuts to middle and lower income taxpayers.

Third, and perhaps most controversial, labor has supported foreign policy initiatives that further its understanding of "advancing the basic idea of freedom for all people everywhere." In operational terms, this has tended to sometimes make the labor movement virulently anticommunistic to the point that it has been aligned on some foreign policy issues with political conservatives who oppose its domestic programs.

Inevitably, any organization or movement manifesting such a broad threefold political orientation will be forced to deviate from its general objectives on occasion. This is more a matter of practical politics than of inconsistency. The AFL-CIO as a union of unions projects solidarity among the unions affiliated with it on many issues. But sometimes these constituent groups simply disagree with one another. Some recent examples include: the split between some unions over support for a bill aimed at protecting

TERMS **Bill** A proposed law is a "bill" from the time it is introduced in Congress until its passage by both houses. Then it becomes an "act" which only becomes a law if the President signs it.

Medicare The national health insurance program for the elderly and the disabled.

Medicaid The federally aided, state operated and administered program which provides medical benefits for certain low-income persons in need of health and medical care.

the union pension funds through greater federal regulation; the deep division within the American Federation of Teachers over whether or not day care facilities should be organized as part of the schools; and the successful opposition to federal land use planning legislation by the United Brotherhood of Carpenters despite support for its passage by the AFL-CIO.

Even labor's overall idealism and its primary self-interest are not always harmonious. For instance, while labor may be broadly committed to a better environment, it nevertheless supported both the Alaska pipeline and the development of the supersonic transport plane because jobs were involved. Similarly, the United Auto Workers, which has long been viewed as progressive and committed to social welfare, has favored the relaxation of auto emission standards. While this might help sell more automobiles by keeping prices down, it would surely contribute to air pollution. Presently "acid rain" is an environmental issue of the sort that divides labor.

Over the years, however, the AFL-CIO has done relatively well in keeping the broad labor coalition together, though some major unions, including the United Mine Workers and the Teamsters, have left its ranks. Perhaps its general success has been due to the fact that its broad orientation and its specific self-interests often mesh nicely. Thus, it has been observed that better schools create construction and teaching jobs; better housing also requires building; and, social welfare programs generally create greater consumption, which may be translated into more jobs at better pay.

POLITICAL ACTION   Overall, labor translates its broad objectives into specific political action in two ways. One is through electoral politics. The Committee on Political Education (COPE) plays a variety of roles in this context. As its name implies, part of its mission is to inform or educate members of unions affiliated with the AFL-CIO about political issues and candidates for public office. It does this at all levels of government. One of its techniques is to rate members of Congress in terms of votes for or against the interests of workers. It also sponsors analyses of political issues and produces reports on matters of public policy. COPE also seeks to register voters and influence them to cast their ballots for prolabor candidates.

However, COPE's activities go well beyond informing voters, rating legislators, and endorsing candidates. It also makes financial contributions to candidates' electoral campaigns. Federal election laws allow "Political Action Committees" to make contributions to candidates for federal office, but the funding must be reported to the Federal Election Commission. Labor as a whole gives millions of dollars in this fashion during each election cycle. The vast majority of labor's funding and endorsements go to Democratic Party members, but to view organized labor as merely an adjunct of that party is too simplistic.

The AFL-CIO does not support every Democratic candidate. Rather, it is generally aligned with the Democrats because, historically, they have been more prolabor and more pro–welfare state than have the Republicans. Nevertheless, when labor finds a Democratic candidate wanting, it may very well withhold endorsement and financial support. One striking example in recent memory was the 1972 election, when the AFL-CIO, which was much closer to McGovern than to Nixon on most economic issues, refused to endorse McGovern because of differences on such issues as foreign policy, "permissiveness" in general, and sexual deviance. More recently, COPE's threats to grant or withhold financial support on the basis of key legislative votes in Congress has touched off an acerbic debate on the appropriateness of such an approach. Some view it as self-defeating since, as in the 1972 election, it may lead to the election of more candidates who are hostile to labor. It also appears too crude and heavy-handed to members of Congress. On the other hand, in the late 1970s, COPE's director pointed out that "we want them [candidates for Congress] to understand they can't take our support for granted; we're putting them on notice."

COPE's frustration with some of the candidates it supports is symptomatic of a more general problem facing labor since it aligned with the Democrats during the post–New Deal period. The AFL-CIO can influence the party; but the party can also influence labor—especially since nowadays, organized labor seems to have no other partisan organization to which to turn on a national basis. One strategy labor may pursue to break out of this dilemma is to support prolabor candidates in *primary* elections, thus exercising greater influence on candidate recruitment and selection. It followed this approach in 1984 by endorsing Walter Mondale at an early stage. But there are potential risks in doing this generally. Backing a losing candidate in a primary could be quite awkward in terms of future influence with whomever is eventually elected. Moreover, when labor puts itself on the electoral line, it runs the risk of not being able to deliver its members' votes. Perhaps nothing has harmed labor's political influence so much in recent years as the growing belief that the leadership's political stance no longer dominates the typical member's voting behavior.

Many believe that labor needs to refine its political image.

Rather than appear to be selfishly motivated, labor might do better by being better understood. It has often been pointed out that the meaning of unions is not widely understood. Nor is the beneficial effect that unions have on everyone's standard of living widely appreciated. This is a key, perhaps, to why labor has done better in promoting general social welfare and civil rights legislation than on some items of crucial and specific importance to itself such as the 1977 common situs bill and the 1978 labor law reform bill.

Another means of translating broad political orientations into specific action is through lobbying efforts. The AFL-CIO maintains a "legislative department" that performs this function. It is viewed as highly professional and potent, though it seems to be most influential in issue areas, such as civil rights, that are of less *direct* importance to labor's legislative program. The hallmark of AFL-CIO lobbying in Congress seems to be their lobbyists' numbers and physical presence. They explain labor's position on a variety of bills and seek to win members of Congress over to their position on bills supported by labor. In practice, they often provide members of Congress with the text of bills drafted by the AFL-CIO legislative department. Labor's lobbyists may work closely with sympathetic staff of congressional committees to facilitate the movement of a bill through the legislative process.

AFL-CIO lobbyists make an effort to retain credibility by not engaging in a "hard sell," but rather by explaining labor's position in comprehensive, informed, and logical terms. To this end, the legislative department's activities are kept separate from COPE's campaign funding operations. Despite their many successes, however, labor's lobby seems to be developing a losing image. It has failed where it counts most: on Taft-Hartley in 1947; on efforts to repeal it in the 1960s; and on granting public employees greater political rights, common situs, and labor law reform in the 1970s.

Inevitably, in a nation such as the United States, labor's political influence will be related to two general factors. One is the size and unity of its membership. Declines have occurred in both of these dimensions and it is not clear that labor can fully recoup its losses in view of the changing nature of the American economy. However, a second dimension offers almost limitless opportunities. Labor can exercise moral suasion by advocating causes which benefit not only its members and leaders, but also promote social justice. Historically, its record in this regard is strong—at least as strong as any other major interest group in the society. And certainly it should be at the peak of its influence when it reminds the society and governmental leaders of their moral obligations. A striking example of this occurred when the AFL-CIO Executive

Council called upon Americans to accept the "inescapable moral responsibility to do all that it can to aid the Vietnamese refugees who are now entering our country." Because it found "a meanness of spirit unworthy of the American people" in the words of some political leaders regarding the refugees, it asked union members everywhere "to make these refugees of communist aggression welcome in their communities." Now that's moral leadership!

REVIEW QUESTIONS

1. Can the "decline" of the labor movement in terms of proportion of workers who belong to unions be interpreted as a success in some ways? Have workers become so well off that they no longer need collective bargaining?

2. Has the political action of the AFL-CIO tended to replace the "voluntarism" associated with its original outlook? Has the AFL-CIO more or less embraced "welfare unionism" by lobbying for legislation that protects and advances workers' economic and social status?

3. How and why do social divisions in the United States make it difficult to achieve labor "solidarity"?

4. Why has the "sun belt" been resistant to unionization?

5. In what ways does collective bargaining seem suitable to the "postindustrial" age? In what ways unsuitable?

6. Would you join a union? Why or why not?

7. What are the major differences between the public employee and the private employee in terms of unionization?

8. Has the Democratic Party coopted the AFL-CIO? Has the AFL-CIO coopted the Democratic Party? What does their continuing association portend for the labor movement?

FOR ADDITIONAL READING

Bracy, John, Jr., August Meier, and Elliott Rudwick, eds. *The Black Worker and Organized Labor.* Belmont, CA.: Wadsworth, 1971.

Estey, Marten. *The Unions,* Second Edition. New York: Harcourt, Brace & Jovanovich, 1976.

Foner, Philip S. *Organized Labor and the Black Worker.* New York: Praeger, 1974.

Gersham, Carl. *The Foreign Policy of American Labor.* Beverly Hills, CA.: Sage, 1975.

Greenstone, J. David. *Labor in American Politics.* Chicago: University of Chicago Press, 1977.

Hutchinson, John. *The Imperfect Union.* New York: E. P. Dutton, 1970.

Juris, Hervey A. and Myron Roomkin, eds. *The Shrinking Perimeter.* Lexington, MA.: Lexington Books, 1980.

Levine, Marvin J. and Eugene C. Hagburg. *Labor Relations in the Public Sector.* Salt Lake City: Brighton, 1979.

Parmet, Robert D. *Labor and Immigrator in Industrial America.* Boston: Twayne Publishers, 1981.

Shafritz, Jay M., Albert C. Hyde, and David H. Rosenbloom, *Personnel Management in Government,* Revised and Expanded Edition. New York: Marcel Dekker, 1981.

Shafritz, Jay M. *Dictionary of Personnel Management and Labor Relations.* Oak Park, IL: Moore Publishing, 1980.

van de Vall, Mark. *Labor Organizations.* Cambridge: Cambridge University Press, 1970.

3 The Evolution of Labor Law

Prologue
Equal Rights at Work

Congressman Howard "Judge" Smith of Virginia was 81 years old when he "invented" sexual harassment. As chairman of the House Rules Committee in 1964, "Judge" Smith was one of the most powerful men in Congress. And as unlikely a hero as the women's movement will ever have.

Smith was a classic southern conservative bigot. He totally opposed all civil rights efforts, but with a deceptive grace. In 1957 he was able to stall the Civil Rights Act of that year by leaving Washington, reportedly to inspect a "burned barn" on his farm in nearby Virginia. Upon learning of Smith's absence, which prevented the Congress from moving on the legislation, the Speaker of the House, Sam Rayburn, remarked, "I knew Howard Smith would do almost anything to block a civil rights bill, but I never suspected he would resort to arson."

Sex discrimination in employment was by no means a significant concern of the civil rights advocates of the early 1960s. Its prohibition only became part of the Civil Rights Act of 1964 because of "Judge" Smith. As the leader of the South's fight against civil rights, he added one small word—sex—to prohibitions against discrimination based on race, color, religion, and national origin. He felt confident this amendment would make the proposed law ridiculous and cause its defeat. Smith was an "old style" bigot: to his mind the one thing more ridiculous than equal rights for blacks was equal rights for women.

The "sex discrimination" amendment was opposed by the Women's Bureau of the Department of Labor, by the American Association of University Women, and by most of the Congress' leading liberals. They saw it as nothing but a ploy to discourage passage of the new civil rights law. The major support for adopting the amendment came from the reactionary southern establishment of the day. Because President Lyndon Johnson insisted that the Senate make practically no changes in the law as passed by the House, there was no discussion of sex discrimination by the Senate. The momentum for a new civil rights law was so great that Smith's addition not only failed to scuttle the bill, but went largely unnoticed.

The legal foundation for the modern women's movement was passed with almost no debate or media attention, and with the support of the most reactionary members of Congress. Could Smith and his supporters have realized the true impact of what they were doing, they would have certainly sought to withdraw the amendment before the final vote. But this was 1964; nobody then could have imagined the outcome.

Although the sex discrimination prohibition was included in the new civil rights law almost in secret, word quickly got out. The new law brought into being the Equal Employment Opportunity Commission to enforce its various provisions. During the first year of the new commission's operation, over one-third of all of the complaints it received dealt with sex discrimination in employment. Over the next two decades, "Judge" Smith's unintended gift to the nation's women became the judicial reference for countless court cases and out-of-court settlements. Today, thanks to Smith, there are hardly any jobs from which a woman can be legally barred if she can perform as well as a man. And vice versa.

When the Civil Rights Act of 1964 prohibited sex discrimination in employment, there wasn't anybody who would have said or implied that the new law had anything to do with sexual harassment. The phrase "sexual harassment" wasn't even in the language. Yet today, for all legal purposes, sex discrimination includes sexual harassment. A few courageous women enlarged the meaning of the law because they were mad enough about unwarranted sexual pressures to "go public" and test their novel interpretation of sex discrimination in federal court.

When a federal district court judge ruled that it was sex discrimination to abolish a woman's job because she refused her male supervisor's sexual advances, the Court of Appeals affirmed that sexual harassment was sex discrimination when a woman's job "was conditional upon submission to sexual relations—an exaction which the superior would not have sought from any male." The Court of Appeals has even held an employer liable merely for tolerating a working environment conducive to sexual harassment.

In 1980, after the federal courts decided that sexual harassment was sex discrimination, the Equal Employment Opportunity Commission—the federal agency responsible for enforcing sex discrimination prohibitions—took formal action. It issued legally binding rules clearly stating that an employer has a responsibility to provide a place of work that is free from sexual harassment or intimidation. And a company can be held responsible for sexual harassment by its employees whether or not supervisors knew of the harassment.

The Civil Rights Act of 1964 was the most far reaching regulation of labor relations since the National Labor Relations Act of 1935. It is a good example of the kind of protective legislation for which working men and women have long fought. It is also a good example of how the federal courts make public policy—how they can take a piece of legislation and make it out to be something that nobody ever thought it would be.

THE CONTINUING EVOLUTION OF LABOR LAW AND REGULATION

Law has long been an important feature of labor relations in the western world. One could even view the religious idea of keeping the Sabbath, or the Lord's day, holy as a labor contract. During the Dark Ages, when the bubonic plague created a serious manpower shortage, attempting to hire away another employer's workman by offering higher wages was a serious offense. Even before the advent of the industrial revolution, England had defined the relationship between master and servant in **statutory** terms. Later, as the industrial revolution proceeded, virtually all nations found it necessary to exercise legal controls over behavior in the workplace. As the United States was no exception, American labor relations have long taken place within the framework of law. Courts, judges, and legislatures have been instrumental in determining the evolving character of labor relations. In the process,

TERMS   **Statutory**   Referring to laws passed by legislatures. A statute is such a law.

they have adopted new policies and discarded older ones in an effort to resolve what is the great dilemma of modern capitalist societies: how can each person vigorously pursue economic self-interest without violating the interests of society as a whole? What kinds of economic behavior are acceptable expressions of self-interest, and what kinds are to be construed as a violation of the public interest?

U. S. Supreme Court Justice **Oliver Wendell Holmes** captured the crux of this dilemma in the context of American labor relations by framing the issue as follows: "One of the eternal conflicts out of which life is made up is that between the effort of every man to get the most he can for his services, and that of society, disguised under the name of capital, to get his services for the least possible return." When looked upon in this light, it is evident that virtually anything an individual working person (or combination of workers) does to raise wages can be construed as antisocial. On the other hand, the American economic system is clearly premised on the notion that each person should have the freedom to choose to work for one employer or another and should be allowed to promote his or her economic self-interest by seeking higher pay. The law first addressed this dilemma by delineating illegal and legal labor practices. Then the law sought to establish a framework through which disputes between labor and capital could be peacefully resolved in the public interest. But the law's evolution did not come easily or even peacefully.

Early unionization efforts were hampered substantially by the law. The "law" of labor relations in the last century was almost entirely what is known as common law; that is, law made by judges applying what they perceive to be the fundamental principles embodied in previous judicial decisions. These principles of common law are not to be found in statutes; they are the reflections of the fundamental political, economic, and social values of the society at large, as distilled through legal reasoning. The common law's virtues also tend to be its vices. Because it is flexible in defining illegal behavior, it can punish antisocial acts that have not been foreseen by legislatures and are therefore not specifically prohibited by statute. At the same time, however, it places great emphasis on what a court or judge thinks is "antisocial" and punishable. In a famous

TERMS   **Oliver Wendell Holmes** (1841–1935)   Associate Justice of the U. S. Supreme Court from 1902 to 1932. He was a strong advocate of judicial restraint who was known as "The Great Dissenter" because of his often brilliant dissenting opinions.

passage, **Jeremy Bentham** addressed this aspect of common law as being equivalent to "dog law":

> When your dog does anything you want to break him of, you wait till he does it, and then beat him for it. This is the way you make laws for your dog: and this is the way the judges make law for you and me. They won't tell a man beforehand what it is he should not do—they won't so much as allow of his being told; they lie by till he has done something which they say he should not have done, and then they hang him for it.

Bentham went on to explain that the judiciary's response to the charge of administering "dog law" was more or less, "watch our cases, and you will understand common law." But Bentham's England was not a federal government. In the United States, watching the common law required watching it in every state, and perhaps at the federal level as well. For the common law could vary remarkably from one state to another, and this presented a major barrier to the organization of a *national* labor organization or trade union as well as to the development of a national labor policy.

It is against this background that the evolution of American labor law is best understood. First, movement from common law to statutory law was required so that workers, unions, and employers could hope to know what their rights were. Second, movement from state to federal statutory law would be required if national unions and nationwide corporations were to have fruitful labor relations. And all the while, the law, common and statutory, would have to draw lines between acceptable selfish economic behavior and unacceptable antisocial economic behavior.

It is fair to say that the common law was rather tough on labor. In England, it flatly adhered to a double standard, making business combinations in restraint of trade acceptable while at the same time making illegal the efforts of labor unions to advance their economic interests through collective action. In the United States, the situation was more varied, but still hostile to unionization.

TERMS   **Jeremy Bentham** (1748–1832)   A utilitarian philosopher who held that self-interest was the prime motivator and that a government should strive to do the greatest good for the greatest numbers.

From the Cordwainer's decision in 1806 until the Massachusetts case of *Commonwealth v. Hunt* in 1842, combinations of workers—that is, unions—by their very existence were considered to be illegal criminal conspiracies under common law. Unions were viewed as combinations in restraint of trade intended to visit economic harm upon their employers, or perhaps upon other workers—organized or unorganized. There is of course a great deal of truth in the charge that unions can have the effect of restraining trade. The closed shop, the strike, boycotts, and bargaining for a fixed wage scale on behalf of a group of employees all restrain trade. But Judge **Lemuel Shaw** in 1842 ruled that was not sufficient reason to consider them criminal conspiracies. Rather, according to Massachusetts common law, the test of criminality involved a weighing of means and ends: combinations to advance one's economic status were not automatically illegal, but they had to advance this interest through the use of legal means.

This is "dog law" at its best (or worst), because it boils down to the right to have a union as long as it does not pursue unspecified illegal ends by unspecified illegal means. Nevertheless, this 1842 case marked a general turning point in labor relations law. Henceforth, unions were generally legal; but any of their "normal" activities might be considered illegal in any particular **jurisdiction.**

This situation invited the various state courts to develop differences of opinion, which is precisely what they did. The difficulties of regulating labor relations through common law can be seen by comparing the situation in two states: Massachusetts and New York. In the 1880s they were both industrial, they both had major sea ports, they both had large populations, and presumably, both had competent judges. Nonetheless, they developed rather polarized common law interpretations of the rights of unions.

Massachusetts evolved what might be called the "illegal purpose" doctrine under which the lawfulness of an act by a union depended upon the union's intent. Thus, even though the means were legal, the act could be considered illegal depending upon its

---

TERMS   **Lemuel Shaw** (1781–1861)   The Chief Justice of the Supreme Judicial Court of Massachusetts from 1830 to 1860 who wrote the landmark decision of *Commonwealth v. Hunt* (1842).

Jurisdiction   The geographical area within which a court, public official, union, etc., has the right and power to operate.

purpose. Under this approach, it was not the activity but rather the purpose or intent with which it was undertaken that was at issue. So it became not a matter of what a union did, but why it did it that the court had to decide. After divining the union's intent, the court then had to determine whether its intent was illegal; that is, was it sufficiently antisocial to be punishable?

The New York approach, in contrast, was much clearer in its standards and provided unions with greater room for collective action. The New York judges tended to adhere to one of two lines of reasoning. The first was that collective action by unions in pursuit of economic gain was lawful, unless it involved action that was *specifically* illegal. For example, a physical assault on the employer would be an illegal action, but an economic assault, such as a strike, would be legal. A second line of reasoning followed the Massachusetts fixation with intent, but allowed intentional harm to others if justified by the union's desire for economic self-advancement and self-protection.

The differing Massachusetts and New York approaches reflected basic differences over what the policy of the law with regard to labor relations should be. Different states could choose their own policies as long as the economy was not truly integrated on a national basis. But these common law policies date from the 1880s and 1890s. The cross-continental railroad system had been largely built and further improvements in transportation were in the offing. Soon, raw materials and finished products would cross state lines many times before reaching their final destinations. The differing state labor relations policies would clearly become an obstacle to economic development in the future. Given the situation it was inevitable that the federal government would have to become involved. Federal labor laws, laws that would be the same in each state, would be necessary in the future; and federal law could only come by statute.

THE INJUNCTION   Ironically, the first major federal law aimed specifically and comprehensively at labor relations, the Norris-LaGuardia Act of 1932, sought not only to overcome the vagaries of state common law at some points, but also to curtail a very abusive device—the judicial injunction against labor actions. Although Bentham may have suggested that the judges were totally free to make their "dog law," this was not altogether true. Sometimes they had to contend with juries, and juries by the 1900s might have been friendly to unions. The AFL at this time was certainly mild-mannered enough to warrant some sympathy from the common man. So what was a conservative, antiunion judge to do when union activities threatened an employer's physical property? For immediate relief, he could issue an injunction.

An injunction is a judicial device issued to prevent someone from harming another in some irreparable fashion. It is used when it appears that the harmful behavior is illegal and is issued by a judge, without benefit of a jury. The injunction is usually temporary at first, pending a fuller judicial consideration of whether the irreparable harm is in fact illegal. If it is determined to be illegal, then the injunction is made permanent. For example, if two farmers have a dispute over their property line and one wants to cut down all the trees in the disputed area, there is a situation in which irreparable harm (the loss of the trees, soil erosion, change in the water table) and illegal behavior (trespass) might occur. A court could issue a temporary injunction against the farmer proposing to play lumberjack and make it permanent if it turns out that he or she does not own the land in question. The virtue of the injunction is that it protects one from a loss that cannot be replaced after the fact through an award of money damages. In other words, the farmer who lost his trees could be compensated, but he could not be **made whole** in his lifetime because it simply would take too long for the trees to grow back.

Enough of trees. In the context of labor relations the injunction can be used to prevent a union from destroying an employer's property. In the heat of a strike, windows, buildings, machinery and so forth might be damaged. An employer might reasonably seek legal action through an injunction to prevent such happenstances. Arguably, the employer could be compensated after the fact, but the participating employees and union were unlikely to have sufficient funds to pay for the damage. Moreover, replacement of machines and buildings might take so long that the employer's business would lose customers and truly be irreparably injured.

By the 1890s, the courts and employers had discovered how useful the injunction was to curtail virtually any threatened or real show of economic and organizational force by unions. Criminal prosecution and civil suits for damages were cumbersome and took too long. Besides, they deprived judges of control over unions because they could never be sure that juries would convict. But the

TERMS   **Make Whole**   A legal remedy that provides for an injured party to be placed, as near as may be possible, in the situation he or she would have occupied if the wrong had not been committed.

injunction was a device that could insure swift justice, and the courts had complete control over it. The earlier idea that the irreparable injury had to be to physical property was largely discarded and injunctions were issued to prevent harm to what amounted to no more than business "interests." Moreover, judges were prone to issuing injunctions without hearing from the union and not paying particular attention to whether the action involved was actually illegal. Under these conditions, and for the right people, these temporary restraining orders (injunctions) were "for the asking." In this way, strikes, boycotts, picketing, and other concerted union actions could be prevented or stopped in short order.

But the injunction was only one step in the exercise of judicial power over union activities. Union leaders and members who violated an injunction could be held in **contempt** of court. And contempt of this kind was punishable by imprisonment without a jury trial. Moreover, ignorance of the existence of an injunction was no excuse for violating it. Many courts were prone to make a temporary injunction permanent with a minimum of **due process**. One mitigating factor was that the efficacy and uses of the injunction varied from state to state. However, even federal judges were inclined to use the device against union activities when interstate commerce was involved.

This discussion of legal policy prior to the enactment of the major federal labor relations statutes helps to illustrate a number of points against which the further development of labor law must be considered. First, the common law was useful in defining legal versus illegal union activity. The fact that it varied from state to state allowed experimentation and permitted the more liberal courts to try to draw a line between acceptable self-interested economic behavior and antisocial behavior. Second, the common law did not prove particularly helpful in erecting a framework for positive and peaceful ongoing labor relations. Third, the injunction demonstrated the difficulties of leaving labor relations up to judges. They were too inclined to favor employers, which made effective collective bargaining tenuous by depriving labor of its most effective tools. Overall, the common law approach was given

TERMS   **Contempt**   A willful disobeying of a judge's command or official court order.

Due Process   The due process clause of the U. S. Constitution requires that "no person shall be deprived of life, liberty, or property without due process of law." While the specific requirements of due process vary with new Supreme Court decisions, the essence of the idea is that individuals must be given adequate notice and a fair opportunity to present their side in a legal dispute and that no law or government procedure should be arbitrary or unfair.

ample time to demonstrate its utility. However, it was the judgment of the federal government during the 1930s that this approach had failed.

THE LANDMARKS OF LABOR LAW

The purposes of federal labor relations law can be stated simply: (1) to define the rights of labor and the rights of management, (2) to create a legal and administrative framework for ongoing labor relations in the public interest, and (3) to seek to assure that unions are democratic organizations free of corruption. The ultimate purpose is to strengthen the national economy.

The Sherman Anti-Trust Act of 1890

The Sherman Anti-Trust Act of 1890 was a congressional reaction to the growth of monopolies in heavy industries during the 1880s. It prohibits contracts, combinations, or conspiracies (price fixing is an example) that restrain trade or commerce. It is still unclear whether Congress ever intended the act to apply to unions, but in the judicial climate of the times this result was perhaps all but inevitable. The U. S. Supreme Court seized the opportunity to use the act against the United Hatters of America Union, which had organized a **boycott** against retailers selling nonunion-made hats. The case, *Loewe v. Lawlor* (1908), usually referred to as the Danbury hatters case, made secondary labor boycotts (that is, boycotts of the seller or user of a nonunion product rather than the actual employer of nonunion labor) illegal.

The Clayton Anti-Trust Act of 1914

The Clayton Anti-Trust Act of 1914 was the response of the Congress to labor's lobbying efforts to gain a statutory exemption from the Sherman Act. It was hailed at the time as labor's **Magna Charta** because it would have enabled labor to engage in activities which restrained trade as long as they were lawful and peaceful. Indeed, the act says that labor is not a "commodity or article of commerce" (section 6). However, through a peculiar line of

---

TERMS   **Boycott**   The refusal to do business with, and the attempt to stop others from doing business with, a company. In labor law, a primary boycott involves a union and an employer while a secondary boycott involves companies that do business (usually buying from) the union's employer.

Magna Charta   This was the charter of liberties that English nobles forced from King John in 1215; now the term is also used to refer to any document offering fundamental guarantees of rights.

reasoning, the Supreme Court held, in *Duplex Printing Co. v. Dearing* (1921), that the Clayton Act permitted only what was legal under the Sherman Act! In other words, at best the Clayton Act merely affirmed the legality of labor unions; it did not convey to them the right to engage in concerted action that restrained trade. Here is another example of the federal courts taking a piece of legislation that "everybody" thinks means one thing and deciding that it means something else.

The Railway Labor Act of 1926

The railroads had long been a focal point of labor difficulty. Moreover, there was no doubt of their importance to interstate commerce and the nation's economic development. If stable labor relations were desirable anywhere, it was here. Congress responded with a series of statutes beginning in 1888 intended to create a positive framework for resolving railroad disputes and facilitating collective bargaining. The Arbitration Act of 1888 encouraged voluntary arbitration by a presidentially appointed three-man board. The **Erdman Act** of 1898 banned interstate railroads from discriminating against union members. Additional statutes defined some labor-management rights and provided for public intervention in resolving disputes that could not be settled by the unions and employers themselves. The Railway Labor Act of 1926 placed many of these provisions in a single statute. It included protection of the right of railroad employees to unionize and created a positive obligation for employers to engage in collective bargaining with these unions. The act, which was amended in 1934 to include the airline industry, served as a model for more general federal collective bargaining legislation during the 1930s and 1940s. Its provisions are quite similar to those of the National Labor Relations Act (discussed later).

The Norris-LaGuardia Act of 1932

Back in 1896, Justice Holmes issued one of the commonsensical observations, reducing a complex issue to a few syllables, for which he later became famous. He observed that in the conflict between capital and labor, "combination on the one side is patent and powerful. Combination on the other is the necessary and desirable counterpart, if the battle is to be carried on in a fair and equal way." It took the federal government until 1932 to come to the

TERMS   **Erdman Act of 1898**   Ten years later this act would be declared unconstitutional by the Supreme Court in *Adair v. United States* (1908).

same conclusion. The Norris-LaGuardia Act took the point of view that an imbalance of power between labor and employers was damaging to the economy as well as to concepts of fundamental fairness. Consequently, it guaranteed labor's right to organize and to seek to negotiate contracts through their representatives. The act outlawed the so-called **yellow dog contract** through which employers required workers to agree that they would not join or support labor unions. It also severely limited the power of the federal courts to issue injunctions against labor actions such as ordinary strikes, picketing, and boycotts. While the act did not establish an administrative framework for continuing government intervention and oversight in the labor relations process, this would come three years later.

The National Labor The National Labor Relations Act of 1935, popularly known as
Relations Act of 1935 the Wagner Act, remains the federal government's most general law for establishing and maintaining a framework for collective bargaining in private industry. The act followed the general patterns already emerging under the Railway Labor Act and the Norris-LaGuardia Act, but it went much further.

In 1933, Congress passed what was at the time considered the backbone of the New Deal plan for economic recovery—the National Industrial Recovery Act (NIRA). Section 7(a) of the act guaranteed labor's right to organize and engage in collective bargaining. But two years later the Supreme Court declared most of the act unconstitutional on the grounds that it delegated legislative power to executive branch agencies in violation of the **separation of powers.** It is debatable whether the NIRA was comprehensive enough to provide a lasting framework for labor relations. Nevertheless, by the time it was declared unconstitutional, the nation was ready for a comprehensive federal collective bargaining statute. It came in the form of the Wagner Act, which did the following:

1. Guaranteed the right of employees to form and join unions, to engage in collective bargaining through their designated

TERMS   **Yellow Dog Contract**   So called because only a cowardly "yellow dog" would sign one.

Separation of Powers   The arrangement under the U. S. Constitution whereby executive powers are exercised by the executive branch, legislative powers by the legislative branch, and judicial powers by the judicial branch. In some contexts, however, the different branches may share their powers.

representatives, and to participate in concerted coercive activities including primary strikes and primary picketing (that is, striking and picketing directly against the employer, rather than another party doing business with the employer).

2. Defined unfair (meaning illegal) labor practices for employers as those including:

   a. Interfering with, restraining, or coercing employees in the exercise of the rights mentioned above;

   b. Dominating or interfering with the formation of a union (included establishing or seeking to establish a **company union**);

   c. Discriminating against employees or applicants because of union membership, unless a closed shop or other **union security** arrangement had been negotiated with the union;

   d. Taking **adverse action** against an employee who filed an unfair labor practice charge against the employer, or testified against the employer in conjunction with the administrative procedures of the act;

   e. Refusing "to bargain collectively with the representatives of his employees."

3. Defined unfair labor practices for unions that might be tempted to use strong-arm tactics. They were forbidden to force or require "any person to cease using, selling, handling, transporting, or otherwise dealing in the products of any other producer, processor, or manufacturer, or to cease doing business with any other person." It also placed some limitations on picketing as a means of forcing employers to grant recognition to a particular union.

4. Included some exceptions for specific industries, primarily construction, with regard to union efforts to require the employer to hire unionized craft workers.

TERMS **Company Union** A union organized, financed, or otherwise dominated by an employer.

Union Security Generally, any agreement between an employer and a union that requires every employee in the bargaining unit, as a condition of employment, to be a member of the union or to pay a specified sum to the union for its bargaining services.

Adverse Action Any personnel action considered unfavorable to an employee, such as discharge, suspension, demotion, etc.

Forms of Union Security

1.   The Closed Shop. The employer agrees to hire only union members. The closed shop had been the normal relationship in the printing, construction, longshoring and certain other trades. The union finds jobs for its members and employees for the employer in need of them. The Taft-Hartley Act outlaws such agreements in all businesses in interstate commerce.

2.   The Union Shop. The employer may hire non-union members but such workers must join the union within a specified period of time, usually 30 days, and must maintain union membership while employed. The great bulk of union security clauses are union shop clauses.

3.   The Union Shop with Preferential Hiring. The employer must hire union members if available but may hire non-members if union members are not available. Non-members must join the union within a specified period of time and maintain union membership. This is also outlawed by the Taft-Hartley Act.

4.   The Modified Union Shop. Employees who are not union members at the time of signing the contract need not join the union, but all workers hired thereafter must join.

5.   Maintenance of Membership. All employees who are members of the union after a specified time after the contract is signed and all who later join the union must remain members in good standing during the life of the contract. Usually a 15-day withdrawal period is provided during which members may withdraw from the union if they choose.

6.   Preferential Hiring. The employer agrees to hire union members if available, but no one need remain a union member if he does not wish to.

7. The Agency Shop. The employees must either join the union, or, if they choose not to, pay to the union the amount of dues paid by union members.

Source: AFL-CIO.

The National Labor Relations Act also established the National Labor Relations Board to oversee the implementation of its provisions. The Board makes decisions on charges of unfair labor practices and rulings on the appropriateness of **bargaining units**. It also oversees **authorization elections** and certifies the results.

From a policy perspective, the National Labor Relations Act (NLRA) was a critically important development. It reaffirmed the position taken in the Norris-LaGuardia Act that greater equality in the strength of labor and management was necessary. The NLRA asserted that the inequality of the two sides and the patchwork pattern of collective bargaining were presenting a barrier to the flow of commerce and the nation's economic recovery as well as to further economic development. Thus, federal policy, which was earlier made by federal judges, was shifted fundamentally and on a continuing basis from hostility to collective bargaining to encouragement, indeed—requirement—of it. The constitutionality of the act was upheld in *NLRB v. Jones and Laughlin Steel Corp.* (1937).

With some exceptions, the act applies to any person or industry engaged in "commerce." Under the Constitution, this necessarily had to mean commerce among the states, or with foreign nations or Indian tribes since the federal government does not have power over other commerce in general. However, the national integration of the economy and recent Supreme Court doctrine

---

TERMS   **Bargaining Unit**   A group of employees, both union members and others, that have been recognized as appropriate for representation by a union for the purposes of collective bargaining. All of the employees in the bargaining unit are subsequently covered in the labor contract that the union negotiates on their behalf. Bargaining units may be as small as a handful of workers in a local shop or as large as the workforce of an entire industry.

Authorization Election   A poll conducted by the National Labor Relations Board (or other appropriate agency) to determine whether or not a particular group of employees will be represented by a particular union.

pertaining to "interstate commerce" have given the act very broad application.

The Taft-Hartley Act of 1947

The Taft-Hartley Act of 1947, formally the Labor-Management Relations Act, represented an important effort to restrain the rights and activities of labor unions. It was passed by Congress over a veto by President Truman and has always been strongly opposed by organized labor. The act followed a wave of major strikes that shook the economy in 1946. The strikes were related to the rapid demobilization of the nation's World War II military forces and the transition from wartime production. In addition, there were the pent-up demands that resulted from the sacrifices made by labor and its cooperation with management during the war. Nevertheless, the National Association of Manufacturers, the U.S. Chamber of Commerce, and other business groups were ready to seize the moment in seeking to convince a Republican controlled Congress and the public in general that organized labor had grown too strong. Consequently, it was "agreed" that labor was impeding commerce and threatening the nation's economic health and stability.

The Taft-Hartley Act amended the National Labor Relations Act in several respects. It outlawed the closed shop in general. It authorized states to pass so-called **right-to-work laws** that limit the kinds of union security arrangements that can be negotiated through collective bargaining. It enlarged the number of unfair practices that can be committed by labor. New prohibitions included the coercion of employees or others to join a union, failure to engage in collective bargaining, seeking to force an employer to recognize a union that was not **certified** by the National Labor Relations Board, and seeking to force an employer to pay for work not actually performed—**featherbedding.** The provisions against

TERMS   **Right-to-Work-Laws**   State laws that make it illegal for collective bargaining agreements to contain maintenance of membership, preferential hiring, union shop, or other clauses calling for compulsory union membership. Section 14(b) of the Taft-Hartley Act gave states the option of prohibiting the union or closed shop; twenty states have done so.

Certification   A formal determination by the National Labor Relations Board (or other appropriate agency) that a particular union is the majority choice of, and thus the exclusive bargaining agent for, a group of employees in a given bargaining unit.

Featherbedding   Any labor practice that requires an employer to pay for more workers than are truly needed for a job, or pay for work that is not

Why President Truman Vetoed the Taft-Hartley Bill

The amended Labor-Management Relations Act of 1947, better known as the Taft-Hartley Act, was sent to the White House for my signature on June 18. Two days later I vetoed the act. The veto message listed the objections to it: The bill was completely contrary to our national policy of economic freedom because it would result in more or less government intervention into the collective-bargaining process. Because of its legal complexities the act would become a source of time-consuming litigation which would encourage distrust and bitterness between labor and management. The bill was neither workable nor fair. The Taft-Hartley bill would go far toward weakening our trade-union movement by injecting political considerations into normal economic decisions. I reminded the members of the Congress of the recommendation for a step-by-step approach to the subject of labor legislation in my message on the state of the Union and had suggested the specific problems which we should treat immediately. What had been laid before me was a bill proposing drastic changes in our national labor policy first, before making a careful, non-partisan investigation of the entire field of labor-management relations.

The Senate overruled my veto on June 23, and the Labor-Management Relations Act of 1947 became the law of the land. I had done all within my power to prevent an injustice against the laboring men and women of the United States.

Source: Harry S. Truman, *Memoirs: Years of Trial and Hope*, Vol. II (New York: Doubleday, 1956), pp. 45–46.

secondary actions (including boycotts) were strengthened, a "no strike" clause became a mandatory subject for bargaining, and the Federal Mediation and Conciliation Service was created.

The act contained two additional provisions of great importance. In a mundane but almost revolutionary development, it made labor contracts enforceable in federal courts. More spectacularly, it provided for federal injunctions against strikes threatening to cause national emergencies. Such strikes can be prohibited for an eighty-day "cooling-off" period during which intensive federal efforts at resolving the dispute can be undertaken.

The Landrum-Griffin Act of 1959

Formally called the Labor-Management Reporting and Disclosure Act, the Landrum-Griffin Act of 1959 represented further regulation of labor union practices. In some ways the act demonstrated what Samuel Gompers feared most during the early days of the AFL. He thought that if labor became involved in politics, government would eventually become involved in the internal affairs of labor unions. That is precisely what the Landrum-Griffin Act does. It was enacted following a series of highly publicized congressional hearings on corruption and **racketeering** within labor unions. The act seeks to regulate the use of union funds and requires that unions engage in extensive reporting to the Department of Labor concerning their finances and administrative operations. It also seeks to establish democracy within union structures by requiring unions to adopt organizational constitutions and to conduct elections for union officials on a regular basis. Concomitant with these objectives, the act provides union members with a "bill of rights" to enable them to participate in union meetings, nominate candidates for union office, and campaign for them. Furthermore, the act strengthened federal provisions against secondary boycotts by prohibiting what are called "hot cargo" provisions. These are clauses in contracts providing that the employer would not discipline employees for failing to handle cargos that were the product of unfair labor practices or were from an employer whose work-

TERMS   performed. Featherbedding provisions in labor contracts usually have their origin in work rules that were once efficient but have become obsolete due to newer technology. Union leaders have often insisted on maintaining the older practices in order to protect the jobs of threatened workers. While the Taft-Hartley Act prohibits featherbedding, this prohibition has not been very useful because of the legal subtleties of defining featherbedding practices.

Racketeering   A broad term for using a union leadership position as a base for illegal or unethical activities.

force was on strike ("unfair labor practice" in this context might mean having been produced by nonunion workers).

PROTECTIVE LEGISLATION

The preceding discussion has concentrated on the development of national policies concerning collective bargaining and the passage of the various statutes that form the basic framework for labor relations throughout the United States. But while the Wagner Act and related statutes support unionization and collective bargaining, they do not guarantee any particular set of outcomes or conditions in the workplace. Consequently, the process of collective bargaining might fail to assure rights considered so fundamental by the government (and presumably by society), that all workers need direct protection through legislation. As a result, a number of "protective" laws have been enacted.

The Fair Labor Standards Act of 1938

The Fair Labor Standards Act of 1938 is the minimum wage and hours law. It originally provided for a minimum wage of 25 cents per hour and established the normal workweek as forty hours (with

TABLE 3-1.
FAIR LABOR STANDARDS ACT MINIMUM WAGE RATES

Legislation	Hourly Rate	Effective Date
Act of 1938	$ .25	Oct. 24, 1938
	.30	Oct. 24, 1939
	.40	Oct. 24, 1945
Amendment of 1949	.75	Jan. 25, 1950
1955	1.00	Mar. 1, 1956
1961	1.15	Sept. 3, 1961
	1.25	Sept. 3, 1963
1966	1.40	Feb. 1, 1967
	1.60	Feb. 1, 1968
1974	2.00	May 1, 1974
	2.10	Jan. 1, 1975
	2.30	Jan. 1, 1976
1977	2.65	Jan. 1, 1978
	2.90	Jan. 1, 1979
	3.10	Jan. 1, 1980
	3.35	Jan. 1, 1981

Source: The U.S. Department of Labor, Employment Standards Administration.

"time and a half" for overtime). It contained strong child labor prohibitions as well. The essential thrust of the act was to assure decency in the workplace in the sense of outlawing unconscionable exploitation, and to make sure that enough adults were able to earn a wage that would enable them to function as consumers, thereby creating demand and stimulating the economy. The act has been amended many times in order to make its coverage more inclusive and to periodically raise the minimum wage. The Supreme Court has held, in the case *National League of Cities v. Usery* (1976), that the act cannot be applied to state and local government employees. Thus, police and firefighters cannot take advantage of the act's overtime provisions.

The Equal Pay Act of 1963   The Equal Pay Act of 1963 prohibits employers from paying workers covered by the Fair Labor Standards Act a wage differential based on gender. Thus, in principle, women cannot be paid less than men for doing the same work. Nevertheless, since some occupations, such as nursing, tend to be "sex segregated," women may still fail to be paid equally for work of **comparable worth.** This has emerged as a major issue in public employment. Many argue that wage rates in sex segregated occupations ought to reflect the nature of the job skills, levels of education, and so forth; rather than just the pressures of supply and demand in the labor market.

The Civil Rights Act of 1964   As amended by the Equal Employment Opportunity Act of 1972, the Civil Rights Act of 1964 prohibits discrimination based on race, color, religion, national origin (ethnicity), or sex (which the federal courts have expanded to include sexual harassment) in most public and private employment. The act applies to discrimination by unions as well as by employers. It is enforced by the

TERMS   **Comparable Worth**   Providing equitable compensation for performing work of a comparable value as determined by the relative worth of a given job to an organization. The basic issue of comparable worth is whether Title VII of the Civil Rights Act makes it unlawful for an employer to pay one sex at a lesser rate than the other when job performance is of comparable worth or value. For example, should beginning librarians with a master's degree be paid less than beginning managers with a master's degree? Historically, librarians have been paid less than occupations of "comparable worth" because they were considered "female" jobs. Comparable worth as a legal concept and as a social issue directly challenges traditional and market assumptions about the worth of jobs.

Equal Employment Opportunity Commission and the federal courts.

The Occupational Safety and Health Act of 1970

The Occupational Safety and Health Act of 1970 created the Occupational Safety and Health Administration (OSHA), which has been embroiled in controversy virtually since its inception. OSHA tries to eliminate hazards from the workplace, including noxious materials and unsafe physical conditions. In the view of many, OSHA has spent too much time seeking to eliminate minor hazards and has given the appearance of harassing employers. Yet, its job is staggering and many of the questions it faces—such as how many parts per million of a substance in the air at the workplace constitute a health hazard—are extremely technical. There is no doubt that OSHA has been a thorn in the side of employers; nor is there any doubt that it has made the nation's workplaces far safer.

The Vocational Rehabilitation Act of 1973

The Vocational Rehabilitation Act of 1973, administered by the Department of Labor, requires federal contractors to "take affirmative action to employ and advance in employment qualified handicapped individuals." It also prohibits discrimination against employees with chronic health problems, such as cancer.

The federal government has also enacted a number of laws which seek to provide some assurance of financial stability for workers. Unemployment insurance, disability insurance, and retirement income security (pensions) are leading examples. While the provisions of the many statutes are too complex to address here, it is important to note that they are part of the **safety net** created during the New Deal and afterward to guarantee that each member of our society will have a minimum level of economic security. The federal government in the Employment Act of 1946 even asserted that it had an obligation to promote full employment. This was tempered somewhat by the **Humphrey-Hawkins Act** of 1977 which asserted that it was national policy to reduce

TERMS **Safety Net** President Ronald Reagan's term for the totality of social welfare programs which, in his opinion, assure at least a subsistence standard of living for all Americans.

Humphrey-Hawkins Act This act explicitly states that it is the "right of all Americans able, willing and seeking to work" to have "full opportunities for

unemployment to only 4 percent by 1983. These ideals and statutes have not worked perfectly; some people continue to fall
through the net, some miss it altogether. Yet, when viewed retro-
spectively against the federal government's attitude toward labor
in the nineteenth century, they are testimony to the remarkable
progress labor has made in gaining financial protection and rights
in the workplace.

TRENDS IN PUBLIC
SECTOR LABOR LAW
REFORM

While the legal framework for labor relations in private industry is
generally set, public sector labor law is still evolving. Collective
bargaining is still relatively new for public employees. Of course,
there have long been public sector unions. The postal employees
began to organize in the 1880s. By 1906 the AFL had granted a
charter to the National Federation of Postal Clerks. There were
even job actions against the federal government in the distant
past—one of which was a strike in the Philadelphia Naval Shipyard in 1839. But these are isolated examples. Until the 1960s
public policy was overwhelmingly opposed to the organization of
public sector unions and to collective bargaining between governments and their employees. The reasons for this opposition explain
why labor law in the public sector is substantially different from
that of the private sector. Even the initial barriers to public sector
unionization were different.

Sovereignty

Sovereignty is the concept that there must be a single repository of
supreme political authority and power in a society; for example, a
traditional king is a sovereign. In the United States the people are
sovereign and government is considered their agent. But sovereignty presents serious problems to public sector collective bargaining—at least in theory.

First of all, it makes it impossible to consider the collective
bargaining process as negotiations between co-equal partners. Justice Holmes' concept of equality in the battle between combinations of labor and capital, upon which the Norris-LaGuardia and
Wagner Acts are based, makes little sense in the public sector.
What does it mean to say that a public sector union is the equal of
the employer, i.e., the government? Would anyone consider the

TERMS   useful paid employment." However, the discussion of the act in the *Congressional Record* (December 6, 1977) states that "there is clearly no right to sue for
legal protection of the right to a job."

National Association of Letter Carriers to be the equal of the United States government?

Second, a strike against the agent of the sovereign can be viewed as an extremely antisocial act, aimed at harming the society itself. This is all the more so when the governmental function that is struck directly deals with the exercise of sovereignty, such as policing. The chaotic and disastrous Boston Police Strike of 1919 led many to conclude that strikes by public employees were merely preludes to anarchy.

Third, there are many matters in public employment that involve considerations of working conditions *and* public policy. For example, should there be a civilian review board to examine police activities? Should police be able to bargain over the conditions under which they will be permitted to use deadly force? Should teachers be able to bargain over school calendars and the number of pupils per classroom? Should prison guards be able to negotiate the conditions in prisons? Generally speaking, our society prefers to make these and other public policies through its political institutions, rather than through collective bargaining between its government and a private association.

The courts and state statutes have gradually eroded the importance of sovereignty as a barrier to collective bargaining by public employees. But even as recently as 1968 it was used by the state of Nevada to prohibit collective bargaining with its public employees. More importantly, though, contemporary restrictions on the scope of bargaining in the public sector can be traced to concerns that stem directly from the matter of sovereignty. In essence, collective bargaining demands that the sovereign sacrifice some of its authority; but this has not been done quietly, cheerfully, or even completely.

Separation of Powers   With whom should organized public employees bargain? The separation of powers doctrine puts some aspects of working conditions under legislative control (wages, for example) while others are considered executive functions (discipline, for example). One of the stickier problems in public sector labor relations is finding a meaningful line between labor and management in order to determine how, if at all, management is to be represented concerning its demands regarding working conditions. When public employee unions engage in collective bargaining with nonelected (and possibly apolitically appointed) public managers, who may be also protected by a merit system, the extent to which the political community has ceded its sovereignty becomes abundantly clear.

The Absence of Free Markets   For the most part governments do not produce goods and services that are bought and sold in a free market economy. Instead, they obtain the largest share of their revenue from taxation. This means that ordinary market competition cannot serve as a brake on the demands of labor for higher wages and fewer hours. While governments do, sometimes, go broke, they do not price themselves out of the market in any simple sense. Consider that governments face free labor markets for employees which prevent them from paying too little in wages and fringe benefits. But there is no comparable market which prevents them from paying too much. Remember, a strike against a public employer may not disrupt the flow of revenue into the public treasury since this revenue is derived largely from taxation, rather than from the sale of a product or service. Since tax revenues that are collected are not likely to be returned if a government fails to provide services, strikes in the public sector are not typically direct economic weapons. Their only real goal is often to be disruptive and to indirectly cause economic losses through lost sales tax revenues.

The Nature of Government Activities   Governments are in the business of providing societal regulation and critical services. They also provide **public goods** that are shared by the society as a whole. Because disruption of such services as police and fire protection can exact a heavy toll on a society, it appears that the adversary model of labor relations found in the private sector is inappropriate in public employment. The public employee is seen as a public servant, not as an adversary of the political executive, the elected official, or the people in general. Of course, some governmental functions such as trash collection and hospitals can also be privately provided. But historically, those emphasizing the differences of the public sector have focused on the characteristics of the employer (sovereignty, lack of market competition, etc.) rather than on the functions of the employees.

The Legal Situation   In the past it was frequently thought that because public employees were protected from arbitrary treatment by merit systems and civil service regulations, additional protections through collective

---

TERMS   **Public Goods**   Things found free in nature or things typically produced by government that cannot be separately parceled out to individuals since no one can be excluded from their benefits. Examples include national defense, clean air, public safety, etc.

bargaining were unnecessary. While there was some merit to traditional approaches, they were unable to stop the demand of public employees that they be allowed to engage in effective collective bargaining. Generally speaking, public officials responded to this demand in three stages. First, citing sovereignty, they sought to simply prohibit collective bargaining. When this failed, employees were given the right to organize and **meet and confer** with the representatives of the government on matters pertaining to the workplace. The meet and confer approach failed because it set in motion forces that could not be constrained. Once employees organized, they wanted to have a more direct impact on working conditions. Today, public policy in most large jurisdictions is in the third stage; this allows collective bargaining, but seeks to modify the private sector model somewhat in order to make it a better fit for the special conditions of public employment.

While there are national laws that regulate labor relations in the private sector, there is no comparable national law for the public sector. The federal government has a collection of laws and executive orders that govern collective barganing with is own employees. About half the states have either "all inclusive" laws dealing with collective bargaining with their employees or have laws that separately regulate labor relations with virtually every category of state and local public employee. In the rest of the states, laws cover limited categories of employees, or there are no laws at all on the subject of collective bargaining.

This patchwork of law, while reminiscent of conditions in private industry before the 1930s, can best be understood as a reflection of the concept of sovereignty. Some states still consider public employment policies so critical to the ability of the state to maintain order and services that no portion of that policy can be subject to bargaining with public employee unions. It also appears that any comprehensive effort by the federal government to regulate public sector collective bargaining procedures at the state level would be in violation of the **Tenth Amendment,** which conveys a

TERMS   **Meet and Confer**   A technique of determining conditions of employment whereby the representatives of the employer and the employee organization hold periodic discussions to seek agreement on matters within the scope of representation. Any written agreement is in the form of a nonbinding memorandum of understanding.

Tenth Amendment   "The powers not delegated to the United States by the Constitution, nor prohibited by it to the States, are reserved to the States respectively, or to the people."

measure of sovereignty to the states. As previously mentioned, the Supreme Court has even held in the case of *National League of Cities v. Usery* (1976) that federal efforts to extend the Fair Labor Standards Act to state and local government employees were prohibited by state sovereignty.

The variations in the state governments' treatment of public sector collective bargaining mean that a public employee's rights may vary greatly from jurisdiction to jurisdiction. While this is a considerable inconvenience for public sector unions, it does enable the states to experiment with differing collective bargaining arrangements in an effort to find an approach that best fits their particular conditions.

Another major public sector difference is that, with the exception of eleven states, all strikes by public employees are illegal. While the desirability of permitting such strikes has long been debated, there has been little overall agreement. However, some states, such as Alaska, Pennsylvania, and Hawaii, have decided that some public employee strikes can be tolerated; but these strikes are regulated by state and local administrative procedures to assure that they do not endanger the public health and safety. Meanwhile, those states that still prohibit strikes are trying to make this restriction more enforceable. In the past, illegal strikes by public employees took place partly because the penalties against them were not credible. The jailing of union leaders and the levying of huge and unrealistic fines seemed just as likely to encourage labor solidarity as to stop strikes. More recently, penalties have been scaled down and selectively applied. New York is an example. Among other penalties, striking public employees are fined two days pay for each day on strike and reverted to probationary status—which makes a possible dismissal easier. The striking unions also stand to lose their dues checkoff rights, which can be a serious financial blow.

The main problem posed by outlawing the strike is that it is such an integral part of the American way of collective bargaining.

TABLE 3–2.
STATES WHERE PUBLIC EMPLOYEES HAVE A LIMITED
RIGHT TO STRIKE

Alaska	Ohio
Hawaii	Oregon
Idaho	Pennsylvania
Illinois	Vermont
Minnesota	Wisconsin
Montana	

Without it, labor may be unable to demonstrate its strength and management may fail to take union demands and proposals seriously. So it is argued that collective bargaining without the underlying threat of a strike can become a charade. The public sector has been working to get around this problem by seeking a substitute for the strike. Here is another area where public sector practices are at variance with the private sector. In private industry arbitration over interests—that is, substantive working conditions such as wages and hours—is uncommon. But in the public sector, interest arbitration, which has labor and management submit disputes to an impartial arbitrator or panel for resolution, seems to be gaining popularity. If arbitration of interests proves generally successful, there is no inherent reason why it could not be more widely used in the private sector as a means of avoiding costly and disruptive strikes.

It should always be kept in mind that the scope of bargaining in the public sector is often far more limited than in private industry. For example, most federal employees cannot bargain over something so central as wages and hours. Matters of public policy that are also matters of working conditions such as safety and **contracting-out** may also be outside the scope of bargaining.

Modern labor relations in the federal government began in earnest in 1962 with President John Kennedy's issuance of Executive Order 10988. Procedures were modified by subsequent executive orders and were put on a statutory footing by the Civil Service Reform Act of 1978. This act also created the Federal Labor Relations Authority which oversees collective bargaining among most federal employees. A major exception is the U. S. Postal Service. The Postal Reorganization Act of 1970 contains no management rights clause and consequently allows an unrestricted scope of bargaining for postal workers. This act, in another concession to the private sector model, requires that labor relations in the postal service be overseen by the National Labor Relations Board. In effect, postal workers have all of the rights of private sector union members—except the right to strike.

TERMS   **Contracting-Out** Having work performed outside an organization's own workforce. While many unions recognize management's right to occasionally contract-out a job requiring specialized skills and equipment not possessed by the company or its employees, the unions oppose the letting of work that could be done by the company's own workforce. In particular, unions are concerned if work normally performed by its members is contracted-out to firms having inferior wages or working conditions or if such action may result in reduced earnings or layoffs of regular employees.

In the states, New York's **Taylor Law** (1967) is often considered a model of a comprehensive public sector collective bargaining law. It delineates the rights and obligations of labor and management, relies on a Public Employment Relations Board for administrative oversight and rulings on the act's requirements, prohibits strikes, and provides a schedule of penalties for strikers as well as their unions. Hawaii could also be taken as a model for other states because of the comprehensive character of its statute. Its law specifies the bargaining units that public employees fall into, provides for strong union security arrangements, and allows strikes under certain conditions.

Finally, it should be noted that in some areas the public and private sectors are learning from each other's experience in an effort to find the best collective bargaining model for a given situation. The health care industry provides a good example. In 1974 the Congress passed the "Health Care Amendments" to extend federally protected collective bargaining rights to private, nonprofit hospital and other health care employees, who had been excluded from the network of federal regulations by the Taft-Hartley Act. These 1974 "Amendments" apply a modified version of the National Labor Relations Act's procedures to the health care industry. Congress specified that mediation of disputes would be mandatory and required that a union proposing to strike a health care facility give management at least ten days advance notice. In this way strikes might be avoided through mediation and, if not, the damage to the public health that might be incurred would be somewhat mitigated by the advance warning.

ADMINISTRATIVE
AGENCIES

The contemporary pattern of labor relations in both the public and private sectors relies on administrative agencies to provide ongoing supervision of the collective bargaining process. Generally headed by a board of from three to five members, these agencies make rulings on unfair labor practices, on the appropriateness of bargaining units, and, sometimes, on the proper interpretation of a contract or the extent of the scope of bargaining. They also oversee representation elections and certify the winners as the exclusive bargaining agents for all of the employees in a bargaining unit.

The National Labor Relations Board is the prototype of administrative agencies dealing with labor relations. It is headed by

TERMS   **Taylor Law**   This is formally the Public Employees' Fair Employment Act. It governs the unionization of state, county, and municipal employees.

five members (one of whom is designated chair) who are appointed by the President for five-year, staggered terms with the **advice and consent** of the Senate. This bipartisan board hears complaints of unfair labor practices and investigates, prosecutes, and adjudicates them when necessary. It also supervises elections and makes rulings on bargaining units. Its General Counsel oversees the handling of unfair labor practice complaints and represents the NLRB before the courts. The NLRB handles some fifty thousand cases a year through its more than thirty regional offices. While routine cases are resolved at the regional level, the board itself acts as an **appellate** body and will hear certain appeals in panels of three members. Appeals involving nonroutine matters and important new principles are heard by the entire board.

The NLRB model has been adapted to the public sector by the federal government and several states. The equivalent agency for federal employees is the **Federal Labor Relations Authority.** In the states such agencies are generally called Public Employment Relations Boards (or PERBs). Typically, their functions parallel those of the NLRB, as do the methods by which they are appointed, their terms of office, and their administrative procedures. One important difference in the public sector is that binding arbitration over interests may be used instead of strikes as the final means of resolving disputes. When this is the case, the PERB may have a role in overseeing the use of arbitration and even the substance of the arbitrators' rulings when they raise serious issues about the scope of bargaining or public policy.

While a labor relations board exists to oversee and supervise the process of collective bargaining, another type of agency is used to intervene in disputes in an effort to resolve them. They are typically called "mediation and conciliation" services, as in the Federal Mediation and Conciliation Service. The federal government also has an agency of this type specifically for collective bargaining with federal employee unions, the **Federal Service Impasses Panel.** Some states have equivalent agencies. These agencies,

TERMS   **Advice and Consent**   The constitutional right of the U.S. Senate to advise the president on treaties and major presidential appointments and to give its consent to these actions (by a majority vote for appointments; two-thirds for treaties).

Appellate   A higher court that can hear appeals from a lower court.

Federal Labor Relations Authority   This is headed by a chair and two members appointed on a bipartisan basis to staggered five-year terms. It replaced the Federal Labor Relations Council.

Federal Service Impasses Panel   This is located within the Federal Labor Relations Authority.

TABLE 3-3.
THE LABOR RELATIONS LEGAL SYSTEM

Sector	Legal Base	Administrative Agency
Private industry	National Labor Relations Act, as amended	National Labor Relations Board
Railroads and airlines	Railway Labor Act, as amended	National Mediation Board
Postal Service	Postal Reorganization Act of 1970	National Labor Relations Board
Federal government	Civil Service Reform Act of 1978	Federal Labor Relations Authority
State and local government	Public employee relations acts	Public employment relations boards

generally speaking, become involved in collective bargaining in one of two ways: they may be invited by the parties to help resolve the dispute or a statute may require that an agency be notified of a dispute and afforded an opportunity to intervene. In either event, mediation by such agencies tends to be successful in the vast majority of instances in which it is used.

REVIEW QUESTIONS

1. What economic, political, and social factors may have contributed to the hostility of the "common law" toward labor organizations in the first half of the nineteenth century?

2. The injunction is still used against illegal strikes in the public sector. From a public policy perspective, how desirable is the injunction in this context? What limits do you think should be placed on its use?

3. How does the separation of powers in the United States complicate the development of a coherent national policy for labor relations?

4. Is the relationship of collective bargaining legislation to protective legislation related to the differences between business unionism and welfare unionism?

5. Can the same general model of collective bargaining be applied to both the public and private sector? What modifications, if any, seem appropriate for the public sector?

6. What are the benefits and problems associated with reliance on administrative agencies to oversee collective bargaining?

FOR ADDITIONAL READING

Bok, Derek C. and John T. Dunlop. *Labor and the American Community.* New York: Simon & Schuster, 1970.

Feldacker, Bruce S. *Labor Guide to Labor Law,* Second Edition. Reston, VA: Reston Publishing Company/Prentice-Hall, 1983.

Ferman, Louis A., ed. *The Future of American Unionism.* Beverly Hills: Sage, 1984.

Herman, E. Edward and Alfred Kuhn. *Collective Bargaining and Labor Relations.* Englewood Cliffs, NJ: Prentice-Hall, 1981.

Mills, Daniel Quinn. *Labor-Management Relations,* Second Edition. New York: McGraw-Hill, 1982.

Myers, Howard A. and David P. Twomey. *Labor Law and Legislation,* Fifth Edition. Cincinnati: South-Western Publishing Co., 1975.

Schlossberg, Steven I. and Frederick E. Sherman. *Organizing and the Law,* Revised Edition. Washington, DC: The Bureau of National Affairs, Inc., 1971.

Taylor, Benjamin J. and Fred Witney. *Labor Relations Law,* Fourth Edition. Englewood Cliffs, NJ: Prentice-Hall, 1983.

Wykstra, Ronald A. and Eleanor V. Stevens. *Labor Law and Public Policy.* New York: Odyssey Press, 1970.

4

Who Has What Rights

President Harry S. Truman had a problem in 1952. We were in the midst of the Korean War and the American steel industry was about to be shut down by a strike. A prolonged strike would seriously impair defense production, hamper the war effort, and—if it lasted long enough—even endanger the lives of the front line soldiers.

Because of federal wartime price controls, the steel companies had to get government approval for the price increase which they felt was needed to meet the union wage demands. While the President was quite willing to grant "a reasonable price increase," he felt that the steel companies' requests were "entirely out of reason"—far more than was necessary to meet wage demands.

The President initially referred the dispute to the **Wage Stabilization Board.** While this delayed the strike, the Board was unable to gain a settlement. After a delay of more than three months, the strike was scheduled for April 9, 1952. Truman waited until the afternoon of the day before the scheduled shutdown. Then he issued Executive Order 10340 authorizing Secretary of Commerce Charles Sawyer to seize the steel mills. While "government seizure" sounds ominous, it did not mean confiscation in this case; merely that the government would assume temporary custody.

TERMS   **Wage Stabilization Board**   Established in 1950; abolished in 1953.

The very same people who worked for and managed the steel plants would continue to do their jobs. The only point of the seizure was to insure uninterrupted production.

As Truman told the American people in a radio address: "With American troops facing the enemy on the field of battle, I would not be living up to my oath of office if I failed to do whatever is required to provide them with the weapons and ammunitions they need for their survival."

The steel companies obeyed the seizure order under **protest** and promptly took the issue to court. With almost unprecedented speed the case reached the Supreme Court. In *Youngstown Sheet and Tube Co. v. Sawyer* (1952) the justices ruled, six to three, that the President had exceeded his constitutional powers. The court did not deny that a president has the inherent power of seizure in cases of national emergency. But Congress had specifically considered the possibility of this kind of dispute when it debated the Taft-Hartley Act just a few years before and, in the opinion of Justice Felix Frankfurter, "chose not to lodge this power in the President." While Congress did not write statutory prohibitions on presidential seizure during industrial disputes, it had "expressed its will to withhold this power from the President as though it had said so in so many words."

The President could have invoked the eighty-day "cooling-off" period provided for in the Taft-Hartley Act and then gone to the Congress to ask for legislation to deal with the looming emergency if no settlement was reached. But Truman chose to ignore the provisions of the Act—perhaps because it had been passed over his **veto.**

When the court's decision reached the President on June 2 he immediately canceled the seizure order and the strike commenced. On June 10 he formally asked Congress for authority to again seize the steel plants and return them to production; but Congress took no action.

The strike ended on July 24 after lasting fifty-three days. And it ended only after Truman allowed government price controllers to grant a substantial increase in the price of steel, which was

TERMS   **Protest** Not agreeing with the legality of an action taken against you, but complying with it while reserving all legal rights to challenge it.

Veto Latin word meaning: "I forbid." The President of the United States can refuse to authorize (veto) any measure sent to him by Congress. If he does so, he rejects the entire measure. Unlike some state governors, a president does not have an "item veto" which allows for the rejection of portions of bills. Of course, the Congress can override a veto with a two-thirds vote.

exactly what he wanted to avoid in the first place. In the American labor relations game, every player's rights are limited by law— even those of the President of the United States.

REGULATING LABOR RELATIONS

American collective bargaining has been transformed from a patchwork of practices regulated by a variety of common law interpretations to a statutorily based system of rights and responsibilities that define the contemporary nature of labor relations. This transformation took well over a century and is still continuing. Indeed, several states still lack comprehensive labor relations statutes for dealing with their public employees. While collective bargaining is overwhelmingly regulated by law and administrative rules, many ambiguities remain. This chapter will focus on the basic concepts and issues of labor relations law and will deal with these matters as they relate to the interaction of unions and employers. Chapter 8, which covers the organizational structure of labor unions, will deal with the legal rights of individual employees vis-a-vis their unions.

Labor relations are defined and regulated in several ways. First, they may be defined by contracts or voluntary agreements between the union and the employer. Second, they may be defined by statute, as in the case of the National Labor Relations Act of 1935. Third, they can be defined by administrative **regulation** and **adjudication,** as in the case of the **rules** propounded and the cases decided by the National Labor Relations Board. Fourth, the **judiciary,** especially at the federal level, has played an important role in defining and refining labor relations law.

Many people would think that most of the rules governing contemporary labor relations come from the Congress or state legislatures. Surprisingly though, most of labor relations law evolves through administrative action. The National Labor Relations Board is the most important administrative agency in this regard, although the Federal Labor Relations Authority and similar public

TERMS **Regulation** A government control on the behavior of people or organizations that is decided upon by administrative agencies such as the National Labor Relations Board.

Adjudication The formal giving, pronouncing, or recording of a judgment for one side or the other in a legal case.

Rule A regulation made by an administrative agency.

Judiciary The courts in general.

employment relations boards at the state level are equally important in their own context. The NLRB often hands down rules or adjudicates cases that cause Congress or the federal courts to react in some fashion—sometimes to rewrite the law, sometimes to overrule the agency, and sometimes to uphold it. But it is generally the NLRB's initial action that fixes the agenda of efforts to further develop labor relations law.

The NLRB's actions can be divided into two broad categories: adjudication and rule-making. First and foremost, the NLRB engages in adjudication. It hears complaints of unfair labor practices and in the process determines what are the rights and obligations of unions and employers toward one another. It also makes rulings with regard to the appropriateness of bargaining units, and the legitimacy of elections for exclusive representation. Developing labor law through adjudication has several advantages over passing statutes or issuing administrative regulations, but it also tends to make the legal principles underlying the set of rights and obligations somewhat obscure—and possibly somewhat arbitrary and capricious. Generally speaking, adjudication is considered to have the following advantages:

1. It is incremental because it proceeds on a case-by-case basis. This is highly desirable when it is impossible to establish in advance all the principles that should govern a body of activity. Labor relations, which involves literally thousands of employers and millions of employees in myriad relationships, is precisely the kind of activity for which it would be impossible to list, in advance of actual events, regulations for each and every interaction.

2. It is highly desirable where the legitimacy of matters turns on factors of intent, such as "good faith." Adjudication seeks to determine the motives of employers and unions when they engaged in activities that were later challenged. Often, the legal acceptability of their actions will be dependent upon their motives.

3. It is advantageous when the enforcement of a general legal principle involves weighing several criteria in the context of a specific situation. For example, when an employer fires an employee who is active as a union organizer, it may be necessary to determine whether the employer had legitimate reasons for the discharge, whether it was motivated by hostility toward the unionizing activities, whether other factors were involved, and to what extent any or all of these factors contributed to

the employer's decision. Similarly, the determination of an appropriate collective bargaining unit often involves weighing and balancing a number of criteria.

4. It is flexible. Adjudication makes it easier to abandon policies that have grown to be undesirable. It also allows the administrative agency to fashion a remedy specifically for the case at hand.

It seems fair to say that adjudication, whether by an administrative agency or a court of law, is literally the central determinant of labor relations regulations in the United States. However, adjudication does have its limitations. Some of these have proven quite frustrating:

1. Adjudication can lack uniformity. Different panels of the NLRB have reached different conclusions on essentially the same sets of facts and same principles. In theory precedents should be followed, but by the same token flexibility is prized. Consequently, when a new decision deviates from past rulings, one can never be sure immediately whether it represents a policy change or an **aberration.** Additionally, if it is a policy change, its scope may depend upon decisions in future cases.

2. Adjudication exists mainly as **case law** that is not easily accessible or understandable. Even lawyers who specialize in labor law—and who carefully study the decisions of the NLRB—still come to different conclusions on the principles involved and what the NLRB will allow or disallow in the future. In short, adjudication smacks of "dog law"; it is often only after the fact that one finds out what one should not have done—and then it may be too late.

3. Adjudication is also problematic when the decisions arrived at are tied heavily to a peculiar, perhaps unique, set of facts. It has been said that **"hard cases** make bad law." They do so because the adjudicators are pulled in one direction by the set of facts, but may have difficulty legally justifying their sympathy for one party or the other.

TERMS   **Aberration**   A temporary deviation from what is considered normal.

Case Law   All recorded judicial and administrative agency decisions.

Hard Cases   Cases where fairness may require judges to be loose with legal principles; that's why "hard cases make bad law."

For all these reasons, contemporary labor law is incredibly complex and difficult to understand. Quite frankly, many NLRB decisions and those of similar agencies for the public sector are sometimes all but impossible to understand, especially if considered in the abstract. The agencies themselves often flip-flop on very fundamental principles. For example, the NLRB had flip-flopped on the question of whether union **propaganda** in a representation election can be so misleading as to render the election unfair. First it said no, then yes, then no again, and then yes again! In other areas, such as picketing and boycotts, the distinctions upon which the legality of an activity turns are so judgmental and subtle that confusion abounds.

Administrative regulation of a field of activity such as labor relations can also be through rule-making. Rule-making is essentially "legislation" by an agency. The rule will have the force of law as long as (1) proper procedures have been followed in making the rule, (2) the rule is within the statutory authority of the agency, (3) the rule does not violate the Constitution or other statutes, and (4) it is not arbitrary or capricious. Rule-making has the advantage of affording interested parties an opportunity to present their views. It can also be clearer than adjudication in its specifications and principles. Rule-making also tends to be prospective, rather than retrospective, looking forward rather than looking backward. While the NLRB and other labor relations agencies issue rules, the bulk of their activity in defining the rights and responsibilities of unions and employers has been through adjudication.

CONCERTED ACTIVITY   It is within the framework of labor related statutes, administrative rules, and agency and judicial adjudication that the basic concepts defining rights and responsibilities have been developed. While these concepts are fairly simple to explain in the abstract, they can be excruciatingly difficult to apply in practice. Perhaps the most basic of these concepts is that of concerted activity; that is, any organized activity by a union to further some collective purpose. Concerted activity can be divided into five main categories, each defined by the issue over which it is undertaken:

1. *Economic Issues.* This is concerted activity which seeks to protect or enhance the economic status of the employees represented

TERMS   **Propaganda**   The totality of publicity designed to spread ideas or persuade people of something.

by the union. It can involve efforts to gain higher wages, fringe benefits, or the like. It can also involve trying to preserve work for the employees and a host of other matters. The rights of unions and the employees they represent may depend on whether the concerted activity is economic. For example, "economic strikers" can be replaced, but not fired, whereas another category of strikers—those protesting an unfair labor practice—can be neither replaced nor fired. Picketers also have different rights when seeking specific economic advancement, rather than other objectives.

2. *Recognition.* This is concerted activity undertaken by a union to gain the right to exclusively represent a group of employees in a collective bargaining relationship with their employer. Again, rights and responsibilities may depend upon whether the union is engaged in recognitional activity or some other kind of concerted effort. For example, the National Labor Relations Act places special time limitations on picketing for recognitional purposes.

3. *Unfair Labor Practices.* Unions may protest unfair labor practices by engaging in concerted activity, such as strikes, picketing, and handbilling to force the employer to abandon practices that the union believes are both unfair and illegal.

4. *Information Dissemination.* Unions may also engage in concerted activity to publicize information about an employer's practices or products.

5. *Contract Interpretation.* Unions can engage in concerted activity to force an employer to adhere to the union's interpetation of a contract, if there is no clause in the contract prohibiting such activity. Generally speaking, nowadays, unions agree to forego striking to enforce a contract in return for the employer's agreement to submit disputes over the interpretation of the contract to arbitration.

Concerted activity cannot occur in isolation. Unions must necessarily picket or strike against someone. So an equally important basic concept is the *target* of concerted activity: Primary activity is union activity against the employer of the employees the union represents or seeks to represent; secondary activity is targeted against an employer other than the one for which the employees represented by the union work. For example, a union may believe the best way to prevent the primary employer (let's call it "A") from engaging in an unfair labor practice is to picket another employer ("B") who does business with the primary employer

("A"). The target of the picketing would be the second employer ("B"); the object would be to convince it to stop doing business with the primary employer ("A") as long as the latter engaged in the practice to which the union was opposed. For instance, a union representing bakery employees might give out handbills at a fast food restaurant to inform customers that the hamburger buns they were about to consume were made by an employer paying substandard wages. The point would be to put pressure on the fast food place, whose employees are not represented by the union, to alter its business relationship with the primary employer; that is, the producer of the buns. Presumably, if faced with the loss of the opportunity to supply its buns to the public through the fast food outlet, the primary employer might change its labor relations

---

Examples of Union Conduct Which Violate the NLRA Are:

Threats to employees that they will lose their jobs unless they support the union's activities.

Refusing to process a grievance because an employee has criticized union officers.

Fining employees who have validly resigned from the union for engaging in protected activity following their resignation.

Seeking the discharge of an employee for not complying with a union shop agreement, when the employee has paid or offered to pay a lawful initiation fee and periodic dues.

Refusing referral or giving preference in a hiring hall on the basis of race or union activities.

Source: National Labor Relations Board.

practices. Unfortunately, the distinction between primary and secondary activity is not always clear. Nevertheless, the right to engage in concerted activity often depends upon whether the activity is of primary or secondary nature.

This gets even more complicated when you consider primary objects and secondary effects. It will often be the case that a union engaging in a primary concerted activity will cause secondary effects. For example, a union engaged in primary picketing may appeal to the employees of the suppliers of the primary employer not to cross the picket line. If the employees of the firms that deliver supplies to the primary employer refuse to cross the line, those supply firms cannot sell their products and presumably are economically harmed. This is called a secondary effect since the

---

Examples of Employer Conduct Which Violate the NLRA Are:

Threatening employees with loss of jobs or benefits if they join or vote for a union or engage in protected concerted activity.

Threatening to close the plant if employees select a union to represent them.

Questioning employees about their union sympathies or activities in circumstances that tend to interfere with, restrain or coerce employees in the exercise of their rights under the Act.

Promising benefits to employees to discourage their union support.

Transferring, laying off, terminating or assigning employees more difficult work tasks because they engaged in union or protected concerted activity.

Source: National Labor Relations Board.

concerted activity is not aimed at the suppliers per se—and is certainly not intended to harm them—but rather is a consequence of primary concerted activity against the primary employer. While a great deal of secondary activity is illegal, primary activity having secondary effects may be acceptable.

These concepts and definitions are not easily grasped. Nevertheless, they are crucial to an understanding of rights and responsibilities in contemporary labor relations in the United States. As the chapter goes on, we will try to show their application to a wide range of common labor relations activity.

THE RIGHT TO STRIKE

It has long been held that there is no constitutional right to strike. Consequently, strike activity can be regulated—indeed prohibited—by law. In general, the right to strike depends upon who the employees are and what their objectives may be. Most private sector employees have a comprehensive right to strike. Those working in private health care facilities must provide ten days notice of intent to strike to both the employer and the Federal Mediation and Conciliation Service. Most public employees do not have a right to strike. Eleven states do permit public employee strikes, but each subjects them to a variety of regulations. Strikes can fall into any of several categories.

Economic strikes are for better wages and other economic benefits, including the preservation of work within the bargaining unit (that is, to prevent contracting-out or the introduction of new technology). Under federal provisions, as interpreted by the NLRB, economic strikers can be replaced, but they cannot be fired. This sounds like a bit of legalistic sleight of hand, but the point is that a replaced striker has a right to be recalled if and when a vacancy for which he or she is qualified occurs. The right to be recalled was established through adjudication by the NLRB in the **Laidlaw** case and a recall list is sometimes called a "Laidlaw" list. An economic striker who is not replaced is entitled to reinstatement when the strike ends. However, the employee returns either under the terms of the contract negotiated by the

TERMS   **Laidlaw**   Also known as the *Laidlaw-Fleetwood* doctrine because the Supreme Court held in the case of *NLRB v. Fleetwood Trailer Company* (1967) that if a striker has been replaced and no suitable employment is available, the status of the striker as an employee continues until he or she has obtained "other regular and substantially equivalent employment." Until then, the striker remains on a preferred hiring list, unless there is a "legitimate and substantial business justification" for not hiring him or her at all.

union with the employer during the strike or, if the strike has failed, unconditionally.

Unfair labor practice strikers are employees protesting an employer's alleged unfair practices. Such employees cannot be permanently replaced and retain a right to reinstatement with full seniority and benefits, should they so apply for it. If such an employee's position has been abolished during the strike, the employee has a right to reinstatement in a similar position.

Sympathy strikes are strikes by employees who have no particular dispute with their own employer, but want to express sympathy for either (1) other employees of the same employer, or (2) employees of another employer with whom their employer has an economic relationship. An example of the first case would be a situation in which the clerical employees in a university struck in sympathy with the custodial employees who were engaged in an economic or unfair labor practice dispute with the same university. The second case is the familiar refusal to cross a picket line. In either event, the general rule is that sympathy strikers have the same status as the strikers with whom they are sympathetic. In other words, if the strike is an unfair labor practice strike, then the sympathy strikers are considered unfair labor practice strikers. If it is an economic strike, the sympathy strikers are considered economic strikers, with their rights defined accordingly. One caveat here is that sympathy strikers who honor an unlawful secondary picket line are unprotected.

Some strikes are in violation of the labor contract. Employees engaging in such strikes, despite a no-strike agreement in the contract, are subject to dismissal for misconduct. The union itself may be liable for damages to the employer caused by such strikes, depending on the degree of union involvement. Such strikes without union involvement or sanction are called "wildcat" strikes. There is one kind of wildcat strike that is legal. Federal labor relations legislation gives employees the right to refuse to work under unsafe conditions. This right overrides a no-strike clause in a contract. The test of the legality of the action is whether the employees undertook it in good faith based on the objective evidence of conditions available to them at the time. Consequently, even if it turns out that conditions were safe, but the employees reasonably and in good faith believed otherwise, the strike is considered legal.

PICKETING   Unlike the right to strike, picketing has enjoyed broad constitutional protection as a form of freedom of expression. In *Thornhill v. Alabama* (1940) the U. S. Supreme Court held that an Alabama statute prohibiting all picketing was unconstitutional because it violated the **first** and **fourteenth amendments.** The Court reasoned that peaceful picketing gave the state no valid reason for imposing such a drastic ban. Since that time, however, both the Court and labor relations laws have recognized that picketing differs from other forms of speech in that it involves a physical presence that can serve as a physical or psychological barrier to entrance to an employer's private property. Consequently, picketing can be subject to certain kinds of regulations that do not apply to other forms of expression. Generally speaking, some forms of picketing are considered unfair labor practices, some are subject to state regulation as a means of maintaining peace and order, while others continue to enjoy strong constitutional protection.

Organizational and Recognitional Picketing

In theory organizational and recognitional picketing are distinct. But in practice they are so similar that it is frequently impossible to discern a difference. Consequently, it is sensible to treat them as one category. Organizational picketing is aimed at convincing or perhaps psychologically coercing employees to join a union; recognitional picketing is intended to force the employer to grant the union exclusive recognition as the bargaining agent for a group of employees. In general, organizational or recognitional picketing will be considered an unfair labor practice under federal law when:

1. The employer has already properly recognized another union as the exclusive agent;

2. A representational election has taken place within the past year;

3. The union has not filed an election petition within thirty days after the picketing started; or

4. Another union has properly been certified by the NLRB as the exclusive agent.

Recognitional picketing is permitted for a maximum of thirty days. However, this period may be shortened by the NLRB, if

TERMS   **First Amendment**   The U.S. constitutional amendment that guarantees freedom of speech, religion, press, assembly, and the right to petition the government.

Fourteenth Amendment   The U.S. constitutional amendment that forbids the states from depriving any person of due process or equal protection under law.

the picketing is harming the employer's ability to operate its business.

Publicity Picketing

Publicity picketing seeks to truthfully advise the public that an employer does not employ members of a union or have a contract with a union. The point is that some consumers may refuse to use the products or services of a nonunion employer. Publicity picketing can continue indefinitely, so long as it is truthful, *unless* (according to the National Labor Relations Act) it induces "any individual employed by any other person in the course of his employment, not to pick up, deliver or transport any goods or not perform any services." In other words, if employees of firms doing business with the primary employer (the one being picketed) refuse to cross the picket line, the publicity picketing becomes an unfair practice. Although the law says "any individual," in practice the NLRB does not employ such a rigid restriction. Rather, it adjudicates each case on its own merits. However, the more employees of secondary employers who refuse to cross the publicity picket line, the more likely the line is to be considered unlawful. This is true even if the picketers urge those making deliveries and so forth to cross the line.

Area Standards Picketing

Here the picketers demand that the primary employer pay "area standards" wages; that is, wages that are paid to union labor by other employers in the same geographic area. The picketers do not demand to be recognized as the exclusive agent, perhaps because recognitional picketing is subject to restrictions and the union might fear losing a representational election. On the other hand, the picketers want to be treated as though they are the exclusive agent demanding what the employer should pay. Consequently, this form of picketing is so close to recognitional picketing that it is subject to stringent regulation. Namely, the union must (1) not demand, or recently have demanded, recognition; (2) avoid any propaganda that suggests it seeks recognition; (3) have evidence that the employer is actually paying less than area standards; and (4) have picket signs that indicate that it is engaged in area standards picketing rather than recognitional picketing. The NLRB generally adheres to these conditions stringently.

Picketing in Support of a Strike

Striking employees frequently set up picket lines in order to induce customers, suppliers, strike replacements, and other employees of the primary employer not to deal with that employer. The purpose, obviously, is to apply economic force against the employer in the hope of negotiating a better contract. This type of picketing is generally legal. However, it can be subject to regulation by state law if it is violent, if picketers mass in large numbers, or if they engage in nonviolent practices that present actual physical barriers to entrance to the primary employer's private property. Thus, laying down at a plant entrance to block supply trucks can be prohibited under state law. The more important principle here is that such picketing must be primary. The striking employees of employer A cannot set up a picket line at the facility of employer B, who is a supplier of employer A. The picket line must be at A's facility; if B's employees refuse to cross it when they are sent with a delivery, that is not normally an unlawful or unfair labor practice.

Common Situs Picketing
What if there are several employers working at the same site? This is common in the construction industry and in shopping centers. Where will the picket line go? This is referred to as the "common situs" problem. Common situs picketing is subject to rather elaborate rules and regulations. In *National Labor Relations Board v. Denver Building and Construction Trades Council* (1951) the U.S. Supreme Court reasoned that primary picketing is illegal if it has both a primary and a secondary object. To be legal it must be confined to a primary object, though it may also have a secondary effect. Furthermore, the court held that each employer at a common construction site should be considered a separate employer. Thus, picketing at the site against one primary employer could not legally have the secondary object of shutting down the entire project or involving other employers directly in the dispute. This decision led to the elaborate system of gates that is now frequently used at construction sites. In general, unions are allowed to set up picket lines at the gate used by the primary employer. If there is only one gate to the entire construction project, picketing may take place there. Otherwise, it must be confined to the gate used by the primary employer. However, this is by no means the end of the story.

Sometimes it will turn out that the primary employer is at a secondary location. This happened in the Moore Dry Dock case of 1950. There the union had a dispute with a shipowner whose ship was at a dry dock being repaired by another employer. In order to picket the primary employer (the shipowner) the union necessarily had to be at the secondary location, the dry dock. The NLRB established the following requirements for such primary picketing at a secondary location to be legal:

1. The primary employer must be engaged in its normal business at the common situs.

2. The picket signs must clearly identify which employer is being picketed.

3. The pickets have to be as close as is possible, within reason, to the site of the employer with whom they have a dispute.

4. The primary employer must have a presence when the picketing occurs. This presence can be in the form of equipment, supplies, offices, etc.

Two additional points should also be mentioned. First, the same general set of rules applies if the employer roves around; that is, if it goes from one location to another on a regular basis. For example, an employer who provides maintenance services, such as typewriter and office machine repairs, roves around. Pickets against such an employer can appear at each site. If the union knows the employer's schedule, it can picket at the various locations only when the employer is actually present. Otherwise, it can picket continuously at any location where the employer normally does business. The second point is that it must be borne in mind that primary picketing of this nature cannot have a surreptitious secondary object. The pickets cannot urge the employees of other employers at the same site to refuse to report to work.

Shopping Centers One of the underlying principles governing concerted labor activity is that while the activity is permissible, it cannot be destructive of private property rights. Obviously, on occasion, it is necessary to balance one interest against the other. Generally speaking, the NLRB will try to reach a solution that permits a balance between effective labor relations activity and the rights of private property. Overall, it is neither one-sided in favor of concerted labor activity nor the employers' property rights. Sometimes, this balance will allow picketing in front of a store in a shopping center, rather than on the periphery.

Product Picketing Sometimes the considerations of private property and secondary locations become tangled in a web. In *NLRB v. Fruit and Vegetable Packers, Local 760* (1964), known as the Tree Fruits case, picketers appeared at grocery stores urging consumers to boycott apples from the state of Washington. This is called product picketing. It occurs at a secondary location and is legal as long as the picketing does not urge a total boycott of the store, but rather only a boycott of a specific product. The problem here is that the product may become merged with another so as to effectively call for a total boycott. For instance, if the Washington State apples were used exclusively in Sarah's Hot Pies, urging consumers to boycott the apples by picketing outside Sarah's Hot Pie Shoppes would effectively be urging a total boycott.

HANDBILLING   Handbilling is passing out leaflets urging consumers not to deal with an employer as part of a labor dispute. The employer who is the target of the handbill may be either a primary or secondary employer. In either case, the handbill must be truthful. Where it is aimed at a secondary employer, it must state that the dispute is with another employer. The status of handbilling is unusual because it can urge the consumer to engage in a total boycott of the secondary employer as long as that employer continues to do business with the primary employer. Unlike product picketing, handbilling does not have to be confined to urging boycotts of specific, individual products. The secondary boycott sought by handbilling is considered legal. Various other forms of notice, such as advertisements in the print and electronic media are treated as handbills in this context. The distinction between handbilling and picketing in terms of urging boycotts is derived from the more coercive nature of picketing.

ALLIES   Generally speaking, unions may engage in concerted activity against secondary employers if such an employer is deemed to be the "ally" of the primary employer. The ally relationship is complicated and subject to a number of tests. Frequently, one employer will be viewed as the ally of another if they are substantially owned and managed by the same group of people or corporation. Additionally, where one employer agrees to perform work for another employer who has been struck, and this agreement is a result of the strike itself rather than a normal business arrangement, the employer performing the work becomes the ally of the other.

The distinction between primary and secondary is of general importance to employees in terms of negotiating rights with their employers. Employees can legitimately negotiate the right to honor a picket line against another employer, provided that the picket line itself is legal and not aimed at achieving a secondary object. Employees can also negotiate the right to refuse to handle "struck goods," also referred to as "hot cargoes," provided that if by doing the work the employees would effectively turn their employer into an ally of the employer against whom the strike is aimed. Garment and construction workers have somewhat broader rights in this area.

CONCERTED ACTIVITY TO CONTROL WORK

As noted in Chapter 1, much of the economic development of the United States has involved boom and bust cycles. Historically, workers have borne a heavy burden by these cycles. At times they are required to work extra hours, at other times they are laid-off or discharged for lack of work. In addition, technological change has sometimes made workers superfluous. This, too, has increased the sensitivity of the American labor movement to the need to gain control or leverage over how work will be performed and allocated. The nation's basic principles of labor law also govern these efforts to a substantial extent.

Featherbedding

Featherbedding is trying to convince the employer to pay for work not performed. The National Labor Relations Act prohibits it and makes it an unfair labor practice. However, the antifeatherbedding regulations do not prohibit a number of related practices. Employees can seek to negotiate manning levels. This is sometimes done under the guise of a concern for safety. For example, police unions often try to negotiate the requirement that at least two officers be assigned to a squad car. Their argument is that single-officer patrols are too dangerous. This may be true. However, the net effect is to require the employer to have fewer patrols or more officers. In the latter case, police will have greater protection against lay-offs and more police will be employed.

In the case of police, the issue of featherbedding is not wholly clear. Higher manning ratios probably do increase safety, but they may also be sought to make the jobs more pleasant and to create more work. In other instances, however, such as the reduction of garbage collection crews from three-person to two-person details, the union's effort to maintain jobs is wholly clear. Indeed, "firemen" were standard on the nation's railroads long after steam locomotives disappeared and there was no coal to shovel into the engine's fire!

Bogus Work

Another practice not reached by antifeatherbedding regulations is the requirement of work that is clearly unnecessary. The most celebrated instance of this was in the case of *American Newspaper*

Publishers Association v. National Labor Relations Board (1953). News-paper printers sought to protect the work allocated to their bargaining unit by doing what is referred to as *bogus* work, or work that was totally unnecessary. The newspapers allowed outside agencies to prepare advertisements that would appear in the papers. The printers insisted that they be paid to copy the ads, even though the originals prepared by the outside agency would be used in the final printing process. In other words, the printers wanted to make copies having no use at all! The Supreme Court held that bogus work was not featherbedding because the work was actually performed—albeit to no purpose whatsoever. Bogus work, by the way, must be paid for even if it is not actually performed if the employees are willing to do it. For instance, in the printers' case, the newspapers might decide that they would rather pay for the work, but not have it performed, since its performance might cost more in terms of using up supplies.

Preserving Work

Unions may also seek to preserve or expand the work done by the bargaining units they represent by seeking to compel the employer to agree not to subcontract work. In such instances, the legitimacy of the union's effort will be governed by the primary object/secondary object distinction. If its primary object is to preserve its own work, efforts to negotiate an antisubcontracting clause may be acceptable. On the other hand, an effort to take the work away from a subcontractor that is already performing it can be considered an illegitimate secondary object. In that instance, the union is negotiating with the primary employer to take adverse action against a neutral third party—the subcontractor. It should be noted with emphasis however, that the National Labor Relations Act contains a broad exception to these principles for the construction industry. There, unions can negotiate contracts limiting subcontracting at construction sites to union employers. A broader exception exists for the garment industry, where unions can legally enter into a variety of work-preserving and "hot cargo" agreements.

Asserting Jurisdiction Over Work

Federal labor relations statutes prohibit engaging in concerted activity to force the employer to assign any particular work to the employees in one union, trade, craft, or class rather than to those in another unless the NLRB has already identified those engaging in the concerted activity as the group to which the work should properly be assigned. Nevertheless, unions do seek to gain control over the assignment of work and if they violate the law in the process, the NLRB may intervene to resolve the matter. Unions also seek to resolve jurisdictional disputes voluntarily through arbitration or joint boards of one kind or another. The AFL-CIO maintains an arbitration panel for this purpose. A major reason for government regulation of jurisdictional disputes is that they frequently place the employer in a "no-win" situation. Without regulation, the employer's assignment of work might always lead one union (the losing one) to strike.

Hiring Halls   A "hiring hall" is a system through which unions refer workers to employers. The benefit of this device is apparent in the construction industry, for instance, where a number of employers in a geographic area may be seeking to employ workers with the same crafts or skills for relatively short-term work. The union can refer workers to these employers. In so doing it presumably screens them to assure that they are qualified. Often screening is tantamount to union membership. However, legally speaking, unions operating hiring halls are forbidden to discriminate against nonmembers. Workers must be referred on the basis of objective criteria. Seniority in terms of the number of years of employment in the industry is one such criterion. In practice, however, there is little doubt that hiring halls encourage union membership. They afford the unions prestige and importance in assigning work. The seniority criterion can legitimately be limited to number of years' employment in the bargaining unit (that is, among the group of employees represented by the union). Moreover, union stewards can be given first preference in referrals since their presence on the job is necessary in order to enforce contracts (see Chapter 7). All told, the hiring hall makes obtaining work almost synonymous with union membership in the eyes of some workers.

EMPLOYER RIGHTS   The historical pattern of the development of unionization and collective bargaining in the United States has caused society to pay a great deal of attention to defining the rights of unions to engage in concerted activity or, conversely, placing limits on the scope of their use of economic force against employers. Far less legislative concern has been devoted to the rights of employers to exercise economic force, or the limitations that should be placed on such activity. In general this reflects the place of private property in a capitalist society and economy. It is assumed that the owner of an economic enterprise has the right to run it as he or she sees fit. When employers engage in antisocial activity, common law can provide remedies to those harmed. The legislature can also pass statutes limiting the practice. For example, the Supreme Court said in *United Steelworkers v. Weber (1979)* that in the absence of legislation to the contrary, private employers would be free to discriminate against persons on the basis of their race, religion, gender, or other social attributes. In order to prevent such a practice, Congress enacted the Civil Rights Act of 1964. Consequently, there is an important although subtle difference between the nature of the rights of employers and those of unions. For the most part it is true that in the absence of a statute or judicial decision prohibiting a practice, an employer is allowed to engage in it. For organized labor, however, the tendency is for the union to be prohibited from engaging in a practice unless the law or a judicial ruling specifically allows it. This means that the employer and its management is treated as though it has a broad body of inherent rights to operate the economic enterprise as they see fit. This is why, in part, management can replace economic strikers and why "closed shops" are now illegal. The concept of management rights can place important limitations on the scope of bargaining, since these rights are not treated as mandatory subjects of negotiation (see Chapter 5).

Avoiding Unionization   Despite the broad sweep of employer rights, there are some important limitations. An employer has an absolute right to go out of business. This is true even if the primary or sole objective is to avoid dealing with a union. However, should an employer shut down a facility in order to discourage unionization in another plant or to reap an economic benefit elsewhere, it could constitute a violation of federal labor relations law. The main issue in this area is that of "runaway shops." A runaway shop is an effort by an employer to shift operations from a unionized plant to a nonunionized plant. An elaborate form of runaway is for the employer to close down the business in one place and reconstitute it elsewhere where there is less interest in unionization. Importantly, the legality of shifting business from one geographic area to another depends upon the employer's motives. An employer can legitimately employ "sound business judgment" in moving operations, including the judgment that wage rates are lower in another (and less unionized) part of the country. Such a decision is not negotiable with the union. However, the employer may be required to negotiate with the union concerning the effects of such a change, such as the amount of **severance pay** that will be granted. Even here, however, the employee is not required to reach an agreement with the union. Rather the obligation is to bargain in good faith.

A true runaway shop constitutes an unfair and illegal practice. So does what might be called the "alter ego employer" or "reconstituted corporation." Suppose one corporation sells its business to another. What are the obligations of the second corporation to bargain with the exclusively recognized union? The successor corporation has the right to negotiate its own contract with the union; it need not adhere to that reached by the corporation from which it bought the business. However, an "alter ego" or reconstituted corporation is essentially the original corporation in the guise of a successor. In this case, the alter ego employer is bound by the existing contract even though technically (and legally for some purposes) it is a new owner.

Similarly, an employer should not seek to avoid living within the terms of a contract by forming two corporations, one that is unionized and another that is not. If the NLRB finds that the operations and/or ownership of these two corporations are highly integrated, the nonunion company may be bound to the same labor terms as the unionized one.

Discriminating Against Union Members or Unions   The obligation of employers to engage in collective bargaining also forbids them from discriminating against employees who join or seek to organize a union. Nor can the employer discriminate against employees who testify before the NLRB. Such discrimination is an unfair labor practice. Nor can an employer promote the organizational or recognitional interests of one union over another. The employer faced with a contest for exclusive recognition beween two or more unions must remain scrupulously neutral even though the outcome may have a substantial impact on the employer's business. At one time, some public employers sought to confine unionization to organizations that did not affiliate with national or international unions. Such approaches have been found to be illegal or unconstitutional. The neutrality principle also prohibits an employer from seeking to dominate a union.

TERMS   **Severance Pay**   A lump-sum payment by an employer to an employee who has been permanently separated from the organization. The amount is usually determined by a schedule based on years of service and earnings. About 40 percent of union contracts contain provisions for severance pay.

Bargaining in Good   Finally, it should be mentioned that an employer is required to
Faith   bargain in good faith once a collective bargaining relationship has
been properly established. Good faith does not require that an
agreement be reached, just that the employer genuinely try to negotiate one. The various ramifications of "good faith" will be discussed further in Chapter 5.

EMPLOYEE RIGHTS   Individual employees also have some rights that are connected to
the collective bargaining process. Of course, they also have rights
under statutes which regulate conditions in the workplace, such as
the Civil Rights Act of 1964 and the Fair Labor Standards Act of
1938. In general, under federal legislation affecting the private sector, an individual employee has the right to protest against an employer's alleged violation of a contract. This means that, whether
right or wrong about the violation, he or she cannot legally be discharged or disciplined for engaging in a protest. However, the
matter must be one governed by a contract. Employees also have a
right to the presence of a shop steward in disciplinary proceedings
(see Chapter 7). Private sector employees are neither legally authorized nor prohibited from engaging in some practices, such as
quickie strikes or slowdowns. Hence, when engaging in these concerted activities, the employees are subject to discipline as the employer sees fit. In passing, it should be noted that although private
sector employees have no constitutional protection of their job
rights (other than not being held in involuntary servitude), several
states (eleven as of 1983) have statutory or common law regulations pertaining to "wrongful firings." Thus, an employee who is
discharged for exercising his or her general rights or liberties as an
individual may be afforded some legal protection.

Public employees are in a substantially different position in
terms of their rights. They have some constitutional protections
under the federal and state constitutions. Consequently, in some
contexts, their rights to freedom of speech, association, and privacy
may be greater in practice than those of private sector employees.
The same is true of their general liberty, such as with some aspects
of their off-the-job conduct. For example, generally the public employee has a constitutional right to make a public speech con-
demning his or her employer's operations or policies, as long as the
speech addresses matters of general concern and does not use

TERMS   **Quickie Strike**   A spontaneous or unannounced strike of short duration.

grossly offensive language. Similarly, the discharge of a homosexual from the public sector raises constitutional issues concerning liberty not presented by such a firing in the private sector. In addition, public employees are entitled to certain constitutional due process protections in dismissals under a variety of conditions.

THE PUBLIC'S RIGHTS   The public and the public interest are obviously affected by the nature of the collective bargaining relationship. For the most part, however, the framework of labor relations law that has evolved in the United States is viewed as protecting the public interest by assuring productive, rather than destructive, labor relations. That is why some practices are considered illegal, such as the "closed shop" or most secondary boycotts and "hot cargo" arrangements. Still, the public interest is manifested directly in three legal contexts:

1. Concerted activity that threatens to damage the national security, or public health, safety, or welfare. There are three broad categories of employment situations in which the normal collective bargaining process that prevails in the private sector is considered undesirable. One is under conditions of national emergency, where pursuant to the Taft-Hartley Act of 1947, the president can intervene in a labor dispute to protect the public interest by requiring an eighty-day cooling-off period prior to a strike or lockout. A second is in the health care industry, where notice of intent to strike must be provided ten days in advance to enable the facility to make adjustments and allow the Federal Mediation and Conciliation Service to attempt to resolve the dispute. The third is in the public sector, where strikes are broadly prohibited, and even where permissible, tend to be heavily regulated by governmental administrative agencies.

2. Right-to-work laws provided for in Section 14(b) of the Taft-Hartley Act allow states (and territories of the United States) to enact legislation prohibiting union security arrangements. Under these statutes all union security arrangements can be prohibited. Accordingly, any individual will have the right to work in a bargaining unit that is represented by a union without having to join the union or support it financially. The union is required to represent such employees fairly, and without discrimination, but the employees are not required to support the union. From the union's perspective, this creates a

class of "free riders," that is, workers who benefit from union representation but do not pay for it. From the individual's perspective, however, the "open shop" is a protection of one's basic freedom of association, in this instance the freedom not to associate with an organization to which one is opposed. Incidently, prohibitions on employer discrimination against union members forbid employers from paying union members at a different rate than nonmembers, even if such discrimination were beneficial to the union members. Therefore unions cannot bargain solely on behalf of their members. Any agreement reached must apply to all the employees.

3.   Litigation is always available as a means of protecting the public's interest. But any effort to sue a union or employer for engaging in an illegal practice that is harmful to the public (as represented by its politically elected officials) is likely to face a number of serious barriers. However, there are a few cases on record that at least hold out the prospect of bringing such a suit successfully. The New York State case of *Caso v. Gotbaum* (1971) was caused when New York City employees represented by the American Federation of State, County and Municipal Employees and the Teamsters engaged in a work stoppage at the City's pollution control plants, pumping stations and yards, which resulted in the "discharge of substantial untreated raw sewage into the [East River] and thence into the Long Island Sound and North Shore bays. As a consequence, the bacteria count tripled, and in some places increased much more. Algae disturbances resulted. The waters themselves developed a brown scum appearance." Several public officials from Nassau County and Long Island towns brought a suit against the unions for a permanent injunction against such a work stoppage. They also sought compensatory damages of $1 million and punitive damages of $5 million from the unions. The New York Supreme Court (which is not the state's highest court) admitted that finding a precedent for the case was somewhat difficult. While the elected officials did not win this particular case, suits of this kind remain a possibility.

The purpose of labor laws has been to arrive at a balance between the rights of workers and employers that provides equity, economic stability, and procedural workability. The balance that is struck at any one time or in any given case is subject to change as different attitudes and economic, political, and social conditions develop. In some areas, the balance remains ill-defined; in other areas, rights may appear out of balance altogether. Adjudication

TABLE 4-1.
STATES WITH RIGHT-TO-WORK LAWS

Alabama	Nevada
Arizona	North Carolina
Arkansas	North Dakota
Florida	South Carolina
Georgia	South Dakota
Iowa	Tennessee
Kansas	Texas
Louisiana	Utah
Mississippi	Virginia
Nebraska	Wyoming

by agencies such as the NLRB often generates complex questions in unforeseen circumstances. Indeed, sometimes a case is all but incomprehensible. This is frustrating. Yet, over the years, some basic concepts and concerns such as the ones treated here have evolved and endured. They are products of a wider social, economic, and political environment. No one should hope to be able to resolve any contest of rights in the labor-management relations forum based on these concepts alone. A comprehensive review of the existing case law would be an absolute necessity. Equally true, however, no one can hope to understand the case law and the nature of rights in any specific set of circumstances without grasping the basic concepts. Labor law is ever-evolving, but its continuing development is now based on a solid foundation for determining the rights of the parties involved.

REVIEW QUESTIONS

1. What are the pros and cons of administrative regulation and adjudication in the area of labor relations?

2. What are hypothetical examples of a legal secondary boycott, an illegal secondary boycott, legal picketing, and illegal picketing?

3. Why is handbilling treated differently from picketing? In your judgment is this distinction still sound?

4. Under what conditions might a union legally: (a) urge consumers to boycott a single product in a supermarket, or (b) urge them to boycott the supermarket itself?

5. Why is recognitional picketing treated differently from informational picketing?

6. Do you think the public's interest is adequately protected by contemporary labor law?

7. Do you favor a law allowing picketing by a union against a primary employer at any and all entrances to a construction site? What would the consequences of such a change be?

FOR ADDITIONAL READING

Blackman, John L., Jr. *Presidential Seizure in Labor Disputes.* Cambridge, MA: Harvard University Press, 1967.

Brinker, Paul A. "The Ally Doctrine," *Labor Law Journal,* 23 (September 1972).

Cabot, Stephen J. and Robert J. Simmons. "The Future of Common Situs Picketing," *Labor Law Journal,* 27 (December 1976).

Dershinsky, Ralph M., Alan D. Berkowitz and Phillip A. Miscimarra. *The NLRB and Secondary Boycotts.* Philadelphia: University of Pennsylvania Press, 1980.

Douglas, Leslie. *Labor Law.* St. Paul, MN: West, 1979.

Estey, Marten S., Philip Taft and Martin Wagner, eds. *Regulating Union Government.* New York: Harper & Row, 1964.

Erickson, John. "Forfeiture of Reinstatement Rights through Strike Misconduct," *Labor Law Journal,* 31 (October 1980).

Evans, Hywell. *Government Regulation of Industrial Relations.* Ithaca, NY: New York State School of Industrial and Labor Relations, Cornell University, 1961.

Gregory, Charles O. and Harold Katz. *Labor and the Law,* Third Edition. New York: Norton, 1979.

Smith, Russell A., Leroy S. Merrifield and Theodore J. St. Antoine. *Labor Relations Law,* Sixth Edition. Indianapolis: Bobbs–Merrill, 1979.

5 The Collective Bargaining Process

Prologue
From "Gimme More, More, More!" to "Gimme Back"

When he was twenty-five years old, Samuel Gompers was elected president of his local cigarmakers union. Two years later, in 1877, he was blacklisted by employers after leading an unsuccessful strike. For months he sought work. His wife, with five children and another on the way, fed the family soup made of flour, water, salt and pepper. Often they simply went hungry. Sam was increasingly desperate—almost to the point of murder! After a day of futile job seeking, Sam returned home to find that his sixth child had been born; but both mother and child needed a doctor. Sam ran to find one. The doctor, knowing that Sam couldn't pay, refused to come. Sam menacingly assured him that if he did not go, he would never make another move. The doctor, interested in saving a life (his own), went. Nobody could accuse Sam Gompers of not knowing the poverty and desperation of the working class at first hand. Years later, he would often respond to the question "What does labor want?" with his credo: "More, more now, more tomorrow!" He could speak the words with a passion born of experience.

Thanks to Gompers and many other courageous labor leaders, American workers did get more and more and more. So much more that they became the best paid in the world, had the highest standard of living, and, according to **Peter Drucker,** turned traditional thinking about labor and capital "upside-down" when by the 1980s their collective pension funds literally owned half of American industry.

But collective bargaining is a two edged sword; what is won can also be lost. Today's collective bargaining process is based upon statutory law. Previous chapters have shown that the struggle to place it on a firm and relatively clear legal framework was long and arduous. The model for contemporary collective bargaining that has evolved from this struggle assumes that the relationship between management and labor is largely adversarial—but adversarial only up to a point. Most managements want to pay labor as little as possible; labor naturally wants more. Management wants to retain control of the workplace in terms of hiring, firing, promotion, discipline, technology, and so forth; labor wants to gain a voice in these matters to assure that management is not arbitrary or harmful to the interests of employees. What makes collective bargaining possible in this context is that both labor and management have an ultimate harmony of interest; that is, the desire to assure that the firm for which they work—and from which they are both paid—will remain in business. In order to stay in business, it must be competitive with other firms. So it cannot pay labor too much and cannot be managed too inefficiently. Because if it pays too much or is managed too poorly, the **market** will force it out of business. This ultimate harmony of interest, imposed by the marketplace, acts as a brake on the demands of both labor and management.

Sometimes, these "brakes" make it impossible for labor to get more. Indeed, such "brakes" as foreign competition, a lagging national economy, and competing technologies have forced some unions to even concede previous gains in wages and benefits. Such "givebacks" have been common in smokestack industries that have been traditional union strongholds. Yet, the same economic realities which helped labor win more through collective bargaining can, should these realities become unfavorable, force labor to give back some of what it had once won. What in an earlier day seemed

---

TERMS   **Peter Drucker** (1909–   ) A preeminent writer and philosopher of management who is usually credited with having "invented" management by objectives and discovering pension fund socialism (whereby the workers own most of the means of production through the common stock investments of their pension funds).

Market The geographical region in which a product can be sold, the economic and social characteristic of potential buyers, the demand for something, or the price for which it will sell if sold.

like a steady uphill climb to even greater wages and benefits for organized labor has, for some segments of labor, become a roller coaster ride.

Samuel Gompers always counseled his followers during times of stress to "have the courage to wait." He was confident that labor would always get "more" in the end. This philosophic disposition to wait out bad times in the belief that the future would be better was illustrated by a debate he had with a socialist leader in 1914. While the socialist was trying to get Sam to admit that the union movement was too conservative in its goals, Sam cut him short by reminding the socialist that "we [the union movement] go farther than you. You have an end; we have not."

ESTABLISHING THE COLLECTIVE BARGAINING RELATIONSHIP

The first step in the collective bargaining process is establishing a relationship for ongoing negotiations and the formulation of agreements covering conditions in the workplace. These relationships are shown in Figure 5-1. Today, this step is largely regulated by law, and overseen by **administrative agencies** such as the National Labor Relations Board (NLRB). In the past, of course, this first step was a giant one, taking more than a century to become fully accepted. But now, the establishment of the collective bargaining relationship is based on several fundamental principles.

Exclusive Recognition

The collective bargaining process requires an employer to recognize a union as the legitimate **bargaining agent** for the employees in a particular occupation, plant, **position classification,** or other unit of work. Moreover, the process demands that a union be recognized as the "exclusive" agent for such a group of employees. This is the principle of "exclusive recognition" which gives a union the right to be the sole speaker for all of the employees in the unit. Accordingly, no individual employee (or group of employees)

TERMS

Administrative Agency   Any impartial private or governmental organization that oversees or facilitates the labor relations process.

Bargaining Agent   A union organization (not an individual) that is the exclusive representative of all the workers, union and nonunion, in a bargaining unit.

Position Classification.   The process of using formal job descriptions to organize all jobs in a given organization into classes on the basis of duties and responsibilities for the purpose of delineating authority, establishing chains of command, and providing equitable salary scales. The individual position descriptions are called position classifications.

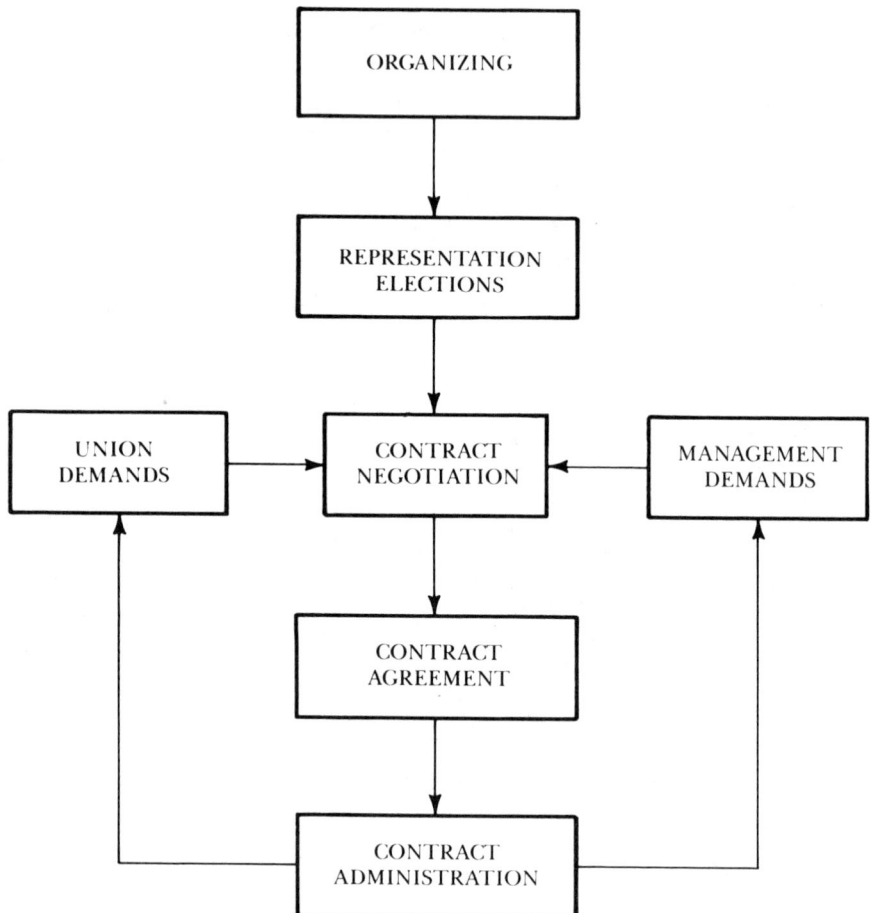

Figure 5-1. An Overview of the Collective Bargaining Cycle

covered by the union contract has the right to negotiate directly with the employer. Conversely, the principle of exclusive recognition prohibits the employer from trying to arrange conditions in the workplace without negotiating with the union. An employer may even be prohibited from discussing certain aspects of work directly with individual employees. While the principle of exclusive recognition gives the union the sole right to represent all employees in a bargaining unit, this carries with it the obligation to represent all employees fairly and equally, even if they are not members of the union. Thus, the exclusively recognized union is precluded by law from discriminating against nonmembers in the bargaining unit.

Contracts between Unions and Employers   Where there is no collective bargaining process, contracts or agreements concerning the workplace are between employers and employees. The establishment of a collective bargaining process changes this to a situation where the work contract is between the union and the employer. The employees are represented by the union, which speaks on their behalf. Consequently, the violation of an employee's rights (or those of the employer) becomes a matter for resolution between the union and the employer, rather than between the employee and the employer. This has many important ramifications, including the development of mechanisms to assure enforcement of the contract which may exclude individual action by an employee. Legally, under this contractural approach, the union intercedes between the employer and the employee— that is, it becomes a full-fledged legal party to the work arrangement. So the legal situation becomes such that employers have rights and interests; employees have rights and interests; and, where the collective bargaining relationship is established, so do unions.

Democracy   It is obvious that the principle of exclusive recognition and the nature of contracts between unions and employers give exclusively recognized unions a great deal of legal authority. No one else can speak to the employer on behalf of the employees such unions represent. No one else can contract with the employer pertaining to conditions in the workplace for the represented employees. Consequently, public policy seeks to assure that unions gaining exclusive recognition actually do represent at least a majority of the employees for whom they purportedly speak. Thus, to be certified as the exclusive agent, a union must show that a majority of employees in a particualr bargaining unit have chosen it as their bargaining agent. This can be done in several ways:

1. A union can solicit membership among the employees and have them sign **authorization cards,** which state that they want the union to be their exclusive bargaining agent. If the union receives authorizations from a majority of the employees in the unit to be represented, it can submit these to the employer. Generally, the employer may extend recognition at this

TERMS   **Authorization Card**   A form signed by a worker to allow a union to represent him or her in collective bargaining.

point. However, if the employer can make a case that the authorization cards were obtained through fraud, coercion, or other unfair labor practices, the employer may refuse to grant recognition. In such circumstances, the NLRB or other administrative agency is likely to be called upon to resolve the matter.

2. An election can be held. If a union cannot gain recognition through a showing of authorization cards, it may be able to do so through a secret ballot election. In general, the election process works as follows: A union petitions the NLRB or other appropriate administrative agency indicating that it has evidence, generally membership or authorization cards, that at least 30 percent of the employees in a bargaining unit want to be represented by it. The administrative agency will then schedule and oversee a secret ballot election. If a majority of employees voting indicate that they want the union as their exclusive agent, the union will be so designated. If a majority select "no agent" (or similar phrase), then the union and collective bargaining have been rejected. In some instances more than one union will be contending to become the exclusive agent. In such cases, if neither union, nor the "no agent" option gain a majority of the votes cast, a run-off election may be held between the two options receiving the highest number of votes. Run-off elections, coupled with the principle of exclusive recognition, have been controversial because they appear to some to be inherently coercive.

3. The employer can initiate an election petition or extend recognition voluntarily. Unionization drives can be disruptive to the workplace. Consequently, an employer might want to resolve the issue of exclusive recognition as quickly as possible. Yet, the current legal framework for collective bargaining prohibits employer-dominated unions, so-called "company unions." The employer may extend voluntary recognition to a union that appears to have majority support, but the employer must do this in **good faith.** Voluntary recognition can usually be challenged before a labor relations agency if it is somehow questionable or tainted by improper behavior. If there are several unions contesting for the status of exclusive agent, the employer may file an election petition with the NLRB, in an effort to resolve the matter and get on with business.

TERMS   **Good Faith**   Honest in fact as well as appearance.

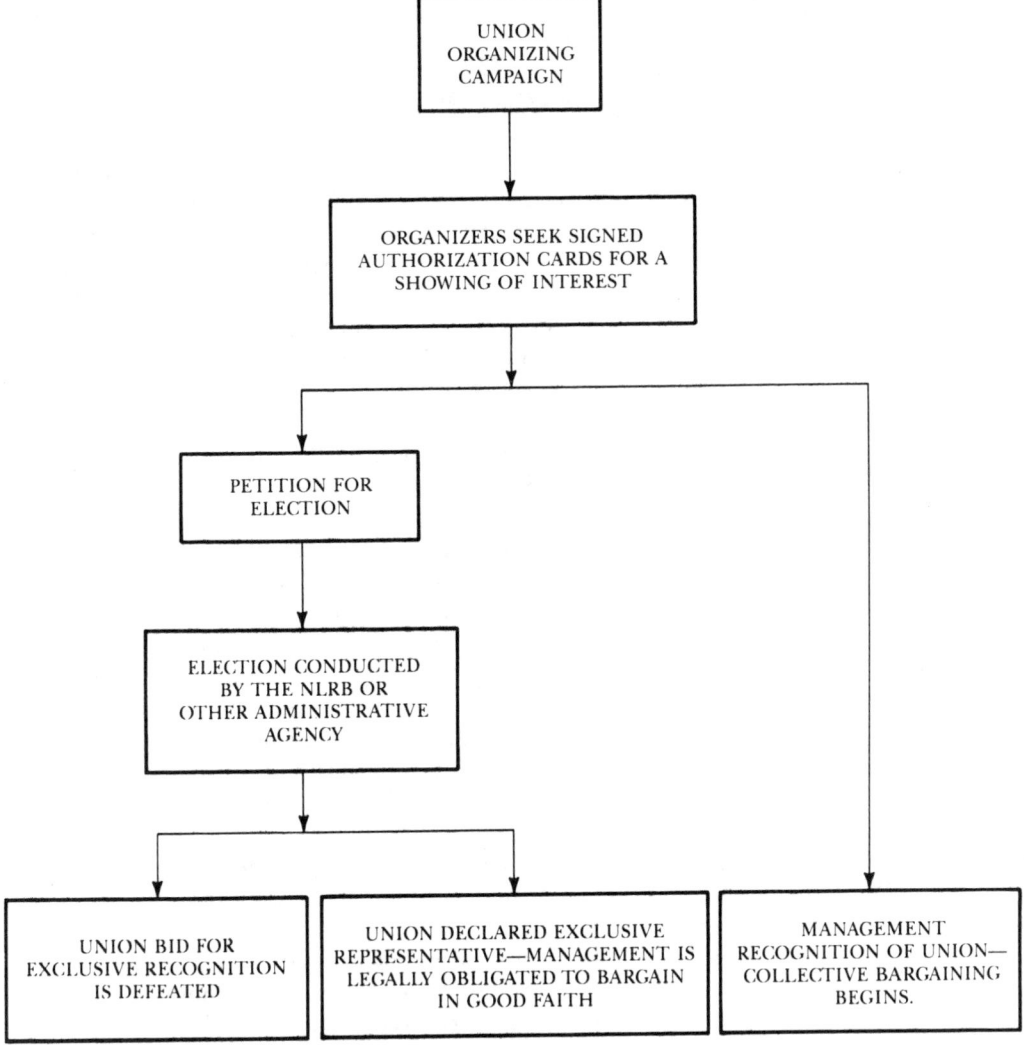

Figure 5-2.   *The Recognition Process*

4. A **recognition strike** or other **job action** might be initiated by
    a union in an effort to convince the employer that a majority
    of the employees in the bargaining unit support it. Such an

TERMS   **Recognition Strike**   A work stoppage whose goal is to force an employer to
formally recognize and deal with a union.

Job Action   A work stoppage or work slowdown, usually by public employees
who cannot legally strike.

action may form the basis for an employer to grant exclusive recognition.

Union drives for exclusive recognition can present problems, no matter what mode of extending it is sought. The primary difficulties involve protecting the principle that the employees must have freedom to choose their exclusive agent, or whether to be represented at all. Coercion is an unfair labor practice. It is unlikely to occur in secret ballot elections, but where authorization cards are solicited or job actions undertaken, it may be a fact of life. If the employer opposes the union, it may file an unfair labor practice charge. Another problem involves the dissemination of information during the union's campaign to enroll support among the employees. Such information can be in the form of picketing or the distribution of literature. In both cases, the activity is likely to be regulated by law. Under procedures established by the National Labor Relations Act, picketing cannot begin more than thirty days before an election petition is filed with the NLRB. The use of the employer's property for organizing activities is also limited by law.

One of the most difficult problems in elections is the nature of propaganda. The NLRB has gone back and forth on the issue of whether factual misrepresentations in campaign propaganda can nullify the results of an election, or taint an election so seriously that it cannot be considered a fair test of the employees' preferences. In a 1962 case involving the Hollywood Ceramics Company, the NLRB held that campaign propaganda could indeed warrant the setting aside of an election. It later abandoned and then subsequently returned to this approach. At the moment, the Board seems to have abandoned it again! Relatedly, employers are allowed to communicate their views on unionization, but they are not permitted to intimidate, threaten, mislead, or seek to coerce employees. The line between legitimate communication and unfair labor practice has been very difficult to draw in this context. The employees' economic dependence upon the employer may lead them to misinterpret the employer's antiunionization statements as threats. If it can be shown that an employer has used an unfair labor practice to thwart recognition, the NLRB may, in turn, certify a union as the exclusive agent (assuming the union has authorization cards from a majority of the employees in the bargaining unit).

Drives for union recognition resulting in elections are inherently disruptive. If a union were to file an election petition, engage in campaigning and picketing, lose the election, and then immediately begin the process all over again, it would place an extreme hardship on the employer. Consequently, public policy incorporates an "election bar," which prohibits electoral activity within a specified period after the last unsuccessful election for recognition. Under NLRB policy this period is twelve months, but in some public sector jurisdictions it may be as long as two years.

Finally, what can be certified, can be decertified. The overriding principle that employees should be represented by agents of their own choosing means that they must be free to switch agents or abandon collective bargaining altogether. Such a process is called decertification; it is the reverse of the certification process. Thirty precent of the employees in a unit would have to show dissatisfaction with the present bargaining agent and file a petition for a decertification election. The results of the election might recertify the incumbent union, lead to the certification of another union, or result in having no union. NLRB regulations require that if such a decertification petition is filed, it should be within ninety to sixty days of the expiration of a valid, written collective bargaining contract. This is called a "contract bar." Its purpose is to prevent decertification too early in the life of a contract (that is, more than ninety days from its termination) or too close to the period in which a new one is under negotiation (within sixty days of its termination). If a contract expires, or no contract is in effect, there is no contract bar. Public sector practices tend to follow the same approach.

NLRB Election Petitions

The National Labor Relations Board will conduct secret ballot elections when any of the kinds of petitions listed below are properly filed with the appropriate NLRB Regional Office:

1. *Certification of Representative.* This petition, which is normally filed by a union, seeks an election to determine whether employees wish to be represented by a union or not. It must be supported by the signatures of 30 percent or more of the employees in the bargaining unit being sought. These signatures may be on separate cards or on a single piece of paper. Generally, this designation or "showing of

interest" contains a statement that the employees want to be represented for purposes of collective bargaining by a specific labor organization. The showing of interest must be signed by each employee, and each employee signature must be dated.

2.   *Decertification.* This petition, which can be filed by an individual, seeks an election to determine whether the authority of a union to act as a bargaining representative of employees should continue. It must be supported by the signatures of 30 percent or more of the employees in the bargaining unit represented by the union. These signatures may be on separate cards or on a single piece of paper. Generally, this "showing of interest" contains a statement that the employees do not wish to be represented for purposes of collective bargaining by the existing labor organization. The showing of interest must be signed by each employee and each employee signature must be dated.

3.   *Withdrawal of Union-Shop Authority.* This petition, which can also be filed by an individual, seeks an election to determine whether the union's contractual authority to require the payment of union dues and initiation fees as a condition of employment should be continued. It must be supported by the signatures of 30 percent or more of the employees in the barganing unit covered by the union-shop agreement. These signatures may be on separate cards or on a single piece of paper. Generally, this "showing of interest" states that the employees no longer want their collective bargaining agreement to contain a union-shop provision. The showing of interest must be signed by each employee and each employee signature must be dated.

4.   *Employer Petition.* This petition is filed by an employer for an election where one or more unions claim to represent the employer's employees or when the employer has reasonable grounds for believing that the union, which is the current bargaining representative, no longer represents a majority of employees.

5. *Unit Clarification.* This petition seeks to clarify the scope of an existing bargaining unit by, for example, determining whether a new classification is properly a part of that unit. The petition may be filed by either the employer or the union.

6. *Amendment of Certification.* This petition seeks the amendment of an outstanding certification of a union to reflect changed circumstances such as changes in the name or affiliation of the union. This petition may be filed by a union or an employer.

Source: National Labor Relations Board (NLRB).

It is obvious that a great deal of effort can go into the process of establishing a collective bargaining relationship. Moreover, a good deal of anxiety is likely to be involved as well. Things do not always go smoothly. Adversary and harmonious relationships between labor and management must be simultaneously maintained. Even in the heat of conflict, each side must scrupulously avoid infringing upon the rights of the other. Consequently, a process that is relatively simple to describe takes on great complexities in practice. The student of labor relations must always be aware that collective bargaining is an anxiety producing process and that each step may involve bitter conflict between the parties. Sometimes this conflict escalates to litigation; sometimes it even spills over into violence. Unfair labor practices and charges are often present and may require adjudication by a labor relations agency. What is described here in a few pages may take months or even years to resolve.

UNIT
DETERMINATION

One of the most difficult aspects of the collective bargaining process is determining appropriate bargaining units. Exclusive agents bargain on behalf of all the employees in a work unit, and the election or authorization processes take place with reference to this unit. It is evident, therefore, that deciding upon the appropriateness of a unit may be tantamount to deciding upon the nature of representation, if any. In other words, by dividing up employees in different ways, and thereby establishing different bargaining units, one can affect which union, if any, is likely to be designated the exclusive agent. For instance, industrial unions generally seek to organize all of the nonsupervisory production and maintenance workers of a particular company. This is often referred to as a P & M unit. Yet, within a P & M unit, there may be several crafts—electricians, painters, plumbers, metal workers, and so forth. These employees may want to be represented on a craft basis, or not at all. Generally, this different outlook has been resolved in favor of the industrial union in manufacturing and mining; but in favor of the craft union in printing, building and construction, and railroads and airlines. Of course, this is only a general pattern and, in any individual case, unit determination may present a very difficult issue. Today, this is especially true in the public sector, where organization and bargaining are relatively new.

While it is possible to identify the general standards used in the private and public sectors for unit determination, the major problem of weighing and applying them in any particular case will remain. The principle to be followed is that there should exist a **community of interest** among the employees to be represented. Otherwise, a single bargaining agent would find it impossible to represent all of their interests equally well. Since the point of collective bargaining in the first place is to represent the workers' interests, this would be an intolerable situation. Misrepresentation is especially problematic since the principle of exclusive recognition prohibits employees from negotiating directly with management. In order to assure representation as best as possible, the following factors are generally taken into account when bargaining units are created:

1. The bargaining history of the industry, trade, or with the employer;
2. The duties, skills, wages, and working conditions of the employees;
3. The organization of the employer's business in relation to the proposed unit, including the geographical location of the plants involved;
4. The form and extent of organization among the employees; and

---

TERMS **Community of Interest** A fidelity to a common purpose that is often the criterion used to determine if a group of employees make up an appropriate bargaining unit.

5. The membership eligibility requirements of the unions involved.

In the public sector, the following criteria might be added:

1. The convenience of the employer;

2. The level of authority of the unit of management with which the union seeks to bargain (for example, the organization of social workers in a department of social services will facilitate bargaining over case loads, but not over civil service regulations and pay); and

3. The agreement of the parties.

Within the framework of these criteria, the employer, the employees, and the union have several choices to make. The employer may want no unionization at all. Consequently, the employer may favor the bargaining unit that is hardest to organize. This may well be one with a limited community of interest among the employees. A larger unit of this nature may be harder to organize than several smaller ones, but once organized, it may be more powerful. Nevertheless, an employer might favor large units because they obviate the need to bargain with many smaller ones. Large units also reduce the risk of being harassed by disruptive strikes by many unions representing small units.

The union is likely to be guided by two criteria: the ability to organize, and the power of the bargaining unit. Generally speaking, smaller units are easier to organize; but unless the employees have skills that are critical to the operation of the business, and not readily replaceable, such a unit will be relatively weak. Larger units also have the benefit of contributing more money to the union's treasury and **strike funds.**

The employees also want bargaining leverage, but it is useless to them if they are not represented well. Consequently, employees want to make sure that there is either (1) a genuine community of interest in the bargaining unit; or (2), if no such community of interest exists, that they are in the dominant faction.

The convergence of these concerns has created some wild variations in the nature of units. In some public sector jurisdictions, there have been collective bargaining units of from one to three employees! Nowadays, however, the trend in the public

TERMS   **Strike Fund**   Monies reserved by a union to be used during a strike to cover costs such as strike benefits to members or legal fees.

sector seems to be toward the larger unit. Public sector employers have an advantage over private sector employers in this regard— they can create the bargaining units by law. This is one of the advantages of sovereignty. Massachusetts presents an interesting illustration. All state workers have been divided into ten units, five of which are for professionals and five for nonprofessional employees. The professional units are: administrative, health care, social/rehabilitation, engineering and science, and education. The nonprofessional units are: clerical and administrative; service, maintenance, and institutional; building trades and crafts; institutional security; and law enforcement.

A bargaining unit is premised on the notion that there will be an exclusive agent to represent the employees in negotiations with an employer. In practice, however, three increasingly common developments substantially alter the concept of the bargaining unit: multi-employer bargaining, multi-union bargaining, and coalition bargaining. The recent history of the workplace has witnessed a tendency in some industries for increasing centralization for collective bargaining on the part of employers and unions. In large measure, this is a function of the increasing size of both companies and unions. Because there needs to be a rough equality in the strength of the two sides in collective bargaining, centralization on the part of one may foster a parallel centralization by the other.

With multi-employer bargaining involving only one union, the employers remain separate economic entities, but they bargain together with the union and seek to reach a single agreement. This approach avoids "whipsawing," whereby the union strikes each employer individually in serial fashion. A whipsaw strike places considerable pressure on a single employer, who is likely to lose business to competitors during the strike. Multi-employer bargaining also enables the employers to share information and in effect hold the price of labor constant among them. Consequently, the employers' behavior may be subject to prosecution under **antitrust** statutes, depending upon the precise nature of agreements and the extent of **collusion** in other areas where competition should be the rule. From labor's perspective, multi-employer bargaining prevents one or a few employers from trying to undercut the wages paid by the others. Finally, this form of bargaining tends to

TERMS   **Antitrust Acts**   Federal and state laws to protect trade from monopoly control, price-fixing, and other restraints of trade.

Collusion   Secret action taken by two or more persons together to cheat another or to commit fraud.

promote labor stability, which is useful for firms seeking to assess the future and decide where to invest resources. Generally speaking, multi-employer bargaining can also accommodate local issues at any given plant or employer.

Aside from being concerned with antitrust violations, those opposing multi-employer bargaining tend to view it as deadening to the collective bargaining process; diversionary in the sense that it tends to hold wage demands constant and focus on other matters such as fringe benefits; and damaging to the influence of local unions. In addition, some economists argue that any collective bargaining practice that tends to reduce wage competition will reduce workers' purchasing power and therefore tend to dampen the economy by reducing demand.

Multi-employer bargaining does not seem to have been anticipated by the National Labor Relations Act. However, the NLRB and the courts are tolerant of it if it is consensual on both sides. No employer or union can be forced to enter into multi-employer bargaining. On the other hand, once accepted by consent of the parties, neither can withdraw except under "unusual circumstances"—a term which currently carries a vague meaning. Multi-employer bargaining seems particularly appropriate in the public sector, where many separate municipalities may be clustered around central cities. It would simplify matters a great deal if collective bargaining for police, firefighters, and other public employees could take place "metropolitan-wide," rather than in each jurisdiction.

Multi-union bargaining, where several unions bargain with a single employer, is less common, but serves some of the same purposes. It must be entered into consensually by all the parties. It is particularly useful in craft settings where the employer might be subject to "round-the-clock" bargaining with multiple unions. Moreover, it prevents a series of strikes that might have the effect of shutting down the entire business operation and causing grave economic harm. Unions may favor this approach where no single one of them is strong enough to exercise substantial power over the employer. The public sector is perhaps a more natural setting for multi-union bargaining since unions cannot legally strike in most jurisdictions and may find greater strength in coordinated bargaining.

"Coalition bargaining" is essentially multi-employer/multi-union bargaining. It has been used for collective bargaining with General Electric and Westinghouse.

One of the concerns that arises when a relatively small bargaining unit merges with a larger unit is that at some point the employees in the smaller unit may be poorly represented and unable to sever themselves from the overall unit. Critics point out that this is an unhealthy aspect of the tendency toward greater centralization of collective bargaining. Yet the alternative is fragmentation in an increasingly integrated and interdependent world economy. Indeed, eventually the "international" union may really become international (aside from Canada) by engaging in collective bargaining on behalf of all of the different nationals employed by today's multinational corporations.

THE SCOPE OF BARGAINING

Once the collective bargaining relationship is established, the next question is what the participants will bargain over. This is referred to as the "scope of bargaining." It is almost always conceptualized as consisting of three broad categories of items: subjects over which bargaining is mandatory, subjects considered illegal or prohibited, and subjects upon which bargaining is permitted but not required.

Subjects over which bargaining is mandatory are designated "mandatory" because the relevant statute or common law makes it an unfair labor practice or breach of good faith to refuse to bargain over them. For instance, the National Labor Relations Act requires bargaining over "wages, hours, and other terms and conditions of employment." Clearly, this is a broad scope of mandatory bargaining items. "Wages" include such matters as overtime pay, supplemental pay, retirement pay, pay for **jury duty,** scheduling of paydays, paid and unpaid leaves of absence, severance pay, salary progression, merit pay, shift **differentials,** and additional pay related items. Hours includes leaves, vacations, starting and stopping times, work schedules, lunch and other breaks, number of hours per week, month, and/or year, hours on call or standby service, and time off for union activities. "Other terms and conditions of employment" is a rather open-ended phrase that is commonly included in collective bargaining legislation. It can refer to such things as the length of the contract agreement, safety, **seniority,**

TERMS   **Jury Duty Pay**   The practice of giving employees leave with pay if they are called to jury duty. Many organizations reduce such pay by the amount the employee is paid by the court for jury service. The Supreme Court has upheld state laws requiring this pay.

Differentials   Increases in wage rates because of shift work or other conditions generally considered to be undesirable.

Seniority   Preference or priority; often, but not always, because the person or thing came first in time. In employment, seniority may be a formal or union security, **grievance procedures,** matters of employee comfort, retirement, pensions, no-strike clauses, staffing and assignment of work, training, insurance benefits, and a host of other matters. Under a scope of bargaining this broad, it would be possible to restructure the nature of relationships in the workplace to a great extent, if both sides were willing to do so. Indeed, managerial authority can be reduced, employee participation encouraged, and **profit sharing** implemented. The fact that an item is mandatory in the scope of bargaining does not mean that the parties must reach ageement on it. Often impasses are reached instead. Depending on legal arrangements, the existence of an impasse may trigger dispute resolution procedures, including mediation and factfinding. In the public sector, where the strike is generally prohibited, arbitration is also commonly used to resolve impasses.

The second category of items in the scope of bargaining are practices considered illegal or prohibited. These are matters that, by law, cannot be bargained. The closed shop is an example. In the public sector a number of matters relating to an agency's mission, budget, ability to hire, fire, and assign employees or contract out work may be prohibited items. These limitations on the scope of bargaining in the public sector are vestiges of sovereignty and the desire not to allow public policy to be made by bargains struck with labor unions instead of by the voting public through their representative political institutions.

Falling between these two categories are items upon which bargaining is permitted, but not required. Either side may refuse to discuss such a matter. To do so is not considered a breach of fair labor practices or good faith. Even if the participants begin to discuss a permitted matter and fail to reach an agreement, the unresolved dispute is not considered an impasse and impasse resolution procedures need not be undertaken. Generally speaking, unless the employer is bound by a contract, it can make unilateral changes in the permitted item area without violating the law. In the case of

---

TERMS   informal mechanism that gives priority to the individuals who have the longest service in an organization. Seniority is often used to determine which employees will be promoted, subjected to layoff, or given other employment advantages.

Grievance Procedure   The specific means by which grievances are channeled for their adjustment through progressively higher levels of authority in both an organization and a union.

Profit Sharing   A plan set up by an employer to distribute part of the firm's profits to some or all of its employees in current or deferred sums based not only upon individual or group performance, but on the business as a whole as well.

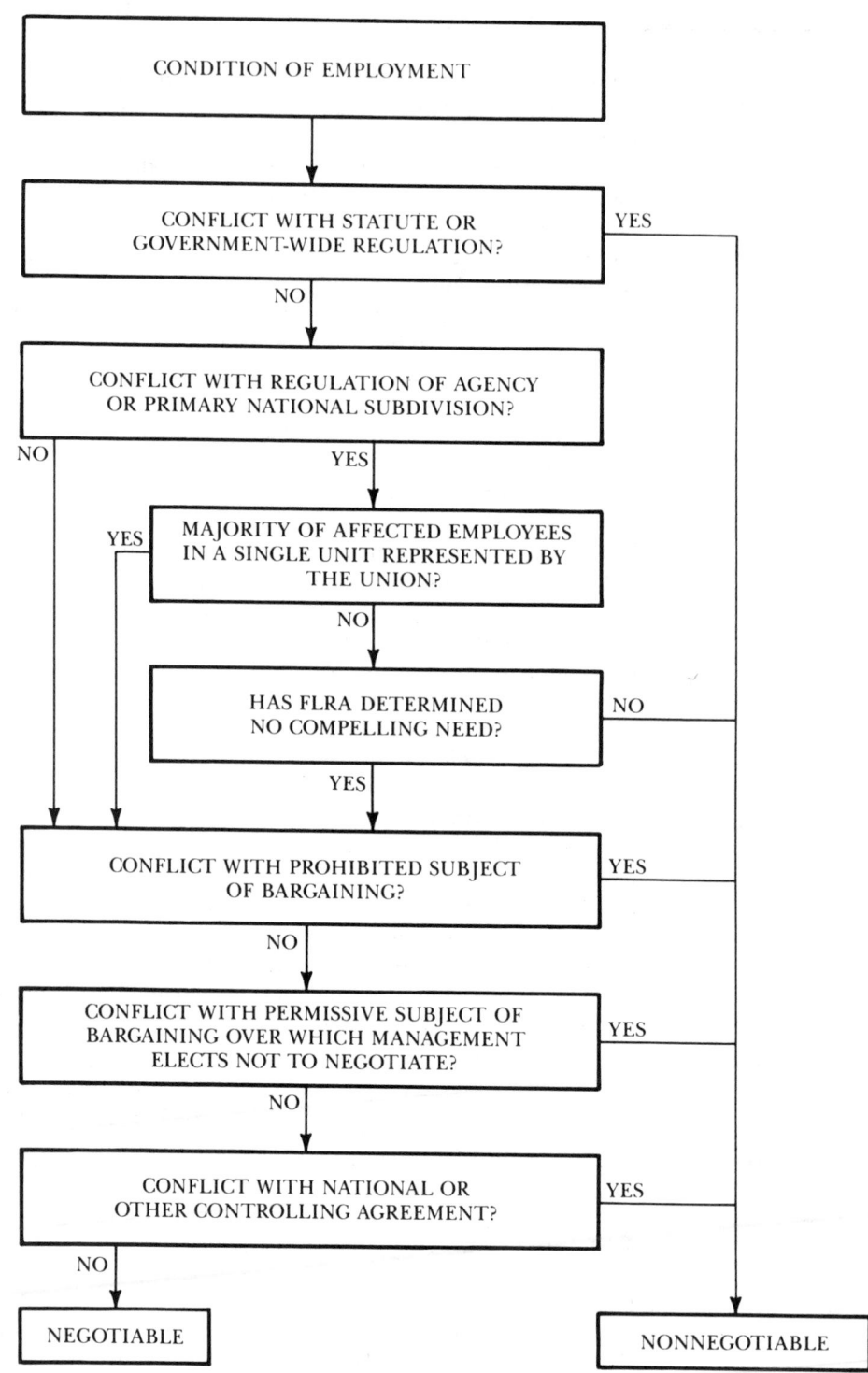

Figure 5-3.   Determining the Scope of Bargaining in Federal Employment

mandatory items, by contrast, the employer must consult with the union before making changes. In the private sector, the permitted area includes matters such as requiring that the union take a poll of its members before calling a strike. In the public sector, the permitted area tends to be more extensive since the mandatory category is often more limited. In the federal government, for instance, permitted items include technology, method of performing work, and the number, types, and grades of employees or positions assigned to a unit. But, under regulations covering most federal employees, only negotiating a grievance procedure is a truly mandatory item.

The different mix of permitted, prohibited, and mandatory items in the public sector often raises perplexing questions about the scope of bargaining. For example, are matters of student discipline best considered working conditions or matters of public policy? What about the number of police officers assigned to a squad car, or the conditions under which a police officer can use deadly force? Decentralization of school systems? The quality and technology of patient care in public mental health facilities? There is no easy way to resolve these questions. Clearly, they are matters of public policy, but they may also be matters of safety that are critical to employees. Different courts, administrative agencies, and other public policy-making bodies have reached different conclusions on such matters. Some believe that the test should be whether the item has a "significant relation" to working conditions as defined within the mandatory or permitted categories. Others take a balancing approach to decide whether the item is mandatory. Under this approach, the question would be the extent to which the item is critical to working conditions versus the extent to which it is critical to sovereignty or matters of public policy generally.

Over the years, the tendency has been to expand the scope of mandatory items in both the private and public sectors. This is in keeping with the basic concept that conditions in the workplace should be codetermined by the employer and the union. One of the things a wide scope of bargaining accomplishes is the need for management to negotiate for its rights, rather than simply assert them unilaterally. And, of course, negotiations take the form of **quid pro quo,** which requires that management give something in return for a union concession on management rights. This might be individual and union security, higher wages, reduced hours, or improved grievance procedures.

TERMS **Quid pro quo** Latin meaning "something for something"; the giving of one valuable thing for another.

GOOD FAITH   Collective bargaining arrangements do not require that the parties reach an agreement. However, they do require that the parties try to reach one and that they treat the collective bargaining process as a legitimate means of defining relationships in the workplace. This is the matter of "good faith," a term that has engendered a great deal of controversy. The problem with the requirement of "good faith" is that it is necessary if collective bargaining is to work, but it is also a state of mind that is difficult, if not impossible, to observe. Consequently, when the parties fail to reach an agreement, or one side feels the other is not taking the discussion of an item seriously enough, it is common to make an accusation of "bad faith." If carried far enough, such a complaint might have to be adjudicated by a labor relations agency, such as the NLRB, or even by a court. The question of good faith is further clouded by the broad rights of the parties to adopt appropriate bargaining strategies and to use economic weapons to try to urge (or compel) the other side to agree to their terms. An aggressive strategy is not, in itself, a breach of good faith; but an obstructionist one may be. In practice, of course, the line between one or the other is very difficult to draw.

One of the more controversial bargaining approaches in this connection was General Electric's reliance on **boulwareism.** Using this strategy, GE canvassed its lowest-level supervisors to determine what employees wanted and expected. These desires and expectations were assessed along with managerial considerations and integrated into a **package.** GE then announced the package publicly and instituted a public relations campaign to demonstrate its reasonableness. When collective bargaining actually began, the company essentially announced that this was its first, last, and best offer. In other words, that it was not prepared to move from the package.

TERMS   **Boulwareism**   Lemuel R. Boulware was the vice-president of the General Electric Company who pioneered this tactic in the 1950s. Because this approach called for management to communicate directly with the workers, circumventing the union, it was challenged as an unfair practice. Boulwareism, as used by General Electric, was found in violation of the National Labor Relations Act in a 1969 ruling of the U.S. Circuit Court of Appeals in New York. The company's appeal to the U.S. Supreme Court was denied.

Package   The total money value (usually quoted as dollars and cents per hour) of an increase in wages and benefits achieved through collective bargaining. For example, a new contract might give employees an increase of fifty cents an hour. However, when the value of increased medical and pension benefits are included, the "package" might come to seventy-four cents an hour.

While GE has abandoned boulwareism, the practice raises many legal and moral questions regarding "good faith." Is such an approach merely a strategy, or is the employer arriving at the bargaining table with a closed mind? Does seeking to find out directly what employees want violate the spirit of exclusive representation? Suppose a union followed a similar approach by stating publicly what it wanted and asserting that it would not accept "a penny less." Would the employer be required to make counterproposals, or could it simply say "no" to the union's proposals? It may be a cop-out to say it all depends upon the terrain and circumstances, but that is the proper answer. Since good faith remains a state of mind, it is not always possible to say what it requires.

Nevertheless, at least two common employer breaches of good faith have emerged over the years. One is an employer's assertion that it does not have the ability to pay for what the union is demanding, without being ready to open its books and demonstrate that this assertion is substantially true. The second is for the employer to alter essential conditions of employment unilaterally at the expiration of a contract. In order to do so in good faith, the employer must first bargain to impasse with the union. Total refusal to bargain is no longer common, but it, too, would be a violation of the requirements of good faith.

In the public sector, an additional matter of good faith has sometimes emerged. Unlike the representative for a private employer, the individual or team negotiating on behalf of a government cannot *bind* the legislature to go along with whatever bargain might be struck. Consequently, there is the possibility that the legislature will reject all or part of the bargain. It may do so in good faith, but it may not use the negotiator for the purpose of "surface bargaining"; that is, trying to knock the union down to a lower position in order to later use that position as the basis for further bargaining. Once again, though, the difficulty lies in determining the intent of the legislative body. Constitutional law and public policy considerations may prevent a government from delegating its authority to a negotiator while collective bargaining requires that its representative have the authority to negotiate. A fine line must necessarily be drawn under such circumstances.

NEGOTIATIONS: STRUCTURES AND STRATEGIES

The point of collective bargaining is to create a process whereby employers and representatives of employees negotiate the nature of conditions in the workplace. Public policy as embodied in contemporary American labor law seeks to facilitate the process of reaching agreements. But the law itself does not specify what those agreements should be in terms of substance. This is up to the parties involved. The structures and strategies they use will have a great deal to do with the outcome of their negotiations. While recognizing that every bargaining situation may have its unique aspects, this section will consider the common wisdom on how parties may facilitate the process of reaching acceptable agreements.

Preparation for Negotiation

Contracts generally run two to three years, although shorter and longer ones are not uncommon. Nevertheless, preparation for the next contract should begin virtually upon the signing of the existing agreement. Some of the matters requiring constant evaluation are relatively technical. Included here would be the cost of **escalator clauses** in retirement systems; the need to rewrite work rules as new technologies are introduced; evaluation of seniority requirements as they affect production and employee security; the possibility and costs of introducing profit sharing, participatory management, or other approaches to incorporating employees into the management of a firm; introduction of **flexi-time,** rewriting the contract to comply better with federal and state laws pertaining to the workplace (such as equal opportunity); and assessing the costs of linking economic benefits to the **Consumer Price Index.**

Less technical preparations involve monitoring noneconomic aspects of the contract, such as the grievance procedures, to determine how they could be improved next time around. Similarly, the specific language of a contract should be considered with a view toward eliminating undesirable ambiguity. Management should also consider how its changing corporate objectives, or a changing

TERMS

Escalator Clause   A provision of a collective bargaining agreement which allows for periodic wage adjustments in response to changes in the cost of living usually as determined by the Consumer Price Index of the Bureau of Labor Statistics.

Flexi-time   A flexible work schedule in which workers can, within a prescribed band of time in the morning and again in the afternoon, start and finish work at their discretion as long as they complete the total number of hours required for a given period of a day, week, or month.

Consumer Price Index   A monthly economic index prepared by the Bureau of Labor Statistics of the U. S. Department of Labor which measures the change in average prices of the goods and services purchased by urban wage earners and their families.

business climate, are likely to affect future negotiations. Both sides should develop plans to deal with a strike or **lockout** should an impasse be reached. In addition, both sides will want to assess what employees doing similar work in similar industries and geographic areas are being paid.

The nature of preparation by management and unions is somewhat asymmetrical. Management will be largely preoccupied with economic costs and matters of managerial rights. It also has many other things to do—mainly running the business—aside from representing the firm in collective bargaining. Consequently, its collective bargaining approach will reflect these other concerns and be integrated with them.

Unions, on the other hand, are in the business of representing employees—that is their chief function. But representation is always political. For example, an industrial union may have considerable difficulties speaking for the employees in a large and diverse bargaining unit. There are many divisions among employees; race, gender, seniority, level of skill, and age are all relevant to employees' desires and demands upon their union. While craft unions tend to have a greater "community of interest," they, too, will have divisions. The union is likely to have full-time **business agents** or other employees and staff to assess employees' desires and integrate them into a bargaining package.

Preparation can be considered successful when it (1) generates knowledge of one's own bargaining case as well as that of the other side; and (2) results in contract proposals that are workable and attainable. Naturally, a successful negotiation will depend upon the economic strength of the two sides, the personal skill and experience of the negotiators, and the adoption of a positive, good faith approach to the bargaining process.

Organization of the Bargaining Process

Collective bargaining is a process that can benefit much from careful structuring. Many observers agree that some structural aspects are crucial in facilitating the ability to reach agreements:

TERMS

Lockout   An employer's refusal to allow employees to work. This is not an individual matter between an employer and a single employee, but a tactic in employer-union disputes. The closing of a business in order to pressure the employees and the union to accept the employer's offered terms of employment is the employer's version of a strike.

Business Agent   A full-time officer of a local union, elected or appointed, who handles grievances, helps enforce agreements, and otherwise deals with the union's financial, administrative, or labor-management problems.

1. Bargaining teams should be relatively small, each consisting of a single spokesperson, through whom communications in full session will take place. The spokesperson will also be the conduit to the media, if it is agreed that the negotiations will be reported to the press. Management's team should include representatives of the divisions that will be affected by the contract, a **personnelist,** and someone competent to assess the costs of various proposals and counterproposals. This is probably the bare minimum for a medium size firm. Larger corporations may need additional staff under the direction of representatives such as these. While officials from the local union will be present, a representative of their international body may serve as spokesperson. Economists, legal counsel, and other staff who can analyze the content of proposals and aid in the formulation of counterproposals should also be present. It is important that the bargaining teams be large enough to evaluate information, proposals and counterproposals efficiently; but if the teams are too large, unnecessary conflict is more likely to develop. The two sides should also be balanced in terms of number of individuals present; pronounced asymmetry can seem overwhelming to the smaller side.

2. The two sides should agree in advance on the timing, location, and length of the bargaining sessions.

3. The format of meetings in terms of exchange of proposals and media coverage, if any, should be established.

4. The format of proposals should be established. Generally, at the outset, these should be in writing. It is useful for the two sides to exchange counterproposals in the first session and then adjourn to consider them. However, one side may not favor simultaneous exchange of proposals.

5. An agenda should be established. For example, economic items might be considered first, other items afterward.

6. If possible, the parties should agree in advance on the acceptability of economic data, such as that available from the Bureau of Labor Statistics.

7. A decision must be made as to whether to treat each item separately, or seek to bargain an entire package at once.

TERMS **Personnelist** One who is professionally engaged in the practice of personnel management.

Adoption of an
Appropriate Strategy

The purpose of collective bargaining is to reach a workable agreement. This requires that the participants ultimately accept the agreement as fair, or at least the best that could be obtained through fair labor practices. In most cases labor and management know that they will be negotiating with one another in the future and recognize their interdependence and shared interests. In any event, it is enforcement that is the crucial test of a contract's workability. Consequently, adopting a strategy for collective bargaining requires deference to the future in terms of living with the contract, the other participant(s), and negotiating subsequent contracts. Ideally, both sides will be governed by these concerns and will engage in what Roger Fisher and William Ury in *Getting to Yes* call "principled negotiations." This approach seeks to avoid the pitfalls of conventional bargaining. One should:

1. *Separate the people from the problem.* Recognize that the problem is arriving at a workable and desirable agreement. Don't let personalities get in the way.

2. *Focus on interests, not positions.* Each side will have different, but often overlapping interests. By focusing on the areas where the interests are compatible, or can be redefined to make them compatible, negotiators can avoid getting locked into initial positions. This is the antithesis of boulwareism.

3. *Invent options for mutual gain.* Explore the possibilities for harmony and compatibility. Although labor and management are adversarial in important respects, it is also important to avoid concluding that they are adversaries in all respects.

4. *Insist on using objective criteria as a means of determining what is acceptable.* Since one cannot expect to dominate in every bargaining situation, it is important that the acceptability of an agreement turn on objective factors, fairly applied. For example, if management and labor have agreed to cost of living increases in principle, it is important to adopt an objective measure of what the increase has actually been.

The "principled negotiations" approach is highly desirable in ongoing labor relations. In practice, it has already been employed in a great number of situations involving experienced negotiators and mature collective bargaining relationships. In theory, it is also well suited to the public sector. Here management and labor both have the same general obligation—to serve the public interest. Moreover, public sector labor relations laws declare that collective bargaining is in the public interest. Therefore, neither side should obstruct the development of a fruitful negotiating approach. Unfortunately, however, it is difficult to apply principled negotiations where one party rejects it and struggles to maintain a "hard bargaining" posture. Ironically, along with the expectation that principled negotiations are characteristic of more mature bargaining relationships, the "hard bargaining" approach is frequently found in the less mature relationships of the public sector where it is actually least appropriate. "Hard bargaining" is not especially productive, despite the fury and the furor it can engender. As Fisher and Ury indicate, it is characterized by:

1. The view that the participants are adversaries.

2. "Victory!" as the foremost goal.

3. Demands for concessions as a condition of a good faith bargaining relationship.

4. Personal attacks on the "opponents."

5. Distrust.

6. Threats.

7. Deception.

8. Demands for one-sided gains as the price of arriving at agreement.

9. Insistence on one's position and viewing it as the single answer to a dispute.

10. The treatment of negotiations as a contest of wills in which various forms of pressure can legitimately be applied.

When confronted with "hard bargaining" situations, negotiators on the other side should try to change the nature of the game. But that may be difficult or impossible, and the two sides will be likely to fall back upon traditional strategies.

Traditionally, management will identify some concrete goals it seeks to achieve through negotiations. For example, these might include a stronger **management rights clause,** a no-strike clause, or a "giveback" of some kind. Management must expect to make concessions, but in traditional bargaining it will view these in a

---

TERMS **Management Rights Clause** That portion of a collective bargaining agreement that defines the scope of management rights, functions, and responsibilities—essentially all those activities which management can undertake without the consent of the union.

quid pro quo fashion. Nothing will be given up without receiving something in return. It is important to note that the union may value some practices, such as a dues **checkoff,** much more highly than will management. This should be taken into account in the quid pro quo balance. Management will also be prepared for a variety of union hard bargaining tactics, such as public grandstanding and threats of strikes. It is often considered best for management to try to gain agreement that bargaining will be over noneconomic items first, since these may be easier to deal with and are less likely to poison the bargaining atmosphere.

Unions face a somewhat different problem in negotiations. Many of them have clauses in their constitutions that require membership approval of negotiated settlements. Under these circumstances, the union negotiators have to win agreement both from management and from union members—no mean feat. Moreover, unions may have less positive inducements to "give" to management in quid pro quo transactions. Management can give higher wages, fringe benefits, and so forth. Labor cannot always "give" more work or guarantee higher productivity. Giving back something won in the past is possible, but difficult for union leadership because of internal union politics. Therefore, in traditional bargaining, labor's strongest card may be its ability to disrupt the employer's enterprise. Strikes can be threatened. Negative publicity can be disseminated to the media and the public. In addition, as Baird, Anderson, and Damas have observed, some of the following cajoling tactics may be used against management:

1. Refusal to move from one's position until management becomes "reasonable";

2. Demands for management's "final offer," in order to obtain a better idea of what management is willing to concede;

3. "Nickel and diming," or trying to squeeze every last bit of concession from management; and

4. Threats to launch a number of "unfair labor practice" charges or file a grievance for even the most minor breaches of the present contract.

TERMS   **Checkoff** A union security provision, commonly provided for in the collective bargaining agreement, that allows the employer to deduct union dues, assessments, and initiation fees from the pay of all union members. The deducted amounts are then delivered to the union on a prearranged schedule. The Taft-Hartley Act requires that union members give written permission for these fees to be deducted.

The outcome of labor negotiations depends upon the maturity of the collective bargaining relationship, the personalities, the past experience, the public relations, and the economic strength of the two sides. Since these factors are hard to measure or assess, generally speaking the outcome of specific, difficult, nonroutine negotiations is unpredictable. This is especially true in the public sector, where an impasse may result in binding arbitration rather than a strike. As we will see in the next chapter, arbitrators use different criteria in making awards, and their actions can be problematic. In the private sector, however, lockouts and strikes—the ultimate tests of economic strength—may be the vehicles through which disputes are eventually settled.

CONTRACT ELEMENTS   Regardless of the outcome of negotiations, most collective bargaining contracts will contain similar clauses. These include:

1. Preamble,

2. Recognition clause,

3. Mutual compliance clause,

4. Grievance procedure clause,

5. Work hours and overtime clause,

6. Vacation and holidays clause indicating eligibility and scheduling procedures,

7. Leave of absence (including sick leave) clause,

8. Seniority provision clause,

9. Entire agreement clause (i.e., "zipper clause," indicating that the agreement constitutes the entirety of the agreed-upon contractual arrangements and that new elements will not be added, by which the agreement is "zipped up"),

10. Savings clause, indicating that if for any reason part of the agreement is illegal, the rest will still be considered binding upon the parties, and

11. Duration of the contract clause.

In addition to these elements, a labor contract may commonly include a management rights clause and a no-strike (during the length of the contract) clause. The management rights clause is a controversial item in some respects. According to one theory, management has all the rights to regulate work and behavior in the workplace that have not been preempted by legislation or by contractual arrangements. Under this interpretation, it is inadvisable to spell out what management's rights are. A second theory holds that management is a trustee for the owners of a firm, or, in the public sector, the public. As such it has no inherent rights, but only those that are necessary for it to perform its trustee functions well. Under the trustee theory, a management rights clause merely confirms which rights management asserts and which ones are shared with labor, that is, subject to negotiations.

The "no strike" clause is a mandatory subject for bargaining in the private sector. In the public sector it is less relevant since strikes are generally prohibited. Generally speaking, the no-strike clause is labor's quid pro quo for management's agreement to submit disputes over the enforcement of contracts to binding arbitration. Presently, over 95 percent of all private sector contracts contain a binding arbitration provision.

The legality of binding arbitration coupled with the no-strike clause was established by the U.S. Supreme Court in **Textile Workers v. Lincoln Mills** and subsequently in what is called the **Steelworkers Trilogy.** These cases established the principle that grievance arbitration will be the final determinant of the meaning of contracts when (1) the parties specify in the contract when arbitration will be used and that it will be binding, (2) the arbitrator actually adheres to the contract, and (3) there are no gross errors or breaches of procedural fairness. Where these conditions are met, the courts will not substitute their judgments on the meaning of the contract for those of an arbitrator.

A no-strike clause coupled with the binding arbitration of grievances goes far to create the appropriate atmosphere for principled negotiations. While the employer is required to relinquish a unilateral right to interpret the contract, labor is also required to abstain from striking when it is opposed to management's administration of the contract. An arbitrator is used instead of the disruptive application of economic power, productivity is maintained, and disputes are settled in a fashion considered legitimate by both sides.

TERMS   **Textile Workers v. Lincoln Mills**   A 1957 U.S. Supreme Court case which held that the arbitration clause in a collective bargaining agreement is the quid pro quo given by the employer in return for the no-strike clause agreed to by a union.

Steelworkers Trilogy   So called because it refers to three 1960 U.S. Supreme Court decisions involving the United Steelworkers of America.

REVIEW QUESTIONS

---

1. Consider the ramifications of the principle of exclusive recognition on: (a) nonunion members in the bargaining unit, and (b) workers belonging to a social or occupational minority in the bargaining unit.

2. Consider a work organization with which you are familiar and discuss the creation of bargaining units from the perspectives of: (a) organizing workers and obtaining exclusive recognition, (b) representing workers, and (c) bargaining effectively with the employer.

3. What kind of items do you believe should be outside the scope of bargaining because they are "management rights"? What aspects of union organization should be kept outside the scope of bargaining?

4. Should the following be within the scope of bargaining in the public sector? Why or why not?

   a. School discipline

   b. Weapons and bullets used by police

   c. Police protective gear (helmets, vests, etc.)

   d. Number of pupils per class

   What principles might guide your answers?

5. How would you turn a "hard bargainer" into a "principled negotiator"?

6. In what ways might the economic, political, and social environment influence the collective bargaining process?

FOR ADDITIONAL READING

Aaron, Benjamin, Joseph R. Grodin, and James L. Stein. *Public Sector Bargaining.* Washington, DC: Bureau of National Affairs, Inc., 1979.

Baird, James, Donald Anderson, and Stanislaw Damas. *Practical Labor Relations for Public Employers.* Wheat Ridge, CO; Colorado Municipal League, 1978.

Davey, Harold W., Mario F. Bognanno, and David L. Estenson. *Contemporary Collective Bargaining,* Fourth Edition. Englewood Cliffs, NJ: Prentice-Hall, 1982.

Fisher, Roger and William Ury. *Getting to Yes: Negotiating Agreement Without Giving In.* Boston: Houghton Mifflin, 1981.

Rubin, Jeffrey Z. and Bert R. Brown. *The Social Psychology of Bargaining and Negotiation.* New York: Academic Press, 1975.

Ryder, Meyer S., Charles M. Rehmus, and Sanford Cohen. *Management Preparation for Collective Bargaining.* Homewood, IL: Dow Jones-Irwin, 1976.

Schick, Richard P. and Jean J. Couturier. *The Public Interest in Government Labor Relations.* Cambridge, MA: Ballinger, 1977.

Walton, Richard E. and Robert B. McKersie. *A Behavioral Theory of Labor Negotiations.* New York: McGraw-Hill, 1965.

6 Resolving Impasses and Strikes

Prologue
Shooting Down the Air Traffic Controllers

Seldom does a strike result in the complete destruction of a union. Of course, the Professional Air Traffic Controllers Organization (PATCO) was an unusual union in many respects. It was one of the very few unions that supported Ronald Reagan for president in 1980. It was the first major union to make **job stress** and **burnout** major issues of collective bargaining. And it overwhelmingly rejected an average annual salary offer of $38,000 in favor of striking.

On July 29, 1981, 95 percent of PATCO's 13,000 members voted to reject the government's final offer. They wanted twice-a-year cost of living increases that would be one and a half times greater than inflation, a four-day, thirty-two-hour workweek without a compensating salary cut, and retirement after twenty years at 75 percent of base salary. As one striking controller put it: "Where are they going to get 13,000 controllers and train them

TERMS **Job Stress** An engineering term applied to humans in reference to working conditions that can overtax an individual's emotional and/or physical ability to cope with them.

Burnout A worker's feeling of mental and physical fatigue that causes indifference and emotional disengagement from his or her job.

before the economy sinks? The reality is, we are it. They have to deal with us."

The government was equally determined in its resolve to keep the planes flying. First, it cut back many scheduled flights and reduced staff at some smaller airports. Then it brought supervisors and some retired controllers back to service and ordered as many military controllers as it could spare to civilian stations. Finally, President Reagan addressed the nation on television. After reminding viewers that it is illegal for federal government employees to strike and that each controller signed an oath asserting that he or she would never strike, he proclaimed: "They are in violation of the law, and if they do not report for work within forty-eight hours, they have forfeited their jobs and will be terminated." Just over one thousand controllers reported back. Most thought that the president was bluffing.

Then the ghoulish wait began. It would only take one mid-air collision and the deaths of hundreds for the situation to radically change to the union's favor. PATCO was loudly critical of the safety of the nation's "fill-in" air traffic control system. The union's president menacingly suggested: "I hope that nothing happens!" He told the Secretary of Transportation: "If passengers are killed, it'll be your responsibility." Luckily, while there were some near misses, no one was hurt.

As the strike continued the President showed he wasn't bluffing. Over 11,000 former controllers received formal letters of dismissal. The union's assets were frozen by the courts, some PATCO leaders were literally hauled away to jail in chains, and the Department of Transportation started formal proceedings to decertify the union.

With its members fired, with practically no public support, and with the "fill-in" system working better every day, PATCO—the union that had broken ranks with labor to support Republican presidential candidate Reagan—called for labor solidarity. The response was lip service. All of the major labor leaders verbally supported the strike and deplored the President's efforts at "union-busting," but they did nothing else. United Auto Workers President Douglas Fraser said that the strike "could do massive damage to the labor movement. That's why PATCO should have talked to the AFL-CIO council"—before they struck. Had any of the other major airline unions joined in the strike, the system would surely have been shut down. But none of these unions felt that they had any obligation to support the controllers in any way that mattered.

In late October 1980 the Federal Labor Relations Authority formally decertified PATCO—the first time that it had

ever done so to any union of government workers. The following December, PATCO filed for bankruptcy. In the end over 11,-
000 controllers who stayed on strike permanently lost their jobs.

ECONOMIC
WEAPONS

The legal and procedural framework for collective bargaining does
not guarantee any particular set of substantive conditions in the
workplace. It is the inherent object of all collective bargaining legislation to establish a process whereby management and labor can
bargain to achieve an agreement that both consider at least "liv-
able." Of course, it is well understood that because the interests of
the two sides are largely adversarial, there is always the possibility
that they will be unable to reach an agreement. Indeed, there is
even a 20 percent chance that a union which has gained exclusive
recognition will never be able to make the further gain of signing a
first contract with the employer. Failure to agree over mandatory
"future terms," and "interests" is called an *impasse*. For the collective bargaining process to function well, some mechanisms must be
developed and used to overcome them.

In the private sector, the main mechanisms for resolving impasses in one way or the other are the economic sanctions that each
side can apply to the other. Labor has the right to strike. Without
labor, the employer cannot produce goods or services or extract resources from the earth. In short, the employer's business depends
on labor—at least in the long term. Moreover, a struck employer
still has **overhead** costs. It may be liable for the nonfulfillment of
contracts with other businesses or customers generally. While the
strike can be quite damaging in economic terms, it is important to
bear in mind that the economic effect of a strike depends upon
many factors. How high are inventory levels? Can the employer
find substitute labor or rely upon mechanization, computer technology, and supervisory personnel for the carrying on of services or
the production of products? Have the employer's customers, in anticipation of a strike, built up their inventories of the employer's
products in advance?

The strike is by no means a perfect economic weapon. Not
only does its success depend on a number of factors pertaining to
the employer's business and specific economic conditions, it also

TERMS **Overhead** The general and administrative expenses of a business that cannot be directly allocated to a particular product or department; includes such
things as power, water, maintenance, rent, real estate tax, etc.

TABLE 6-1.
WORK STOPPAGES: 1947 TO 1982

[Excludes work stoppages involving fewer than 1,000 workers and lasting less than 1 day. Information is based on reports of labor disputes appearing in daily newspapers, trade journals, and other public sources. The parties to the disputes are contacted by telephone, when necessary, to clarify details of the stoppages.]

Year	Number of work stoppages[1]	Workers involved[2] (1,000)	Days Idle Number (1,000)	Days Idle Percent estimated working time[3]	Year	Number of work stoppages[1]	Workers involved[2] (1,000)	Days Idle Number (1,000)	Days Idle Percent estimated working time[3]
1947	270	1,629	25,720	(NA)	1973	317	1,400	16,260	.08
1950	424	1,698	30,390	.26	1974	424	1,796	31,809	.16
1955	363	2,055	21,180	.16	1975	235	965	17,563	.09
1960	222	896	13,260	.09	1976	231	1,519	23,962	.12
1965	268	999	15,140	.10	1977	298	1,212	21,258	.10
1967	381	2,192	31,320	.18	1978	219	1,006	23,774	.11
1968	392	1,855	35,567	.20	1979	235	1,021	20,409	.09
1969	412	1,576	29,397	.16	1980	187	795	20,844	.09
1970	381	2,468	52,761	.29	1981	145	729	16,908	.07
1971	298	2,516	35,538	.19	1982	96	656	9,061	.04
1972	250	975	16,764	.09					

NA Not available   [1] Beginning in year indicated   [2] Workers counted more than once if involved in more than 1 stoppage during the year   [3] Agricultural and government employees are included in the total working time, private household, forestry and fishery employees are excluded.

Source: U.S. Department of Commerce, Bureau of the Census, *Statistical Abstract of the United States, 1984* (Washington, D.C.: U.S. Government Printing Office, December 1983), p. 441.

has considerable costs to labor itself. Workers who engage in a strike for **economic goals** can legally be temporarily or permanently replaced, although (as discussed in Chapter 4) they retain certain rights of reinstatement. While on strike, workers are not paid. Depending on the circumstances, they may also lose their fringe benefits. Additionally, strikes can cause great inconvenience to the public and damage labor's image generally. There is no better example of this than the air traffic controllers strike. For all these reasons, labor may be reluctant to use the strike even though it is its most potent weapon.

TERMS   **Economic Goals**   Better wages, hours, or working conditions. This is in contrast to a strike in response to an unfair labor practice.

The employer, too, has a potent but costly economic weapon—the lockout. A lockout occurs when, as a tactic in a labor dispute, the employer prohibits its employees from working. This is a severe economic sanction for the employees since they lose their pay. They, too, have overhead expenses that must be met—housing, food, clothing, and so forth. Denying them the ability to work can place substantial hardships on them.

Lockouts have been characterized as "defensive" or "offensive." The defensive lockout occurs when the employer prohibits the employees from working in order to speed up negotiations on a new contract and overcome an impasse before the old contract expires. The point of this is to place economic pressure on the employees at a time when reducing work is beneficial, or at least not excessively damaging, to the employer; for example, during a slow season in order to preclude labor from striking later on during a busy season. Remember, because "no-strike" clauses are a **mandatory** subject of collective bargaining, they are to be found in the overwhelming number of contracts. Consequently, workers may have to wait until a contract expires before they can legally strike.

An offensive lockout is simply a matter of the employer placing economic pressure on the workers by denying them employment. This could be in response to a strike, a new wage demand, or for a variety of other reasons. In the past only defensive lockouts were legal under National Labor Relations Board rules; but today, both types are permissible—unless they are used to violate the legal rights of employees or are in support of an employer's unfair labor practice.

The lockout, much as the strike, is a severe but imperfect sanction. Generally, an employer would incur substantial costs during a lockout. No matter how slow the season, the employer still has overhead costs to meet. Lockouts, like strikes, produce anxiety, animosity, hostility, and unanticipated—possibly violent—events. They make labor relations more difficult in the future and may also harm the employer's image and public standing. For the most part, an employer would be better off coping with a slow season through lay-offs, rather than lockouts. Consequently, like the strike, the lockout is an extreme measure.

While strikes and lockouts are not the preferred means for resolving impasses, many believe that their potential use is absolutely necessary for the collective bargaining process to function.

TERMS   **Mandatory**   Those bargaining items that each party must bargain over in good faith if introduced by the other party.

They act as deterrents to both sides in a dispute. Coming to terms is generally less expensive and damaging than engaging in strikes or lockouts. Where these weapons are illegal, as in the vast majority of public sector jurisdictions, there may be less incentive to reach collective bargaining agreements. Indeed, public employees sometimes work for a year or more *without a contract*—a situation that is virtually unheard of in the private sector.

In general, economic weapons exist in the hope that they will not have to be used. But it is their mere existence that makes impasse resolution by other means more plausible.

THE ROLE OF THIRD PARTY NEUTRALS

Voluntary, noncoercive agreement is one means of arriving at a labor contract. Engaging in economic sanctions, such as strikes and lockouts, is another means of eventually bringing the parties to agreement. In addition to these two situations is the possibility that **neutral** third parties can be brought in to resolve impasses. While this sounds simple enough, it presents some complex policy questions. Even the potential of bringing in a third party may weaken the commitment of the two major parties (management and labor) to serious collective bargaining. It has been argued that the introduction of third parties inevitably produces three effects:

1. *The Ritualism Effect.* The availability of third party intervention in a collective bargaining dispute over future interests encourages management and labor to engage in grandstanding, **chest pounding,** and unrealistically hard-line bargaining. In other words, the parties may make statements less directed toward resolving the dispute than convincing some constituency (union members, other managers, the public, etc.) how tough their leaders are. Under these conditions, the give-and-take normally associated with bargaining does not occur. And the "bargaining" that does occur becomes a ritual bearing little relation to the final content of the contract after a third party intervenes.

2. *The Chilling Effect.* While somewhat similar to ritualism, there is an important difference. The chilling effect impels both sides

TERMS   **Neutral**   Not partial to one side or the other; any third party who is actively engaged in labor-management negotiations in order to facilitate a settlement.

Chest Pounding   A simian display of virility.

to make extreme demands, not for the benefit of their constituencies or the public, but because they assume that the third party intervening in the dispute will be inclined to **split the difference.** Hence, in anticipation of third-party intervention, neither side will compromise and actual bargaining will not take place.

3. *The Narcotic Effect.* This encourages both parties to rely upon outside intervention to such an extent that they do not even try to engage in collective bargaining. It is the attitude of, "Why bother? Let George or Georgeanna (the arbitrator, mediator, or fact-finder) do it."

The major problem with all these effects is not just that they undermine the collective bargaining process, but that there is no reason to believe that agreements worked out by third parties will be superior to those arrived at by the two primary parties as a result of serious negotiations. In fact, the intervention of third parties limits the potential for workers, participating through their unions, to determine the conditions of work. In addition, it is probably true that the parties will be more committed to living within the agreement, if they negotiate it themselves.

Despite these limitations on the usefulness of third party intervention, **public policy** supports it under certain circumstances. Most obviously, third party intervention is desirable, if not completely necessary, where strikes and lockouts are prohibited. The best example of this is in the public sector. But third party intervention is also favored as a means of resolving impasses involving railroad employees, between hospitals and their employees, and under conditions of **national emergency.** In addition, public policy supports the use of limited third party intervention simply as a means of avoiding the use of the potent, but damaging, economic weapons.

The major forms of third party intervention are mediation, fact-finding, and arbitration. Each will be considered in turn.

TERMS **Split the Difference** A collective bargaining tactic in which both sides agree to a settlement half way between their bargaining positions.

Public Policy The totality of law and government actions that have the effect of law or guide its interpretation or implementation.

National Emergency A condition determined by the president under provisions of the Taft-Hartley Act.

MEDIATION   **Mediation** is perhaps the most popular and least intrusive form of third party intervention. Under federal law either party to a collective bargaining agreement must inform the other at least sixty days in advance of a desire to modify or terminate it. Within thirty days after notice of this type, a letter must be sent to the Federal Mediation and Conciliation Service and to any appropriate state agency as well. These agencies may offer to mediate the dispute. Alternatively, if mediation is used, the parties themselves may choose a mediator privately.

In either case, mediation appears to be effective although it is difficult to judge because it is used only in disputes that the parties themselves cannot resolve. Mediators tend to be highly professional and well-versed in labor economics and labor relations law. But their success may depend more on their interpersonal skills than upon their technical knowledge.

Successful mediation depends on two general factors. First, the parties must *trust* the mediator. They have to place their faith in his or her integrity and be confident of the mediator's ability. Second, the *timing* of mediation is critical to its success. If mediation starts too soon, the mediator is likely to be used as a go-between by the parties to reduce the demands of one side or increase the proposals of the other. If mediation is used too late, it is likely that the two parties will have hardened their positions to the extent that mediation will promote little compromise. But what is too early and what is too late? Apparently public policy considers the thirty days before the termination of a contract to be about the correct timing. For health care facilities, however, notice to the Federal Mediation and Conciliation Service should be not less than sixty days before the termination of the existing contract. In the public sector, provisions for notification to mediation services vary widely.

How does one mediate? Essentially the mediator tries to reduce the distance between the parties. This can be done by encouraging them to engage in "principled negotiation" (as discussed in Chapter 5). Especially important is removing the personalities from the proposals. Mediation also consists of developing "supposals." The mediator will ask one side, "Suppose they give you this, will you give them that in return?" In this fashion, mediators are able to ascertain what each side is willing to accept, what each can live with, or, in essence, each party's "bottom line."

TERMS   **Mediation**   Outside help in settling a dispute. The person who does this is called a mediator.

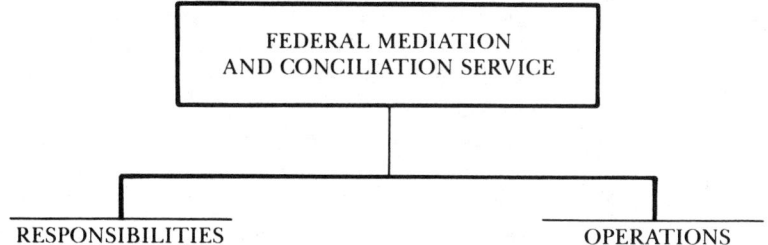

Figure 6-1.   Federal Mediation and Conciliation Service

Once the mediator has a good picture of this, he or she may try to convince one or another party that it has to accept even less. The mediator is also likely to use ingenuity to put together packages that both sides can accept. Even where mediation is not completely successful in bringing the parties to terms, it may reduce the scope of their conflict by resolving some issues. Mediation, by definition, cannot work if both parties do not support it.

FACT-FINDING   Fact-finding is a more difficult process than mediation to describe and to engage in—primarily because there is no standard concept of what the fact-finder's role is. According to some, fact-finding is a misnomer since "fact-finders" do not find facts. According to long-time public sector labor leader, **Jerry Wurf,** "the parties usually know and understand the facts. The problem is that these facts are interpreted from positions of self-interest and therefore lead rational people to conflicting conclusions." On the other hand, sometimes the "facts" of a dispute are so complex that in truth they are not known to the parties—or anyone else for that matter. For instance, part of a dispute may involve the value of a fringe

TERMS   **Jerry Wurf** (1919–1981)   President of the American Federation of State, County and Municipal Employees (AFSCME) from 1964 to his death.

benefit package, what similar employees are paid elsewhere by other employers, or a consideration of the value of a pension twenty years hence. No doubt the parties will have different perspectives on the same facts, as Wurf indicated; but they may also have different facts. Indeed, some observers of collective bargaining make a distinction between "facts" and "true facts" for this very reason.

A second problem in defining the fact-finder's role is that it frequently involves two related but somewhat competitive functions. On the one hand, the fact-finder engages in mediation. He or she seeks to enhance communication between the parties, would prefer to see them reach an agreement on their own, and tries to get them to see proposals that can get them beyond their impasse. But on the other hand, the fact-finder has a quasi-judicial role. Ultimately he or she will have to make a judgment as to what the "true facts" are. This often will tend to make one party a "winner" and the other a "loser." Moreover, the judicial role tends to be far more formal than the mediation role. It involves formal hearings, with the presentation of data and arguments by both parties. Because this is an adversary procedure, it makes it less likely that the parties will be forthcoming and compromising when the fact-finder tries to engage in mediation. Under these circumstances, the fact-finder's success may depend on his or her ability to convince the parties that the two approaches (mediation and judicial) can be separated in his or her mind. This is not an easy task, especially in an atmosphere in which distrust abounds.

A third issue pertaining to fact-finding is whether or not the fact-finder's report on his or her assessment of the facts should include recommendations. Some consider fact-finding without recommendations to be an exercise in futility from the perspective of resolving impasses. In the view of others, fact-finding with recommendations is deficient since either party is free to reject the recommendations. Moreover, although recommendations can center on viable proposals upon which the parties can agree, they can also harden the parties' positions and make agreement more difficult.

Another question with regard to fact-finding is whether the report should be public. Making it public brings additional pressure on the parties. This is especially useful if the impasse is in an economic area or is in an aspect of public employment that is critical to the public convenience, welfare, or safety. In the view of some, however, labor relations disputes are so complicated that the public and the press cannot hope to understand them in more than a superficial fashion. If this is true, making the report public may mislead public opinion.

With all these issues involved in fact-finding it is a wonder that it ever works. However, it *appears* to work *well*, though given the nature of such statistics, it is impossible to say for sure. It is generally believed that 90 percent of the disputes going to fact-finding are resolved, and that of these the fact-finders' reports are the basis for resolution in 60 to 70 percent of the cases.

ARBITRATION   Arbitration is another form of third party intervention. Here, too, there are several forms and variations. At the outset it is important to note that the arbitrator's role is primarily judicial. That is, he or she holds hearings and makes recommendations (often called awards) as to what the resolution of the dispute should be. Arbitration abandons the hope found in mediation and fact-finding that third party intervention can lead the two parties to reach an agreement. Instead, it seeks to establish an agreement for them. In this sense it is an extreme measure that is much at odds with the fundamental assumptions of collective bargaining policies and procedures, which place such a heavy emphasis on self-determination in the workplace through agreements negotiated by management and labor. Moreover, since arbitration is primarily a judicial function, there is a tendency to rely upon a panel of three or more arbitrators, rather than a single individual. This is viewed as a guarantee of greater fairness and a check on the biases or incompetence of any single arbitrator. By contrast, mediation and fact-finding generally do not use panels.

Arbitration can be either voluntary or compulsory, depending upon how the parties enter into it. In the private sector it is always voluntary. However, the parties can agree in advance of the termination of a contract to engage in it if necessary to resolve an impasse. In this sense, should an impasse occur, they are required by previous contractual arrangement to use arbitration. **Compulsory arbitration** is often found in the public sector, where it is used as a substitute for the economic weapons of strike and lockout. Procedures among public jurisdictions vary greatly. Generally, though, when an impasse is reached a labor relations agency will be notified and, if all other available means for dispute resolution have been exhausted, the parties will be *compelled* to submit to arbitration. There may also be some jurisdictions in which the public

TERMS   **Compulsory Arbitration**   A negotiating process in which the parties are required by law or contract to arbitrate their dispute.

employer is compelled to go to arbitration if the union so requests. Voluntary arbitration can be used in the public sector as well.

Arbitration can also be binding or nonbinding. Binding arbitration requires that the parties accept the arbitrators' award or report. Neither party is able to unilaterally reject it and demand to go back to the bargaining table. Both parties will be compelled to live with the award as best they can until the term of the contract expires or, possibly, they can arrive at an agreement as to how it should be modified. Binding arbitration is obviously a drastic step away from **codetermination** of conditions in the workplace by the two parties. This is especially evident where arbitration is over very central issues, such as wages and safety matters.

Nonbinding arbitration is akin to fact-finding with recommendations. It puts pressure on one or both parties to reach an agreement, but it does not require them to do so. The advantages of nonbinding arbitration are not immediately evident. However, it is logically useful in the public sector where matters of public policy and working conditions tend to coincide. Under such circumstances it is a breach of democratic governmental processes to allow a nonelected arbitrator to decide matters of public policy. Making the report nonbinding would place moral and public pressure on the public employer, but would not violate sovereignty or the federal or state constitutions. Similarly, nonbinding arbitration may have some utility in private sector situations where public image and moral force are of particular importance, as in the health care industry.

In theory, arbitration can take any of the four forms indicated: it can be voluntary/binding or voluntary/nonbinding; compulsory/binding or compulsory/nonbinding. Today the weight of opinion seems to be on the side of binding: voluntary for the private sector and compulsory for the public sector, although arguments can be made for any of the types.

Perhaps the best example of voluntary/binding arbitration comes from the steel industry. In 1973 an Experimental Negotiating Agreement (ENA) was reached. Under the agreement, either side could request arbitration over **interests** when a contract

TERMS   **Codetermination** Joint decisionmaking on all aspects of management by both labor and management. Under formal programs of codetermination the union might even have equal membership on a company's board of directors.

Interests Either the terms and conditions of employment or the specific aspects of a labor contract. Interest arbitration is an arbitration of a dispute arising during the course of contract negotiations where the arbitrator must decide what will or will not be contained in the agreement.

impasse was reached. Strikes and lockouts were prohibited by the agreement. In addition, since the arbitration was binding, the **rank and file** membership of the unions involved forfeited the right to ratify or reject the contract. In the view of many labor leaders and unionists, this was a heavy price to pay for better impasse resolution procedures. Still, the logic behind the ENA was that labor relations in the steel industry were so disruptive that both the employers and workers were being harmed. The problem was that steel customers, anticipating the possibility of a strike as contracts expired, began stockpiling inventories. This caused the steel mills to operate on an overtime capacity prior to contract terminations. Afterward, however, the consumers of steel would draw upon their inventories regardless of whether there was a strike or not. Thus, the strike became an impotent weapon and lay-offs a matter of course.

Compulsory/binding arbitration is found in the public sector in a number of states. It is viewed as especially useful where public safety employees, such as police and firefighters, are concerned. For instance, in Alaska, Hawaii, and Pennsylvania, compulsory/binding arbitration is used as a substitute for the strike by essential employees.

Public sector compulsory binding arbitration raises several important issues that have prompted a variety of experiments. One issue is the matter of public policy, as alluded to above. It cannot be emphasized too much that the public sector is different from the private sector in this regard. Politicians, government officials, and, presumably, the public are not willing to delegate governmental power to private individuals (arbitrators) to make public policy. There is little support in society for allowing arbitrators to decide how many pupils can be in a classroom, what kind of bullets police can use, when they can fire their guns, whether firefighters can carry weapons, and a host of other issues. These are viewed as matters of public policy, issues too important to be left up to labor relations arbitrators. Hence, these issues may even be excluded from the scope of public sector collective bargaining; or at least from arbitration.

TERMS   **Rank and File**   A colloquial expression referring to the masses. When used in an organizational context, it refers to those members of the organization who are not part of management. The term is frequently used to describe those members of a union having no status as officers or shop stewards. Rank and file was originally a military term referring to the enlisted men who had to line up in ranks (side by side) and files (one behind the other). Officers, being gentlemen, were spared such indignities.

TABLE 6-2.
TYPES OF IMPASSE RESOLUTION

	Mediation	Fact-Finding	Arbitration
Process	Intervention by Federal Mediation and Conciliation Service or other appropriate third party at request of negotiating parties or on own proffering of services	A procedure for compelling settlement, frequently a final alternative to arbitration	A terminal procedure alternative to or following fact-finding
Subject Matter	Terms of new agreement being negotiated	Terms of agreement being negotiated	Terms of agreement being negotiated (also final step in grievance procedure)
Setting	*Mediator* tries to determine basis for agreement and persuade parties to reach agreement	*Parties* try to persuade fact-finder by arguments	*Parties* try to persuade arbitrator by arguments (same as fact-finding)
Third Party	*Mediator*—a Federal Commissioner of Mediation and Conciliation or other third party	*Fact-finder*—a public employee or a private citizen selected by parties or by an administrative agency	*Arbitrator*—a public employee or a private citizen selected by parties or by an administrative agency
Power Factor	*Mediator* limited to persuasion and ability to find compromise	*Fact-finder* may make recommendations for impasse resolution	*Arbitrator* makes binding decision
Publicity	Confidential process— no public record kept	Quasi-public process with recommendations recorded and reported	Quasi-public process with decisions recorded and reported

Remember, impasses can only result over items upon which bargaining is mandatory. But that is hardly the end of the matter. What if an arbitrator makes an award over wages and fringe benefits? Where is the money needed to pay for them to come from? It could come from user fees (as in public transportation) or from higher sales, property, income, and school taxes. But it could also come from some other function. For example, money may be shifted by the legislature from housing for the elderly to wages for police and firefighters as the result of an arbitrator's award. The problem here is that nobody arbitrates the interest of the elderly in public housing. The elderly can vote and lobby, but they cannot collectively bargain with the government. Public employees can vote, lobby through their unions and collectively bargain—*and* sometimes even have their case arbitrated in a fashion that is binding. In the view of some, this provides public employees with too much leverage over government. It is especially significant in this context that when an arbitrator makes an award in the public sector, he or she is not confronted with all the competing claims upon the public treasury. Thus, he or she does not have to weigh the case of the elderly (or any other group) against that of the fire-fighters. The arbitrator need only be concerned with the case of the firefighters, although there is nothing to prevent him or her from assessing the wider impacts of the proposed award.

ARBITRATION STANDARDS Overall, arbitrators must be concerned with four fundamental criteria in making their judgments. The mix of these factors that will be applied in any particular case of arbitration will depend upon the arbitrator's proclivities, the nature of the dispute, and, if it is in the public sector, the standards (if any) set forth in pertinent legislation. These criteria are: acceptability, equity, the public interest, and ability to pay.

Acceptability Reaching a judgment that is acceptable to the parties is crucial in nonbinding arbitration. Otherwise, the parties might be unwilling to use the award as a basis for resolving their impasse. But even where arbitration is binding, acceptability is of concern because an award that is truly unacceptable to one party will be hard to live with and will generate problems of contract enforcement. It may also further exacerbate poor labor relations and personnel policies. From a personal perspective, an arbitrator will not seek to develop a record of handing down unacceptable awards, since this would eventually mark him or her as incompetent or undesirable. Arbitrators are jointly selected by the parties to a dispute; consequently, they strive to be viewed as neutral. Generally, acceptability depends upon getting the two parties to see that the arbitrator's award reflects the balance of economic power in the dispute. Because arbitration is a substitue for the economic weapons of the strike and lockout, an arbitrator's award may be premised on the approach of saying to the parties: "Look, if there were a strike or lockout in this situation, this is what would happen. . . ." In other words, an "acceptable" award should reflect the bargaining strength of each of the parties to the impasse.

Equity   Equity refers to fairness in the resolution of the dispute. It requires that regardless of their bargaining strength, neither side should be victimized to the benefit of the other. The final award must be fair to both parties in terms of some considerations other than simply their relative economic or organizational strength. Consequently, although equity can coincide with acceptability, it may also require a radically different settlement. What would be some of the factors considered when applying equity as a criterion for making an arbitration award? Comparability with workers in similar jobs with other employers, or with the same employer, is a common concern. In the public sector, comparability often leads arbitrators dealing with a dispute in one city to look at similar cities in determining what is fair or equitable. For instance, in trying to determine what a firefighter should be paid in Chicago, an arbitrator might look at pay scales in Boston or New York.

Comparable worth is a concept related to equity. Here it is assumed that for one reason or another, the labor market price for a type of labor does not reflect the true value of the work that is to be performed. Usually, this issue is associated with gender discrimination and sex-segregated occupations such as nursing. What a nurse is paid according to labor market prices may reflect a number of noneconomic factors, including social discrimination against women. Equity might demand that the nurse be paid not at market value, but according to comparable worth; that is, according to the value of her contribution to the health care facility. In calculating comparable worth, an arbitrator might look at such elements as the level of education, the nature of technical training, the nature of supervision, the exercise of discretion, and similar factors. At the moment, the contest between acceptability and equity in the area of comparable worth is a major issue confronting the economy.

The Public Interest   Collective bargaining is a process of negotiation and dispute resolution between two parties, sometimes with the assistance of third party neutrals. But there is often another party to the dispute, one who does not enter into negotiations directly. This is the "relevant" public—a group of people outside the primary employment relationship who are most likely to be affected by the outcome of the negotiations. In the private sector, the relevant public may be the consumers of a particular product or service. They may also be workers in related industries. In terms of national emergencies, the relevant public may be the population at large. For example, negotiations in the steel industry can affect the price of steel, which in turn may affect the production levels and price of automobiles. Such negotiations may also have a substanital impact on the nation's defense budget and, therefore, upon the taxpaying population. Similarly, collective bargaining in utility companies will affect the ratepayer. Indeed, wage settlements with gas and electric companies may force some individuals to lower their thermostats in winter. Settlements with telephone companies may lead people to talk to their friends and relatives less frequently.

In the public sector, the public interest is generally more obvious. Labor relations statutes may even directly assert that the intervention of third party neutrals is in the public interest. Questions involving labor disputes in public school systems provide a good illustration. Clearly, the public has an interest in school discipline, school calendars, and the number of pupils per classroom, all of which have been subject to arbitration at one time or another. But how is the arbitrator supposed to define and incorporate the public interest into a settlement? There is no pat answer here, which is one of the reasons binding arbitration in the public sector in particular is so problematic. Apparently, in the absence of comprehensive definition of the public interest by a labor relations statute, this important question will be left up to the arbitrator in any given case. Consequently, some observers believe that it is important that the public sector use arbitrators especially trained to deal with its unique conditions and special concern for the public interest.

Ability to Pay   Ability to pay is related to acceptability, but the two are not identical. This criterion is relevant in both the public and private sectors. The last thing an arbitrator wants to do is to drive an employer to bankruptcy through an award that it cannot afford. Indeed, although labor wants higher pay, it, too, wants the employer to stay in operation since workers' jobs depend upon it. This all sounds obvious, but there are some complications. First, it is often very difficult to determine what the employer's ability to pay is. What will a pay hike mean in terms of the price of the final product and its competitiveness in the market? For public employers, what will it mean in terms of tax levels and strength of the tax base?

These are questions that may have no definite answers. Another difficulty with ability to pay as a criterion for dispute resolution is that it can victimize employees. An employer cannot go to a company that supplies pencils or paper clips and say: "I need some pencils and paper clips; but right now I cannot pay you the going

rate for them, so I think you ought to sell them to me for less."
That just isn't the way our market economy works. So why should
the same employer be able to go to its workers and say: "I wish I
could pay you what you are worth; but I can't, so you will have to
take less?" Ability to pay leads to a serious dilemma for arbitrators.
It is not equitable for workers to have to sacrifice because the employer, perhaps as a result of mismanagement, does not have the
ability to pay them what their work is worth. Yet, if the employer
really cannot pay, then the workers cannot be paid. Consequently,
not taking ability to pay into account can lead to seemingly equitable resolutions *on paper,* but unrealistic settlements *in practice.*
Some public sector collective bargaining statutes seek to resolve
this dilemma for the arbitrator by formally requiring that ability
to pay be taken into account. In passing, it should be noted that
sometimes this leaves the public employee in a very disadvantaged
position. Residency requirements may require the employee to live
in the city that cannot pay for his or her services at a fair rate. **Political neutrality** regulations may make it difficult for the same
public employee to do much about the city's governance through
political action. In short, the public employee may feel and be
"stuck"—which is one reason why unionism has become so appealing in the public sector in recent decades.

FINAL OFFER   As the discussion of the criteria that arbitrators generally consider
ARBITRATION   in making awards indicates, arbitration is not a foolproof means of
impasse resolution. Arbitrators can make mistakes. By its very nature, arbitration can undercut the viability of the collective bargaining process between the two primary parties, management
and labor. Consequently, there has been some experimentation
with different forms of arbitration in an effort to improve this type
of third party intervention. For the most part, these developments
have occurred in the public sector, where binding interest arbitration is most common.

A promising new form of arbitration is called "final offer" or
"last best offer" arbitration. The basic concept is to reduce the

TERMS   **Political Neutrality**   The concept that public employees should not actively
participate in partisan politics. The Hatch Acts of 1939 and 1940 restrict the
political activities of almost all federal employees and those in state employment having federal financing. Many states have "little" Hatch Acts which
further limit the possible political activities of public employees.

arbitrator's discretion and authority to establish conditions in the workplace, while at the same time protecting the vitality of the collective bargaining process itself. This is accomplished by requiring labor and management each to submit their final offer to the arbitrator for consideration. The arbitrator is not free to modify these offers, but must accept either labor's or management's offer as the one that will be adopted. This puts a great deal of pressure on the two parties to be reasonable in making their final offers. It should narrow the distance between them substantially and enhance acceptability whatever the outcome. If the process works well, it precludes a poorly thought out arbitration award. In the public sector, it also helps alleviate the problem of the public interest, since this should be incorporated into management's final offer.

There are two varieties of final offer arbitration: "whole package" and "issue by issue." The "whole package" approach requires that the arbitrator choose either management's final offer in its entirety, or that of labor. The arbitrator is not free to choose management's clause on wages, and then labor's on some other topic, such as fringe benefits. It is one side's entire offer or the other's. This limits the arbitrator's flexibility very substantially. By contrast, the "issue by issue" approach allows the arbitrator to choose either management or labor's position on each particular issue. Thus the arbitrator could choose management's final offer on wages, but labor's on fringe benefits; management's on matters of work assignment, but labor's on matters of safety; and so on. This approach enables the arbitrator to exercise more leeway in formulating an award that meets the considerations of acceptability, equity, the public interest, and ability to pay. However, it also allows either of the two primary parties to insert unreasonable offers in any given area, without jeopardizing that party's final offer in other issue areas. This makes grandstanding and posturing feasible, and may detract from the quality of the collective bargaining process itself.

Currently, "issue by issue" final offer arbitration is used for some categories of public employees by Connecticut, Iowa, and Montana. The "whole package" approach is used by Hawaii, Massachusetts, Nevada, and Wisconsin. Michigan and New Jersey use "whole package" on economic issues and "issue by issue" on non-economic issues. Conventional binding interest arbitration is used by Alaska, Delaware, Maine, Minnesota, Nebraska, New York, Oregon, Pennsylvania, Rhode Island, Washington State, and Wyoming for at least some categories of employees and types of issues.

Michigan also uses conventional arbitration under some circumstances, making it a state that uses all three of the forms discussed here.

NATIONAL
EMERGENCY
DISPUTES

The approaches to arbitration mentioned above do not exhaust the possibilities. Another technique that appears to be growing in popularity is a combination of mediation and arbitration, called "med-arb," which engages the third party neutral in both mediation and arbitration. The main idea is to mediate in an effort to resolve the impasse or at least reduce the number of issues going to arbitration. Then, where mediation is unsuccessful, some form of binding arbitration is used.

There is always a **trade-off** between the intervention of third party neutrals and the vitality of the collective bargaining process. Mediators, fact-finders, and arbitrators can be used to avoid strikes; but by their very nature they reduce the responsibility of the two primary parties to collectively negotiate and arrive at an agreement. In general, public policy with regard to the private sector is more inclined to leave the task of arriving at such agreements up to the parties themselves; public sector approaches currently place a higher emphasis on avoiding strikes and using arbitration as a substitute for them. This difference in emphasis is indicated by the procedure for resolving "national emergency" disputes under the Taft-Hartley Act.

The Act's procedures do not prohibit strikes, even though these may be extremely damaging to the economy or national security. Rather, the Act allows the U.S. President to invoke special procedures when a labor dispute "will, if permitted to occur or continue, imperil the national health or safety." He appoints a board of inquiry, to make an investigation of the situation. Upon receiving the board's report, the president can ask the attorney general to seek an injunction to prohibit the strike or lockout. During the period of the injunction the workplace is governed by the previous or still prevailing contract. Management and labor are required to try to resolve the dispute with assistance from the Federal Mediation and Conciliation Service. If after sixty days, no resolution is reached, the board of inquiry is reconvened to bring the president up to date on the dispute. The National Labor Relations Board also polls the workers on the employer's final offer.

TERMS   **Trade-off**   Either the selection of one of several alternatives, or a concession made in response to the other side's concession.

Fifteen days are allotted for this. The NLRB then has five days to inform the attorney general of the results. After this step is taken, the injunction must be dissolved and use of economic weapons may be resumed. The total eighty days during which strikes or lockouts are prohibited is called a "cooling off" period. The main point to be noted here, however, is that even though these disputes can be extremely damaging, the impasse is essentially left up to management and labor for resolution.

WHY UNIONS STRIKE

Strikes are a very common means of resolving impasses. Once a strike is launched, it is either won, lost, or critical in the development of a compromise between management and labor that settles the dispute. In a typical year, there are perhaps about 4,000 strikes involving some 1.5 million workers. These strikes may amount to the loss of 30 million or so idle days for the workers on strike. Yet, when viewed from the perspectives of the economy as a whole, even so many work stoppages and lost days are unlikely to amount to more than three-tenths of one percent of all the nonfarm hours worked in the United States each year. The typical strike involves less than 250 workers. Thus the strike is common, but for the most part conditions in the workplace are determined through other means.

What causes some unionized workers to strike over interests, while others do not? It is embarrassing to observers to be compelled to admit, after much studying and analysis, that most strike activity is simply "unpredictable." Public sector strike activity, in particular, has been subject to comprehensive analysis. Yet it was found that such factors as the nature of the bargaining law, the illegality and penalties attached to strikes, the role of third party neutrals, the degree of unionization, and the amount of earnings were not useful in predicting strikes. Nevertheless, even though we cannot say unequivocally what provokes strikes, we do have a fairly good idea about who strikes and over what issues. In the public sector, it has been found that there is a tendency for employees in the departments of sanitation, streets and roads, and sewage to strike most frequently. Public safety workers also are prone to engage in strikes, as are some categories of hospital workers. The majority of public sector strikes have been short, lasting four days or less. Only a small proportion of such strikes last as long as a month. Interestingly, it appears that the more critical the function to society, the shorter the public sector strike will be. Thus, during the high strike period of 1965 to 1969, police strikes averaged 4.9 days while social service worker strikes averaged 29.4 days. By far the most common issue in strikes is economic interests, including fringe benefits.

Many believe that although the availability of strikes is necessary as a means of forcing management to negotiate seriously, the use of strikes is becoming somewhat outmoded. They observe that the use of economic force can be too damaging and unpredictable in today's economy and, consequently, the strike is viewed as a last-resort means of producing an agreement. Moreover, it is sometimes argued that the fundamental character of the strike is changing due to the maturing of collective bargaining relationships. Violence is sometimes incidental to strikes nowadays, but physical force no longer plays a central role. Rather, the parties tend to view the strike as a continuation of the bargaining process. Indeed, negotiations may avidly continue during the strike. Again, it is important to remember that both sides have an overriding interest in common—the economic vitality of the employer and the concomitant maintenance of the employees' jobs. Another general factor affecting strike behavior is what **Bob Dylan** refers to as "Union Sundown." Because the public's image of unions has changed, they are no longer considered weak underdogs struggling for justice in the workplace. In contrast, many segments of the population see them as too powerful and too greedy. Since organized labor now seeks to achieve many of its goals through political means such as lobbying and electioneering, it cannot be oblivious to its public standing. The days of Samuel Gompers' voluntarism are long gone, as are those during which the evils of big business seemed to be incarnated in the likes of the **Robber Barons.**

Still, strikes do occur and it is possible to identify at least five sets of concerns that promote them. First, it is still the rule in the private sector that workers will not work after a contract has expired. "No contract, no work" remains fundamental to the system of collective bargaining, since the purpose of negotiations is to arrive at agreements to govern the workplace. Sometimes, as negotiations reach the hour for the termination of the existing contract,

TERMS **Bob Dylan** (1941–   ) A writer and singer of "folk" songs who was especially popular with the issues of the postwar baby boom during the 1960s and 1970s.

Robber Barons A label applied to the big business titans of American industry toward the end of the nineteenth century. Now it is also an invidious term for corporate leadership in general.

Medieval America!

In 1909 the female workers in the New York garment industry shirtwaist shops worked under appalling "sweatshop" conditions. They vowed solidarity and thousands took the oath: "If I turn traitor to the cause I now pledge, may this hand wither from the arm I raise!"

As the strike went on (in the end it was a partial success: some improved working conditions; but no union recognition), over 700 girls and young women were arrested. One New York magistrate sentenced a striker with the words: "You are on strike against God and Nature, whose firm law is that man shall earn his bread in the sweat of his brow."

When the great Irish playwright, George Bernard Shaw, heard of this, he wired the Women's Trade Union League: "Delightful. Medieval America always in the intimate personal confidence of the Almighty."

Source: Derived from Irving Howe, *World of Our Fathers* (New York: Simon and Schuster, 1976), pp. 295–300.

the "clock is stopped" and marathon, all night/all day, bargaining sessions take place. There is no doubt that "no contract, no work" places a great deal of pressure on both sides to arrive at an agreement.

Second, as we noted in the previous chapter, the union leader is often in a complicated political position. A strike and the solidarity it promotes may be necessary for the leader to maintain his or her position. The union leader's personality may also be an important factor in a strike. The American labor movement has certainly had its share of characters. John L. Lewis was not to be trifled with; he took his United Mine Workers out on strike in the middle of World War II. Nor was **Mike Quill,** the leader of New York City's Transport Workers Union, who allegedly once denounced an injunction with the words: "Let the judge drop dead in his black robes!" On the other side of the political coin, the union members may reject a contract that the leader supports. This will frequently lead to a strike, if the existing contract has expired. During the 1970s membership rejection ran at about 10 percent of the contracts subject to membership **ratification.** At least two factors, both essentially political in nature, contribute to rejection:

1. The union leaders tend to oversell their ability to dictate conditions to management. In order to justify their leadership and the exclusive representative position of the union, they tend to generate very high expectations. Eventually, the gap between these expectations and reality leads the membership to think it has been "sold out" by the union leader. Many readers will notice a parallel with the election and subsequent performance of United States presidents in this regard.

2. Contract rejection by the membership can be viewed as a technique to compel management to further concessions. The 1968 sanitation strike in New York City and the 1978 coal mine strike were examples of this phenomenon. And, to an extent, both were successful. In the public sector, this ploy raises an interesting problem because management's concessions to labor may also be subject to outside ratification by a legislative body. In some cases, the legislature has used the city's negotiators as "surface bargainers," intending later on to reject the contract and force further concessions from the union. This practice is a breach of good faith and illegal in many jurisdictions, but if used with sophistication, it is hard to identify and challenge.

Third, in the public sector, a strike may be used as a political weapon against public officials. It may be intended to embarrass an official, such as a mayor, who is running for reelection. It may also be intended to show public officials "who's boss." Certainly this was true of the protracted, damaging, and divisive New York

---

TERMS   **Mike Quill** (1905–1966)   One of the founders of the Transport Workers Union and its president from 1936 until his death.

Ratification   The formal confirmation by the union membership of a contract that has been negotiated and signed on their behalf by union representatives.

City school teachers' strike of the 1960s, which was as much over control of the school system as anything else. Other municipal strikes have resembled urban guerrilla warfare: tons of garbage have been left in the streets, buildings allowed to burn, draw bridges left in uncrossable positions, and sewage spewn into waterways and upon public beaches. One of the acute problems in public sector labor relations is the tendency for unions to play a major role in a candidate's election, only to find later on that all their economic demands will not be met. This, too, leads to frustrations caused by a gap between expectations and reality.

A fourth general factor contributing to strikes has been management's efforts to provoke them at a time when unions are relatively weak. It may be too evocative and emotive to call this a "union busting" technique. Perhaps, "union taming" would be a better term. However, today a failed strike can lead to a decertification election and unions are now losing such elections with greater frequency than ever before. A tame union will be an aid to the employer in selling management's view of what conditions in the workplace should be to the employees. It will also be more willing to engage in "givebacks." As union membership has declined and as the nature of jobs has changed so that they can often be minimally performed by supervisors with the aid of high technology, many unions may find themselves simply too weak to sustain a strike. Knowing this, management may seek to push them into one—sometimes successfully.

Finally, strikes are related to the economic positions of the two parties and the employees. An economic weapon can backfire if it cannot be afforded. Unions with limited membership may have difficulty developing large and sufficient strike funds to aid the workers during the length of a strike. Government economic benefits available to workers on strike vary from state to state. Recently, as part of the general trend to reduce government spending, public policy in many places has sought to curtail unemployment benefits and other welfare aids to striking workers. The timing of strikes can also be of great importance. Strikes during periods of economic recession and high unemployment are very risky because they make it easier for the employer to find temporary or permanent replacement workers; and because the public's sympathy is hardly likely to be extended to those people fortunate enough to have jobs but unwilling to work them. Strikes at times when there is high demand for an employer's perishable product or service are more likely to be successful. Such commodities or services are widespread. For example, an airline seat is a perishable commodity. Once it goes unused due to a strike, it can never be sold again. The same is true, of course, of many food products, high fashion garments, and many other products and services in the economy.

COPING WITH
STRIKES

Once a strike occurs, a high premium may be placed on containing and resolving it. Although violence is no longer a central facet of strikes, it is frequently involved in them. No matter how lawbound and common strikes have become, they continue to arouse great anxiety and to stir up emotions. They are both physical and psychological confrontations. There is much at stake. The workers fear for their jobs; the employer fears for its property. Owners, managers, and employees all fear for the continued economic viability of the firm. Events and outcomes associated with strikes are unpredictable. Accidents occur and how the parties will respond to them can never be known in advance. Sometimes physical fighting breaks out between strikers and nonstrikers or strikebreakers. Sometimes those who cross picket lines are subject to harassment and are the objects of violence. In the public sector, a strike by public safety workers can be chaotic and even anarchic. The Boston Police Strike of 1919 still serves as an apt example. But, given all the apprehensiveness that surrounds strikes, can they be contained? How can their destructive side effects be limited? Especially important, can they be resolved before positions harden to such an extent that the strike becomes prolonged to the point that both the employer's or employee's economic interests are damaged beyond repair?

If everyone knew the answers to these questions, strikes would not present the problems that they do. Nevertheless, some considerations can be suggested:

1. Unless the employer's desire is to "bust the union," communication channels should be kept open. Negotiations should continue throughout the strike. The strike itself should not divert attention from trying to arrive at an agreement. Even if no progress is being made, it is helpful to schedule meetings at regular intervals. Although it may be difficult to avoid letting personalities get in the way during a strike, the ideals of "principled negotiations" (discussed in Chapter 5) should be adhered to as best as possible.

2. It may be helpful for the employer and union to set up "rumor control" centers. The anxiety surrounding strikes makes it highly likely that communications and events will be misunderstood. Strikers will also be in contact with one another to a

great extent. Under these conditions rumors inevitably spring up. These can be extremely damaging to the prospects of settling the strike and eliminating violence.

3. Both sides should avoid unfair practices during the strike. Labor should not damage the employer's property or harass its customers. Management should not threaten to close the plant and move elsewhere to avoid disputes, or to fire workers (though they can legally be replaced).

4. In general, public statements should reflect factual information only. Innuendo and threats about even anticipated future events should be kept to a minimum. Speculation about remote possibilities should be avoided altogether. Labor disputes are difficult to understand at times. Attempting to mislead the public to gain its favor is unlikely to resolve the impasse and may lead the other side to retaliate.

5. Since pickets are on the front line of the confrontation, picketing, if any, should be orderly. Unions have a special responsibility to make sure that pickets behave properly and within the law. Management, too, must assure that pickets are not endangered or threatened by its actions. Although a seemingly mundane consideration, pickets should be kept safe from vehicular traffic.

6. Avoid miscalculation. This is always easier said than done. But a miscalculation of the resolve of one side can lead the other side to make some very damaging errors. For example, during the air traffic controllers' strike both sides miscalculated. The president thought that most of the strikers would return to work after his forty-eight hour ultimatum. Because he was wrong, the nation faced curtailed air traffic for many months. The union underestimated the firmness of the government, the public's antipathy toward their cause, the slight measure of support they would receive from pilots and other unions, and the ability of a highly computerized air traffic control system to work without them.

Resolving strikes may be more complicated than containing them. A strike can be resolved by finding a contract formula that is acceptable to both parties—and the economic pressure generated by the strike may impel the parties to do just this. A strike can also be resolved through the capitulation of one of the parties. In this case, the economic and legal situation will be paramount. If the strike hurts the union or the employer sufficiently, that party is likely to meet the other's terms. In the public sector, the application of legislation prohibiting strikes may be a key determinant as well.

One of the more controversial means of attempting to resolve strikes is to hire replacements. The federal government did this in 1981 after the air traffic controllers refused to return to work. Continental Airlines did this in 1983 after their striking pilots refused to return to work for half pay. Legally, the employer is entitled to try to maintain operations during an economic strike and to hire temporary or permanent replacements for the striking workers (the law is different for unfair labor practice strikes). Moreover, the employer can refuse to reinstate a striking worker who has been permanently replaced. Nevertheless, if the strike was legal, such a worker has a right to be placed on a **recall** list and reinstated should a vacancy occur. A reinstated worker retains his or her prior seniority, and is not considered a new employee. The employer can also abolish a striking employee's job, but again the employee must be placed on a recall list.

Although the right to reinstatement exists, it can be problematic. Reinstatement may take a long time. If technology is changing rapidly, it may never occur since the employee may no longer be qualified for any of the jobs the employer has. Permanent replacements can vote in a decertification election at some point. Practically speaking, if the union loses, the replaced striker is likely to have a great deal of difficulty in gaining satisfactory, or any, reinstatement.

Hiring replacements can be risky though. If the union wins the strike anyway, such a move by the employer is likely to poison labor relations for some time to come. In some cases, replacements will not be as skilled as those they are replacing. They may also have to be extensively trained. If replacements somehow cause the employer's product or service to be inferior, it will not redound to the employer's benefit. If they cause accidents, or lead the public to think that the employer's products or services are unsafe, it may be extremely damaging. These considerations vary from industry to industry. Certainly in airline or bus transportation, the last thing a company wants the public to think is that its service is unsafe. In some highly skilled crafts, the option of hiring replacements is precluded by the expense of recruiting and training such people.

TERMS   **Recall**   To rehire employees, usually after a layoff but sometimes after a strike. Union contracts often require that the union be given both notice of the recall and the names of the employees to be recalled after a layoff. This enables the union to determine if employees are being called back in the appropriate order.

What is a Scab?

by Jack London*

After God had finished the rattlesnake, the toad and the vampire, he had some awful substance left with which He made a SCAB. A SCAB is a two-legged animal with a corkscrew soul, a water-logged brain, and a combination backbone made of jelly and glue. Where others have hearts he carries a tumor of rotten principles.

When a SCAB comes down the street men turn their backs and angels weep in heaven, and the devil shuts the gates of hell to keep him out. No man has a right to SCAB as long as there is a pool of water deep enough to drown his body in, or a rope long enough to hang his carcass with. Judas Iscariot was a gentleman compared with a SCAB. For betraying his Master, he had character enough to hang himself. A SCAB HASN'T!

Esau sold his birthright for a mess of pottage. Judas Iscariot sold his Savior for thirty pieces of silver. Benedict Arnold sold his country for a promise of a commission in the British Army. The modern strikebreaker sells his birthright, his country, his wife, his children, and his fellowmen for an unfulfilled promise from his employer, trust or corporation.

Esau was a traitor to himself, Judas Iscariot was a traitor to his God. Benedict Arnold was a traitor to his country.

A STRIKEBREAKER IS A TRAITOR TO HIS GOD, HIS COUNTRY, HIS FAMILY AND HIS CLASS!

---

*Jack London (1876–1916) was the author of novels such as *The Call of the Wild* (1903), *The Sea-Wolf* (1904), and *Martin Eden* (1909). He was also an avid socialist and enthusiastic union supporter.

Resolving strikes in the public sector involves some special considerations. Often these strikes are less economic than political. For example, a city or school system is not immediately harmed economically by strikes if taxes are still collected. Political strikes demand political responses. The major lesson learned in the 1970s in this regard has been to avoid panic and immediate capitulation. Firefighter strikes, transportation strikes, school strikes, sanitation strikes, and others taught municipalities that a strike by public employees does not automatically beget anarchy, chaos, crime, a breakdown of law and order, or any other of the dire consequences so often predicted in the past. Nor does the public automatically side with the union. In fact, in some strikes the public has shown strong determination to put up with inconvenience and support the public officials. This was true in the Atlanta sanitation strike by **AFSCME** and in transportation strikes in New York and San Francisco. Chicago even managed to "tough it out" during a firefighter strike.

In general, it appears that three factors are critical to the public employer seeking to "win" a strike:

1. Public opinion must be rallied to the side of the public employer. Of course, this is easier when the employer has a good case to make and, consequently, if the employer is not behaving in a fashion that is unacceptable to the public. The Memphis sanitation strike of 1967 that provided the backdrop of the assassination of Martin Luther King, Jr., is an example of a situation in which the employer's behavior could not command overwhelming public respect.

2. Legal prohibitions against strikes must be used sensibly. Using the law in an "overkill" fashion is likely to create a public opinion backlash. Rather than replace all workers at once, allow strikers time to return to their jobs. Rather than fire them at the outset, fine them and threaten them with being placed on probation. Replacing workers slowly has been one effective means of breaking public sector strikes.

3. Labor leaders must not be made martyrs. Jailing union leaders, allowing them to be photographed in handcuffs, and the like is not calculated to resolve the strike. Rather, the lesson from New York City's labor strife in the 1960s is that such

---

TERMS   **AFSCME**   The American Federation of State, County and Municipal Employees.

behavior is likely to prolong the strike by enhancing the solidarity of labor and by turning public opinion against the public employer.

Although the potential to engage in a strike is useful and perhaps even necessary for effective labor relations, labor and management should never discount the damage strikes can do to the public economic interest and welfare. In some ways, strikes are antisocial actions that should be reduced to a minimum. Innocent third parties may be harmed by them, as may the nation's economy and even security as a whole. Today, we are too interdependent economically to be isolated from the effects of strikes. Indeed it has been alleged that one reason why the Chicago firefighter's strike failed was that the nonfirefighter friends and relatives of those on strike communicated to the strikers that, quite simply, they ought to be ashamed of what they were doing because it was so threatening to life and property. Strikes among hospital workers and doctors engender the same kind of reaction. Consequently, society as a whole, but especially those involved in labor relations, should continue to seek ways of avoiding strikes and making them less damaging when they occur.

REVIEW QUESTIONS

1. What are the pros and cons of relying on strikes or lockouts to resolve impasses?

2. What are the advantages and disadvantages of mediation, fact-finding, and arbitration relative to one another?

3. Review the different forms of arbitration used in the public sector and consider their benefits and drawbacks.

4. Should interest arbitrators in the public sector be public employees? Licensed by the government? Why? Why not?

5. Do you think the Taft-Hartley procedure for dealing with national emergencies adequately protects the public interest?

6. Review the means of coping with strikes discussed in the chapter. How appropriate would these be in the school or work organization with which you are associated? What might you add to the list?

FOR ADDITIONAL READING

Cullen, Donald E. *National Emergency Strikes*. Ithaca, NY: New York State School of Industrial and Labor Relations, Cornell University, 1968.

Feuille, Peter. *Final Offer Arbitration*. Chicago: International Personnel Management Association, 1975.

Gennard, John. *Financing Strikers*. New York: John Wiley, 1977

Horton, Raymond D. *Municipal Labor Relations in New York City: Lessons of the Lindsay-Wagner Years*. New York: Praeger, 1973.

Levin, Edward and Daniel V. DeSantis. *Mediation: An Annotated Bibliography*. Ithaca, NY: New York State School of Industrial and Labor Relations, Cornell University, 1968.

Simkin, William E. *Mediation and the Dynamics of Collective Bargaining*. Washington, DC: The Bureau of National Affairs, Inc., 1971.

Stern, James L. and others. *Final Offer Arbitration*. Lexington, MA: Lexington Books, 1975.

Paterson, Lee T. and John Liebert. *Management Strike Handbook*. Chicago: International Personnel Management Association, 1974.

7 Contract Management: The Daily Life of Labor Relations

Prologue
Bust the Contract, Bust the Union!

The purpose of collective bargaining is to gain a viable contract between management and labor. If the contract can be legally set aside, collective bargaining could be, in effect, negated. Some companies have found a way to break an otherwise legally binding labor contract with the incidental side effect of possibly busting the union.

In 1978 the Congress passed the Bankruptcy Reform Act. This major overhaul of the federal bankruptcy statutes provided that **insolvent** corporations could undergo a **reorganization** which would transfer ownership to a new corporation made up of old owners and creditors. This procedure, supervised by a federal bankruptcy court, also allowed the business to continue operating

---

TERMS   **Insolvent**   The condition of some persons (or organizations) who either cannot pay debts as they come due or whose assets are less than liabilities.

Reorganization   Any restructuring of a large organization. A reorganization under federal bankruptcy laws allows an insolvent corporation to continue functioning while financial reforms are implemented.

during the process. It is Chapter 11 of the Act that regulates such reorganizations.

While it was not intended at the time of the Act's passage, Chapter 11 has turned out to be a way by which companies in financial difficulty can evade their union contracts. For example, Wilson Foods of Oklahoma City filed for a Chapter 11 bankruptcy in April of 1983 and then cut wages for 6,000 workers from $10.69 to $6.50 an hour. While the union, the United Food and Commercial Workers, struck, it eventually settled for a wage cut of $2.69 an hour.

Companies are increasingly using Chapter 11 to technically become different legal entities that are not bound to the union contract of the original company. The best known instance of this is Continental Air Lines. In September of 1983 it filed for bankruptcy under Chapter 11, dismissed its 12,000 employees, and offered "new" nonunion jobs to about one-third of them at about one-half of their previous pay. The affected unions—the Air Line Pilots Association, the Union of Flight Attendants, and the International Association of Machinists—struck and took the company to federal court, charging that management "engineered" a Chapter 11 reorganization specifically in order to break its collective bargaining agreements. While a federal bankruptcy judge in January of 1984 upheld the reorganization, he also ordered the company to present a settlement offer to the unions. In spite of the bad publicity, the strikes, and the stigma of bankruptcy, Continental has succeeded in staying in business (at about half of its former size) and reducing its per capita labor costs by about half.

A result similar to Chapter 11 can be achieved by "double-breasting" whereby a single management operates two (or more) legally different companies, one union, the other nonunion. This is particularly common in the construction industry and may be spreading. For example, Frontier Airlines in 1984 started Frontier Horizon, a nonunion "discount" carrier whose employees earn about half of the salaries of the unionized Frontier Airlines. Frontier's unionized employees are naturally concerned that their jobs may eventually be "transferred" to the nonunion sister company, leaving them, in effect, laid-off and locked out.

It used to be that a **runaway shop** actually had to run away. Now a company wishing to run away from its union may file for bankruptcy under Chapter 11 or have their lawyers establish a

---

TERMS   **Runaway Shop**   A business that closes and moves away to avoid unionization or the effects of union wages.

parallel nonunion company to which work can be transferred. All in all, labor contracts don't offer the degree of security that they used to.

THE BASIC ELEMENTS OF LABOR CONTRACTS

The formation of unions, their struggles for recognition, the negotiation of contracts, and the resolution of impasses are some of the "sexier" aspects of contemporary labor relations. However, they are not the stuff of which most labor relations now consist. Today, the most important aspect of labor relations in both the private and public sectors is living within the negotiated contract. Indeed, it has been estimated that over a two-year contract period an employer's labor relations specialists will spend only 15 percent of their time on contract negotiation. The other 85 percent will be devoted to administering the contract. This is appropriate for there would obviously be little point in expending so much energy on establishing a system of collective bargaining if contracts were routinely ignored or violated.

Neither employees nor employer's rights would be protected if contracts went unenforced. In fact, it is generally viewed as one of the great accomplishments of the American system of collective bargaining that the negotiated contract becomes the "law" of the workplace. It is still a relatively rare event when an employer seeks to "run away" from a labor contract by filing for Chapter 11 bankruptcy. Of course, in order to be "the law," a contract must be subject to authoritative interpretation and considered binding upon employers, unions, and employees. This chapter will describe the general problems that arise in contract enforcement and the machinery developed to resolve disputes over a contract's meaning and application.

The provisions of labor contracts are generally classified into three categories:

1. Fixed provisions which deal with conditions that are not expected to change during the life of the contract, such as wages, fringe benefits, and union security;

2. **Contingent** provisions which involve areas where change is quite likely, as in personnel matters such as promotions,

TERMS **Contingent** Something that is possible, but not assured, because it depends on future events or actions (known as contingencies) that may or may not occur.

discharges, disciplinary action, lay-offs, and work-scheduling; and

3. Dispute resolution provisions which deal with means of resolving disagreements between the union and the employer over the meaning, the applicability, and the implementation of the contract.

Ambiguous Contract Language

A negotiated agreement inevitably contains ambiguities. There are two types of ambiguity—patent and latent. Patent ambiguity exists where language is unclear on its face. Examples of patently ambiguous language that you may find in some negotiated agreements include such phrases as:

reasonable time for representation duties, or

equitable distribution of overtime.

Patently ambiguous language finds its way into labor agreements for a variety of reasons. Among the more common of these reasons are the following:

Compromise—Many provisions in a contract are arrived at through compromise at the bargaining table. This often results in compromise or ambiguous contract language.

Flexibility—If the union proposes that employees receive four hours advance notice of an overtime assignment, supervisors will often prefer to modify this to where employees will *normally* receive four hours advance notice. The phrase *normally* introduces an ambiguity in the contract, but it provides more flexibility in administering the agreement than if the phrase were deleted.

Workability—Discipline for *just* and *sufficient* cause is a relatively ambiguous phrase but it is sometimes more workable than a detailed listing of offenses and penalties.

Whatever the reasons for patent ambiguity in a contract, it is important to realize that the ambiguity was intentional. There is often a rich bargaining history surrounding these phrases and the negotiators may have an understanding of how these clauses are to be administered that transcends the written agreement.

Latent ambiguity occurs when language that appears clear on its face is rendered obscure by unforeseen circumstances. A contract clause stating that "employees will be assigned overtime in order of their position on the seniority roster maintained by the supervisor" appears to be clear on its face. If, in attempting to administer this clause, supervisors find that there is no seniority roster, it is difficult to determine whether overtime should be assigned first to the individual with the earliest service computation date, the greatest amount of time-in-grade, etc. The quoted language does not provide an answer and the ambiguity results from the unforeseen absence of a seniority roster.

Latent ambiguity is generally unintended and there is often no bargaining history to guide the parties on how to administer these clauses.

Source: Raymond R. McKay and Ralph Smith. *Supervisor's Guide to Labor Relations in the Federal Government* (Washington, DC: U.S. Office of Personnel Management, 1982), pp. 20–21.

Implementing and enforcing contracts is generally most problematic in the area of contingent provisions. Here change is likely to occur; it may be governed by the wording of the contract. However, that wording may not be clear. It may involve language that was used to smooth over different understandings of the practices that would govern the workplace when the union and the employer were engaged in negotiation. For instance, management may have thought the right to discipline employees was incorporated into a management rights clause, while the union may have thought that a protection against disciplinary action except for just cause required that it be consulted prior to such action being taken. Similarly, definitions of seniority relative to workplace, work unit, or trade may purposely be left vague to enable a union to avoid alienating some groups among its members, such as younger employees, members of minority groups, or women. Moreover, even if the wording of the contract is ambiguous, conditions that neither party foresaw may arise, leading them both to agree that the contract as worded is not workable, but disagreeing as to what should be done. Indeed, almost an infinite number of problems can arise as a result of contractual language that must be interpreted in a number of changing situations. Finally, it is always possible that a supervisor or foreman will simply ignore the language of a contract in making a work assignment, allocating overtime, or engaging in some other activity. In such instances, a mechanism for enforcing the contract is necessary.

WHY GRIEVANCES ARISE

Disputes over the meaning, application, and enforcement of a contract are referred to as "grievances." These can be of at least three types, although two are most common. One is an "individual grievance," an instance in which an employee feels that he or she is being treated unfairly. A second involves the union and relates to enforcement of part of the contract as a whole, rather than its application to one particular employee. A disagreement over holiday pay might be an example. Another possibility, though somewhat unusual, is a grievance by the employer against the union on the grounds that the union has violated the contract. Examples would include union support of a **wildcat strike** or dissemination of negative publicity against the employer.

Individual grievances are by far the most numerous. These involve myriad situations where individuals believe they are being treated unfairly in violation of the contract. The largest single category involves disciplinary action. Employees are frequently

---

TERMS   **Wildcat Strike**   A work stoppage not sanctioned by union leadership and usually contrary to an existing labor contract. Unless it can be shown that unfair employer practices were the direct cause of the strike, the union could be liable for damages.

protected against **arbitrary,** capricious, or discriminatory discipline by a contract clause limiting management's right to discipline an employee except for just cause. But what is just cause? The same behavior can be interpreted differently in different circumstances. For instance, in some work areas extreme profanity is "normal" and accepted; in others it presents "just cause" for discipline. **Absenteeism,** tardiness, dress, grooming, and **insubordination** present similar examples. In some places acceptable standards are different than in others.

Even where there is just cause for discipline, there may be a dispute over whether the extent of disciplinary action was justified. Should the employee who repeatedly curses at the supervisor be discharged or is this penalty too extreme, at least as a first effort at disciplining the employee? Then there is the issue of nondiscriminatory application of discipline. Should the employee of twenty years' service in good standing be fired uttering his or her first profane word during all that time, if the employee of three months' tenure is dismissed for the same iteration? What if they both have stolen something from the employer? When does "progressive discipline" become arbitrary or discriminatory? The questions and issues can go on and on—and they do. There are literally thousands of grievances involving discipline every year in public and private workplaces covered by collective bargaining agreements.

Discipline, however, is not the only area where disputes over the meaning of the contract and its application to individuals arise. Promotions, the assignment of overtime and "dirty work," and matters of leave all generate a number of grievances. So do matters of safety, work scheduling, and a host of other aspects of the employment relationship. In order to get the flavor of individual grievances look at some of the arbitrated grievances reported by the federal government (and the decisions rendered):

● Did the employer violate the agreement by changing the workweek and requiring the **grievants** to work on Sunday without overtime pay? (Yes)

● Did management violate the agreement when it refused to issue the grievant safety shoes? (Yes)

TERMS **Arbitrary**   An action decided by personal whim that was not guided by general principles or rules.

Absenteeism   The unnecessary, unexcused, or habitual absence from work.

Insubordination   Disobedience to higher authorities in an organization; refusing to take orders from those who are properly designated to give them.

Grievant   A person who files a formal grievance; one who does so "grieves." This person is not in a state of mourning, but one of complaining.

- Was the five-day suspension of the grievant warranted by his use of threatening and abusive language against a supervisor and a fellow employee?(No)

- Did management violate the agreement by requiring male employees to wear neckties? (Yes)

- Was the change of grievant's work location a violation of the agreement?(Yes)

- Did management have just cause to issue a ten-day suspension to the grievant for leaving the job to which he was assigned during working hours? (No)

- Was the grievant forced to take substantially more night shift duty than circumstances required due to personal favoritism of the supervisor? (Yes)

- Did the activity violate the negotiated agreement by unilaterally transferring the grievant in order to remove him from the supervision of his future wife? (Yes)

While thousands upon thousands of other cases could be listed, these should suffice to provide a notion of the range of activities that may lead to grievances. These cases were selected to demonstrate the extent to which management's authority to assign, discipline, transfer, and otherwise deal with employees can be restricted by a negotiated contract. In fact, grievances of this nature carry some obvious lessons for management. First, **foremen,** supervisors, and managers must be thoroughly familiar with the language and requirements of the contract. Ignorance is no excuse for violating an employee's rights. Second, employees must be treated fairly. Favoritism or discrimination must be avoided as it will almost automatically lead to a grievance. Third, exceptions should be made only with the utmost care. The managerial attitude of "Okay, but just this once," is a dangerous practice as far as grievances are concerned. Although it has less appeal, the standard bureaucratic attitude, "If I make an exception for you, I'll have to make one for everyone," is more appropriate insofar as managing under a labor contract is concerned. Fourth, informal work

TERMS   **Foreman**   A first-line supervisor—the first level of management responsible for securing adequate production and the managerial employee who supervises the work of nonmanagerial employees. Present-day foremen work under a fading occupational title. It has fallen victim to the Department of Labor's efforts to "de-sex" the nature of work and has been retired as an officially acceptable job title by the fourth edition of the *Dictionary of Occupational Titles* (1977).

arrangements should be avoided, lest these become "custom and practice" in the workplace that later create grievances if altered. Indeed, "custom and practice" can become part of the contract. Yet, all of this is easier said than done. Managing by contract reduces managerial flexibility in many respects—perhaps so many that traditional management as practiced in the United States becomes dysfunctional, if not impossible. Before considering some ways of reducing grievances and then of handling them effectively when they arise, let's look briefly at some examples of the second type of grievance, that involving the union itself as a party. In the cases listed below the dispute is between the union and the employer, rather than an individual and the employer:

- Should the released time granted to union stewards for the preparation of union grievances be counted as official time? (No)

- Did the union violate the agreement by allowing other locals to occupy the same building? (Yes)

- Did the merit promotion plan reserve to management the right to appoint candidates to career positions without consultation with the union? (No, the union should have been consulted.)

- Did management violate the agreement when it refused to approve the union newsletter for distribution on its premises? (No)

- Did management violate the agreement by refusing to negotiate on staffing? (No, it was required to consult, however.)

Here it becomes critically important that the contract is between these two parties, rather than between the employer and the employees. These grievances concern the treatment of union representatives, union dissemination of publicity, and the scope of bargaining. As in the case of individual grievances, grievances of this type can reduce management's discretion and require it to share the governance of the workplace with the union.

REDUCING THE NUMBER OF GRIEVANCES   In general, both labor and management want to reduce the number of grievances. Their first preference is to resolve matters during contract negotiations, rather than on a day-to-day basis in the workplace. However, occasions do arise when unions will seek to obtain through grievances what could not be won during negotiations. There will also be occasions when employees or a union seek to use grievances to harass individual supervisors. As mentioned above, management can reduce grievances by making sure the supervisory personnel are thoroughly aware of the contract's requirements, and avoid favoritism, exceptions, and informal arrangements. But, there is more to it than this. A positive approach to living with the union must be developed. In large part, this requires recognition of the union leaderships' political situation and a desire not to exacerbate its insecurity. Efforts to "bust" the union, dethrone its leadership, or stonewall it on every turn will probably increase the number of grievances and make life more difficult for all concerned. Baird, Anderson, and Damas, along with most responsible labor relations authorities, recommend the following general guidelines:

1. The union should be advised of important decisions affecting employees before they are implemented.

2. Because all union leaders are inherently political actors, they should be helped to play out their role. This may require "building up" the leader in the eyes of employees from time to time; also helping union leaders save face, when necessary.

3. Deal honestly with the union. Dishonesty (which is usually found out) breeds distrust which will surely result in grievances and disharmony.

4. Always have open channels of communication. This helps avoid misunderstandings and prevent minor problems from becoming major ones.

5. The most comprehensive possible personnel records should be kept. They are often needed to prove management's reasonability in its dealing with individual employees. Unions generally have no particular interest in supporting unsound grievances.

6. Be careful not to interfere in the internal affairs of unions.

7. Representatives of management should not get too friendly with union leadership. This could taint the leadership in the eyes of the members. And remember, if you ask the union for a favor, you are inviting the union to ask for one in return.

In addition, foremen and supervisors should be encouraged to appreciate the role of the union **steward.** The steward's function is

---

TERMS   **Steward** A local union's most immediate representative in a plant or department. Usually elected by fellow employees (but sometimes appointed by union leadership), the shop steward handles grievances, collects dues, solicits new members, etc.

to assure that the contract is followed and that employees are treated fairly on the local level. Stewards, like union leaders, may have to represent diverse groups of employees. They may feel under pressure to test management and try to win concessions beyond the content of the contract. While management should encourage its representatives to resist these efforts, they should be careful not to personalize the situation. Efforts to "get" the steward are an excellent prescription for poor labor relations. In fact, harmonious and mutually respectful relationships between supervisors and stewards (and middle managers and local union leaders) are crucial to efficient and effective collective bargaining. Such constructive relationships serve well to notify all parties of possible problem areas and often lead to considerations of ways of resolving problems in a mutually satisfactory fashion.

First-line supervisors should always keep the following in mind: (1) grievance resolution is one of their most important responsibilities, (2) because worker-manager relations are to some degree inherently adversarial, grievances are normal happenstances rather than personal criticisms, (3) quickly passing the buck or capitulating will eventually make it difficult or impossible to engage in effective supervision, and (4) grievances should not be thought of as being failures on management's part—they are simply a natural aspect of work and of dealing with other people.

The reduction of disputes over the requirements of contracts as they pertain to the treatment of individual employees or the rights of a union is a valuable objective. But what if, after all the rules are followed, and all possible efforts are made at harmonious labor relations, such disputes still occur? How should they be handled? This question can usually be answered by examining an organization's dispute resolution or grievance **machinery.**

DISPUTE RESOLUTION MACHINERY

Individual grievances can be defined and handled in a variety of ways because there is always the question of whether a grievance should be confined to an alleged breach of the specific wording of a contract, or, alternatively, broadened to cover more general employee complaints and "gripes." In the first case, a grievance could be defined as a suspected violation of a provision of a labor contract which adversely affects workers covered by its provisions. The broader approach would hold that a grievance is any dispute

TERMS **Machinery**   The totality of the methods, usually enumerated in a collective bargaining agreement, used to resolve the problems of interpretation arising during the life of the agreement.

between a worker and his or her employer. The major virtue of the broader approach is that it enables the grievance procedure to serve a **human relations** function, by allowing employees to express their generalized complaints and requiring that management become cognizant of them. The narrower approach, on the other hand, protects managerial authority and discretion in the workplace. In many cases, a compromise definition between these two general approaches will be used.

Grievances can be generated in any of three ways:

1. Individual employees have the right to present grievances to employers and to have them adjusted, if the employer is willing to accept the employee's point of view. However, the provision of the Taft-Hartley Act which allows this does not entitle an individual employee to use the complete grievance machinery provided for in the union contract, which very frequently ends in binding arbitration. Rather, it simply serves notice that while the union is the "exclusive representative," the individual employee has the right to complain directly to management. Nevertheless, a union representative may legally be present at any time that an individual complaint is adjusted. Consequently, one approach to defining the grievance is to confine it to the individual employee.

2. The union is allowed to file grievances, on behalf of its own rights or those of the employees it represents. Where this approach is used, the individual employee may not be able to move beyond the first step in the grievance machinery without union representation. When the union itself has a grievance it may be an instance where it was not consulted on a change in personnel procedures, or on a new interpretation of the contract, or when its functionaries are excluded from various kinds of meetings. It may also find itself in a situation where the issue is essentially a class action, affecting a high proportion of the employees in the bargaining unit. Generally speaking, grievance procedures pertaining to matters involving the union as a party are limited to two formal steps. The union representatives meet with the appropriate management functionary for labor relations and seek to resolve the matter. If this fails, the next step is grievance arbitration. However, such

TERMS   **Human Relations**   The discipline concerned with the application of the behavioral sciences to the analysis and understanding of human behavior in organizations.

disputes often involve a great deal of informal interaction between the parties. They may also result in litigation.

3. Management may have a right to file a grievance against the union.

No matter what form the specific grievance process takes, some overriding principles are generally viewed as crucial to its success. First, the system must result in the prompt adjustment of grievances. It does little good to drag them out while both the supervisor and the aggrieved employee must continue to work with one another. Second, grievances must be resolved on their merits. It should be the principle that is involved, not the individual personalities. Third, it should always be remembered that the objective of the grievance procedure must be to reach fair settlements, not simply to win cases. It is also helpful if supervisors view grievances as an aid in identifying and eliminating problems in the workplace. Both sides must also be willing to devote adequate time to gaining an understanding of the working of the grievance machinery and to dealing with actual grievances. Moreover, both sides (but especially management) must be prepared to lose. Finally, both sides must view the grievance process as an ongoing mechanism for improving relations in the workplace on the basis of equality between the union and management.

While the procedural steps for resolving grievances vary from workplace to workplace, a common pattern has developed over the years. A comprehensive procedure would include the following steps:

Step 1.   The grieving employee, the union steward, and the immediate supervisor discuss the complaint orally. This step is considered informal. It can lead to an immediate adjustment, if the supervisor has the authority to do so. Perhaps little but an apology and statement that the supervisor will refrain from repeating the act will suffice if it's a relatively minor matter such as the use of harsh or profane language against the employee. The basic rules for supervisors at this point are:

1. Listen attentively to the employee's complaint. Let the employee tell his or her story without interruption or contradiction.

2. Display interest in the problem. The employee feels an injustice has been done. This feeling will only be

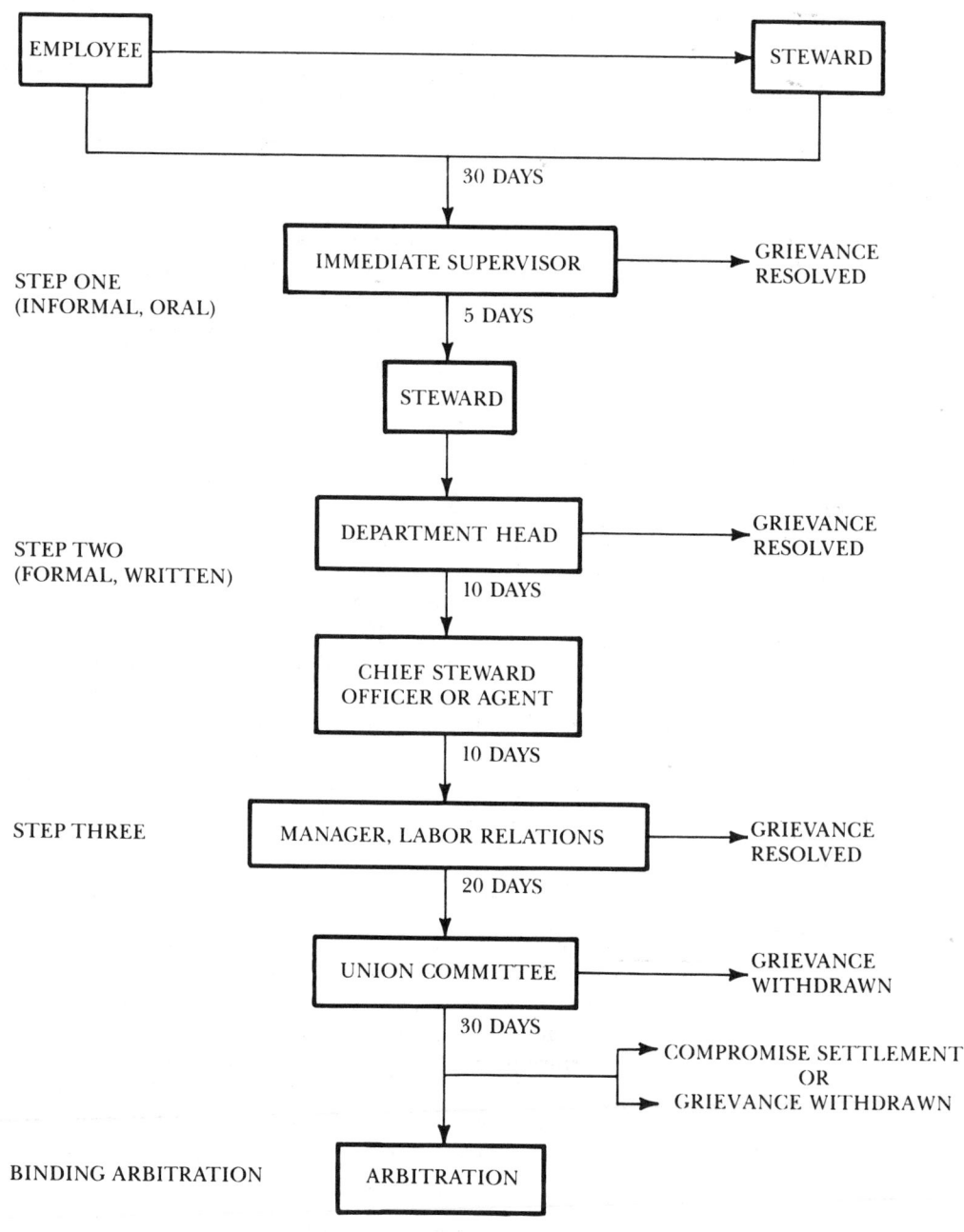

Figure 7-1. *Model Grievance Procedure*

Source: Donald S. McPherson, *Resolving Grievances: A Practical Approach* (Reston, VA: Reston Publishing Co., 1983), p. 32.

intensified if the supervisor dismisses it as a minor matter.

3. Get all the facts and keep records of the employee's statements. It is important to find out when the alleged problem occurred, who was present, what was said, and so forth.

4. Restate the employee's grievance. After hearing the employee's complaint and asking questions to help clarify matters, the supervisor should reiterate the complaint as he or she understands it. The employee should have an opportunity to correct this reiteration. At times, this approach will lead the employee to change his or her perspective on the gravity, import, or even sequence of what occurred.

5. Be timely! At the first stage, however, the supervisor should not take any position on the matter unless it is relatively minor and can be corrected verbally (e.g., by apology). Consultation with superiors, labor relations personnel, and personnelists is desirable before the supervisor makes any significant commitment to the employee.

Step 2. The grievance is taken to the chief steward and departmental superintendent. This is the first level of appeal if the grievant is not satisfied with the results of the informal processes of step one. At this stage the grievance must be turned into a written statement, and a more thorough investigation will be undertaken. Management may make an effort at resolution through adjustment or it may deny the validity of the complaint altogether.

Step 3. If the grievance needs to go further, the union grievance committee and/or local union president and the director of personnel must meet. At this stage the grievance becomes even more highly formalized. In essence, it is submitted to both sides' specialists in personnel and labor relations for resolution. The personnel director should be in a position to evaluate the grievance in terms of whether it is a matter covered by the contract and, if so, whether it has merit. In making a determination, the personnel director may want to (a) consult with managers generally, (b) hold a conference with the grievant, or even (c) engage in further investigation. At this point, the investigation may change its character in some respects. Rather than being an effort simply to find out what occurred and why, the personnel director may begin to develop a **brief** should the matter eventually go to arbitration. If possible, of course, the personnel director will resolve the dispute at this point.

Step 4. This is generally the final step under control of the union and management. It is an appeal by the union grievance committee, local union president, union business agent, or international union representative to a company's vice president for industrial relations (or the equivalent). Again, an effort is made to adjust the grievance. However, a grievance that reaches this stage is likely to involve an important matter of some controversy and the positions of the two sides may already have become well defined and uncompromising. If no resolution is reached at this step, the issue will most likely go to arbitration.

While the procedure outlined above is comprehensive, many private and public employers are inclined to use an abridged version. Generally, however, there will be the same first step effort at informal resolution and at least one managerial review if this fails. Craft unions are particularly prone to favoring a two-step procedure because of their centralized structure and tendency to have considerable strength at local levels.

So far we have stressed the handling of grievances from a managerial perspective. However, grievances present unions with some tricky problems as well. Ideally, union leaders want to be able to pick and choose their grievances in order to be more likely to achieve victories and avoid defeats. Moreover, if they can choose the issues for individual grievances, they may be able to expand workers' rights in the most important areas. Since processing grievances costs money, unions also want to avoid taking on superfluous gripes from malcontented employees. However, the union leader must always seek to show the rank and file that the union works for them and is improving their situation in the workplace. As Sayles and Strauss have found, in order to maximize important victories and minimize defeats, union leaders commonly:

1. Require members to sign grievances;

2. Screen grievances before negotiating with management;

TERMS   **Brief**   A written statement prepared by each side in a formal lawsuit or hearing which summarizes the facts of the situation and makes arguments about how the law should be applied.

3. Do not negotiate without a second union officer being present (so that the situation never becomes one of just "your" word against management);

4. Rely on **precedents** and legalistic interpretations;

5. If possible, pass the buck to the arbitrator; and

6. Involve the international union.

The union's handling of a grievance may suggest that the union's interest may be different from that of the employee ostensibly being represented. This is often the case. The union is a collectivity. The grievant can be a single individual. The objectives of a majority in the union and that of the individual grievant may not be identical. Race, gender, and seniority are among the characteristics that may set off an individual grievant from most other members of the bargaining unit.

This possible **conflict of interest** may raise some problems in handling grievances. Under prevailing labor legislation and Supreme Court decisions the union must represent all members of the bargaining unit equally, without discrimination as to matters extraneous to the strength of the employer's case. Presumably such extraneous matters would include the overall interests of the union itself as well as race, gender, and so forth. The union is not required to pursue a grievance through all steps on behalf of the employee, but it cannot perfunctorily dismiss or arbitrarily refuse to pursue the matter. In short, the union must exercise good faith. Civil rights legislation places further requirements on unions' responsibility to treat all employees fairly. If an employee fails to obtain satisfactory adjustment of a grievance, and it is partly based on a claim of racial or other prohibited discrimination, he or she may move to another forum—a federal administrative agency or a federal court—for resolution of the matter.

ARBITRATION OF
GRIEVANCES

When the parties to a labor contract (that is, the union and the employer) have a disagreement over what the collective agreement requires, they generally try to resolve this dispute through their

TERMS **Precedent** A legal decision on a question of law that gives authority and direction on how similar cases should be decided in the future.

Conflict of Interest Being in a position where your own needs and desires, generally economic, could possibly lead you to violate your duty to a person who has a right to depend upon you.

grievance machinery. But what if there is no such machinery, or what if it fails to achieve a resolution of the matter? In the absence of additional techniques of dispute resolution, the employer would most likely assert its view and implement it. This would violate the principle of equality among the parties to the contract and might even turn the whole collective bargaining process into much ado about nothing. Presumably the union could sue the employer in court for **breach of contract.** But this would be cumbersome, expensive, and time consuming. The union might also resort to a show of economic strength and call a strike to force its view of the contract on the employer. The employer might respond at some point with a lockout to show the union who's boss. This is an excellent scenario for continued labor strife, lost productivity, and economic hardship. During World War II, a better method gained credence. Unions and employers would agree to forego the use of disruptive economic weapons and submit their disputes to binding arbitration. Just prior to the war, in the 1930s, only about 10 percent of all collective bargaining contracts provided for binding arbitration as a means of resolving disputes over the interpretation of agreements. By the mid-1940s, about three-fourths of all contracts did so. By the 1970s the figure had reached 95 percent. Clearly, grievance settlement procedures ending in binding arbitration, where necessary, have become the rule in both the private and public sectors. The quid pro quo is that labor gives up its right to strike during the life of the contract for management's agreement to submit contract disputes to binding, third party arbitration.

Binding grievance arbitration has an interesting legal status. The labor agreement defines a system of rights, obligations, and governance in the workplace. If the contract provides for binding arbitration, it usually indicates that enforcement will not be through the courts, but rather by neutral third parties voluntarily selected by management and union representatives. The critical principle of grievance arbitration is the assertion that the arbitrator is the "officially designated reader of the contract." The arbitrator's only source of authority is from the parties to the contract, and this authority is always limited to the interpretation and application of the terms and conditions of the contract. (Remember that "custom and practice" in the workplace can become part of the contract and therefore within the scope of arbitrability.)

This status has been recognized by the U.S. Supreme Court in

TERMS   **Breach of Contract**   A failure, without legal excuse, to perform any promise or to carry out any of the terms of a contract.

the Lincoln Mills and Steelworkers' Trilogy cases (discussed in Chapter 5). Because of these cases grievance arbitration properly includes all matters that come within the scope of the grievance and arbitration provisions of the contract, excluding only matters specifically and explicitly placed outside these provisions by the contract. Although arbitration is limited to the contract, the arbitrator is permitted to consider **industrial relations common law** as part of the agreement. Thus, arbitrators may consider factors such as productivity, morale, and tensions at work in reaching their decisions. Moreover, an arbitrator's decision is subject only to a very limited scope of **judicial review** which will be restricted to inquiring as to whether (1) the arbitrator followed the contract, (2) the parties agreed that arbitration was to be binding and final, and (3) the process was procedurally regular and fair with no gross errors by the arbitrator. In short, for most intents and purposes, the arbitrator (or panel) is the final judge of a grievance.

Because arbitrators are given great power, questions are often raised about how they are trained and what criteria they employ. In a formal sense, arbitrators need but one qualification—the parties must agree to use them. No special training is actually required. Nevertheless, the function of grievance arbitration has become so prevalent that several organizations now exist to assure that there is an adequate supply of professional arbitrators imbued with certain standards of responsibility. The **American Arbitration Association,** The Federal Mediation and Conciliation Service, and the **National Academy of Arbitrators** have established a *Code of Professional Responsibility for Arbitrators of Labor-Management Disputes.* It provides in part that the arbitrators should (1) disclose their work background and monetary interests, current or past, with any company or union involved in the proceedings, (2) not be influenced by personal relationships in reaching decisions, (3) treat the proceedings as confidential, (4) not delegate decisionmaking to

---

TERMS   **Industrial Relations Common Law**   The total body of law established by judicial precedent that applies to the workplace.

Judicial Review   A court's power to review governmental acts or decisions in order to assess their legality or constitutionality.

American Arbitration Association   A national organization that supplies arbitrators who help settle labor and other disputes through arbitration, mediation, and other voluntary methods.

National Academy of Arbitrators   An honorific organization that seeks to promote the study of, and maintain standards for, the arbitration of labor-management disputes.

another person, and (5) not engage in collusion with the parties for improper purpose. Many arbitrators are lawyers.

Arbitrators must be chosen freely by the parties. Generally they are selected from lists provided by the American Arbitration Association, the Federal Mediation and Conciliation Service, or similar state agencies. Often five, seven, or nine names will appear on the list and the parties to the dispute will alternately strike names off until only one is left—that is their arbitrator. Another common procedure is for labor to select one arbitrator, management another, and those two a third to form a panel of three. The arbitration proceedings are quasi-judicial in nature. Each side presents its "evidence" and arguments. The arbitrator is active in trying to discover facts and many challenge the logic or supporting documentation of the parties. Ultimately, however, the arbitrator must be a neutral judge if he or she hopes to remain employed in this line of work. Thus, the question of standards or criteria for grievance resolution becomes of paramount importance. These have been identified as:

1. Adherence to the contract. If the contract seems explicit to the arbitrator as to what is required, then the grievance is an easy one that probably should not have reached arbitration. Generally, however, the problem is that the contract is in fact unclear.

2. Erosion of the contract. Sometimes the contract will be eroded by constant deviance from its letter and/or spirit. An arbitrator may take this into account.

3. The "custom and practice" of the workplace generally.

4. The effect on employees other than the grievant.

5. **Equity** and reasonability.

An arbitrator may also have to take federal or state laws into account. This raises a question as to the arbitrator's authority. Certainly an arbitrator's decision as to the applicability and content of **civil rights laws** is not likely to be treated as binding on the courts if one side can make a prima facie case that these laws were misconstrued. Similarly, it may not be treated as final and binding

TERMS   **Equity**   Fairness in a particular situation.

Civil Rights Laws   The federal laws passed just after the Civil War and during the last four decades that prohibit discrimination based on race, color, age, sex, religion, or national origin.

by the parties to a dispute. This raises the issue of multiple forums for resolving grievances. According to current federal court rulings, where a grievance involves a matter of prohibited racial, sexual, ethnic, or religious discrimination, the aggrieved employee retains a right to seek satisfaction in a federal or state administrative agency, or in federal court. Many labor relations specialists believe that binding arbitration of grievances will lose its effectiveness if it is not the final forum for resolving disputes. However, they also recognize that people have a right not to be unlawfully discriminated against at work.

The parties to an arbitration hearing can enhance their chances of winning by proper preparation. Having adequate documentation pertaining to the matter in question, its relation to the contract, and its prevalence in the workplace may be especially important. Each side should also develop arguments supporting the reasonableness of its position. Witnesses should be selected with care for their credibility and knowledge. They should also be prepared; that is, the party presenting the witness should rehearse what the witness will say and how he or she will answer questions from the other side. During the hearing itself, exaggeration, reliance on legal technicalities, and lack of cooperation should be avoided. It is also important to concentrate on trying to convince the arbitrator, rather than the other side, of the strength of one's position. **Ex parte** communication—that is, communication with the arbitrator when the other side is not present—must be strictly avoided.

Grievance arbitration in the public sector can present some peculiar problems. Often public sector disputes involve questions of public policy as well as issues of working conditions. What are to police officers matters of safety, for example, may be to a community matters of public policy. For example, the kind of bullets police will use, the conditions under which they may use deadly force, and the number of officers per police car all fit into this category. Educational matters, such as school calendars, the number of pupils in a class, and the nature of disciplinary procedures present similar examples. Generally speaking, an arbitration decision that is primarily a matter of public policy will be vulnerable to suit in court and to being overturned by the judiciary. But precisely what the courts are likely to consider matters of public policy, as opposed to matters legitimately covered by labor agreements, is difficult to say.

TERMS   **Ex Parte**   Latin phrase meaning "with only one side present."

In one case, for instance, a seventh grade public school teacher sought to hold a debate on abortion. He was prevented from doing so by his school board and alleged that this was a violation of the labor agreement which provided for "academic freedom." The contract clause at issue included the proviso that material had to be "appropriate for the maturation level of the group." The New Jersey Superior Court dismissed the possibility of arbitration using the following words: "The American Arbitration Association may be well qualified to 'arbitrate' compensation, hours of work, sick leave, fringe-benefits and the like, but they and their panels possess no expertise in arbitrating the maturation level of a 7th grade student in the elementary schools of Rockaway Township." The major problem, of course, is that decisions of public policy cannot be delegated to private individuals for resolution. They must be addressed by elective legislative and executive officials.

Related problems can occur when the treatment of a public employee involves a grievance that concerns the employee's constitutional rights. Generally speaking, public employees are likely to have more forums in which to present their cases. These include civil service agencies such as the Federal Merit Systems Protection Board (for breaches of personnel law), civil rights agencies (such as the Equal Employment Opportunity Commission), and the courts for resolution of constitutional issues, such as standards of due process and privacy.

As arbitration has evolved over the years, it has become increasingly expensive and time consuming. Generally, the costs are divided between the union and management, although other arrangements are possible. These costs may run into thousands of dollars in lost time, arbitrators' fees, legal assistance, and so on. Consequently some efforts have been undertaken to simplify the arbitration process and reduce its costs. Among these are:

1. Reliance on permanent arbitrators. Here management and labor select an individual to handle grievances under the contract. An appropriate retainer is paid the arbitrator, and perhaps a **per diem** as well. The main advantage of this approach is that the arbitrator gains expertise in the nature of conditions in the workplace and the provisions in the contract. Accordingly, grievances should be handled more rapidly since the arbitrator has much less to learn than an individual brought in

---

TERMS   **Per Diem** Latin phrase meaning "by the day," "day by day," or "each day." Someone who is paid a "per diem" is paid a fixed amount each day.

on an **ad hoc** basis. This approach is used in the steel, automobile, rubber, clothing, and other industries. Smaller employers tend to rely on the ad hoc approach.

2. The use of prehearing briefs to set forth the agreed-upon facts and state the issue in precise terms.

3. Dispensing with transcripts and court reporters, except under unusual circumstances.

4. Expedited procedures, including no transcripts, no briefs, limited time for the presentation of arguments, short written decisions by the arbitrators, and reduced reliance on legal counsel.

5. Bench decisions, or decisions handed down at the conclusion of the hearing, rather than after extended study by the arbitrator.

6. Instant arbitration, or arbitration on the spot with a permanent arbitrator. This is used among actors and longshoremen, where delays in resolving grievances can be highly disruptive to the employer's business.

The major purpose of grievance procedures ending in binding arbitration is to avoid strikes and lockouts over interpretation of the labor agreement. Yet, workers do go out on such strikes and many hours of productive time are lost. In fact, in the mid-1970s, it was found that about 27 percent of all work stoppages occurred under existing agreements. The vast majority of these strikes were of the "wildcat" variety; that is, not sanctioned by the union and also in violation of the agreement. These strikes occur for a number of reasons. Some could be avoided by instant arbitration, particularly in dangerous industries, such as coal mining, where safety matters are critical. Additionally, of course, better management practices can resolve many issues before workers decide to engage in an unfair and **illegal strike.**

Still, such strikes do occur. At present the employer appears to

TERMS **Ad Hoc** Latin phrase meaning "for this special purpose," or "for this one time." An "ad hoc" arbitrator is selected to serve on one particular case. Nothing prevents the arbitrator from being used again and again if both sides agree.

Illegal Strike Any strike that violates existing laws or contracts, that is not properly authorized by the union membership, or that violates a court injunction.

have two main legal remedies for them. One is to seek damages against the union. But here the employer will have to show that the union was somehow instrumental in the strike. A second possibility is to gain an injunction in a federal court against such a strike. Remember, however, the strike has to be in violation of the agreement and the employer also has to agree to arbitrate the issue. Still, these are cumbersome remedies for such strikes. Thus, the wildcat strike continues to present both management and union leadership with an important challenge.

Contract enforcement is the culmination of the drive to establish equality in the workplace. The effort undertaken by the Cordwainers in Philadelphia in the 1790s reaches fruition in the widespread—almost universal—reliance on final and binding arbitration of grievances arising under a negotiated contract. This system creates a "law" of the workplace that treats labor and management equally and seeks to make fairness and equity the rule. It is quite an achievement, and a special contribution of labor relations in the United States to notions of democracy in the workplace.

REVIEW QUESTIONS

1. Identify a variety of ways of reducing the incidence of grievances.

2. To what extent are different interpretations of a contract the result of the need to leave some terms vague in order to reach agreement in the first place? For instance, what is just cause for firing an employee, in your opinion?

3. Does grievance arbitration machinery require management to try to adapt new approaches to dealing with employees—approaches based less on the exercise of sanctions and authority?

4. Looking around your own educational or work setting, what seem to be the major causes of grievances? Specifically, what are the kinds of actions that individuals would be most inclined to grieve over? How could these be reduced?

5. How do you think the costs of grievance arbitration should be apportioned? Should the loser bear all the expense?

6. Do you think the standards of judicial review of grievance arbitration are too broad, too narrow, or about as reasonable as possible? What changes, if any, would you make?

FOR ADDITIONAL READING

Clark, R. Theodore, Jr., and Sandra P. Zemm. *Drafting the Public Sector Labor Agreement.* Chicago: International Personnel Management Association, 1977.

Coulson, Robert. *Labor Arbitration: What You Need to Know.* New York: American Arbitration Association, 1973.

Davey, Harold W., Mario F. Bognanno, and David L. Estenson. *Contemporary Collective Bargaining.* Englewood Cliffs, NJ: Prentice-Hall, 1982.

Elkouri, Frank and Edna Asper Elkouri. *How Arbitration Works,* Third Edition. Washington, DC: The Burearu of National Affairs, Inc., 1973.

McPherson, Donald S. *Resolving Grievances: A Practical Approach.* Reston, VA: Reston Publishing Company/Prentice-Hall, 1983.

Paterson, Lee T. and Reginald T. Murphy. *The Public Administrator's Grievance Arbitration Handbook.* New York: Longman, 1983.

Sayles, Leonard R. and George Strauss. *The Local Union,* Revised Edition. New York: Harcourt, Brace & World, 1967.

Trotta, Maurice S. *Handling Grievances: A Guide for Labor and Management.* Washington, DC: The Bureau of National Affairs, Inc., 1976.

8

Union Structure and Democracy

Prologue
Unions and the Iron Law of Oligarchy

Unions are voluntary associations formed to represent and advance the interests of their members in collective fashion. As in the case of all complex organizations, their formal structure and the nature of their self-governance is the product of a variety of factors and competing forces. Indeed, unions face a very complicated organizational dilemma. On the one hand, since they are established to represent the interests of their members, they must have democratic governance. Otherwise, there is no reason to think that the leadership of a union will reflect the wishes of the rank and file membership. However, on the other hand, unions by definition are formed to present a strong collective voice in dealing with management. Consequently, they must be unified—and unification implies constraints on the liberty of any given individual member to violate or subvert the will of the collectivity (majority) as a whole. For instance, what good would it do for a union to call a strike and have many of its members show up at work anyway? A better prescription for failure would be hard to conceive. Thus, a balance between the rights of the individual member and the strength of the governing body of the union is implied. But the situation is even more complicated.

Over the years many observers have agreed with **Robert Michels'** famous statement that "who says organization says **oligarchy**." His "iron law of oligarchy" holds that majorities within organizations are incapable of governing themselves. After studying the major European political parties and workers' unions early in this century, he concluded that all such organizations are inherently "minoritarian" because only an active minority has the experience, interest, and desire to lead. Consequently, "every party or professional union becomes divided into a minority of directors and a majority of the directed." Even if a new group gained power through democratic processes, this would not alter the oligarchic structure of the organization; it would merely be an exchange of elites.

In keeping with Michels' "iron law," any large organization will tend to perpetuate the domination of a few members, generally those with positions of official authority within the organization's governing structure. Unions are by no means exempt from such tendencies. There is even a good rationale for them. The older unions in the United States are far more than the sum total of their membership at any given moment. They supercede their members; they have played important historical roles; they exist for workers of the past, present, and future. In short they are *institutions* that are valued in their own right for their contributions to the American economic, political, and social systems. Therefore, it would be naive to expect unions to reflect, in a simple sense, the immediate desires of a majority of their present members. It is these themes to which this chapter is devoted, for it is obvious that labor relations cannot be understood without thoughtful consideration of the complicated pressures placed upon unions' structures and governance.

UNION STRUCTURE   The major point of labor unions is to *represent* the will and interests of their members. But in order to do this, unions have to be powerful. A weak union cannot assert the interests of its members vis-à-

TERMS   **Robert Michels** (1876–1936) German-Italian political sociologist whose 1915 analysis of the oligarchical tendencies of large and presumedly democratic organizations, *Political Parties* (Glencoe, IL: Free Press, 1949), remains the classic work on the subject.

Oligarchy   Any form of governance in which power is held by a comparative few.

vis employers. To be powerful enough to attract members and to engage in effective collective bargaining, unions need a governing structure. Moreover, the governing structure must involve an effort to maintain the strong support of the membership. Union constitutions vary widely, yet a pattern seeking to fulfill all these needs tends to emerge.

The governing philosophy of unions is akin to that of other "warring institutions." A heavy emphasis is placed on "unity." Dissent is unwelcome. Indeed, it is viewed as antithetical to the collective purpose of the union. Remember, we refer to *collective* bargaining and rely upon the principle of exclusive recognition and representation. There is little room for the **pluralism** that characterizes American government generally in the governance of unions. Rather, the phrase that captures the philosophical content of the governance of labor organizations best is probably "majoritarian democracy" or "majoritarian rule." Its essence is that the majority of members will determine the course of action for a union and those members in a minority will follow along without complaint. There is no room for a **loyal opposition** in this system of organizational governance. Nor are **checks and balances** necessary.

Power is not viewed as an evil, but as a good; and the more of it the union has vis-à-vis the employer, the better. It is not surprising therefore that very few unions have institutionalized two- or multi-party systems. In fact, elections within unions are often uncontested. Although union members do have rights that they can assert against the union claiming to speak for them, these have come about largely through federal legislation (and will be discussed below). Unions prefer to emphasize the *obligations* that members have. Some of these are rather nebulous. For example, a punishable offense might be engaging in conduct not becoming a "union man." Others, however, seek to protect the incumbency of union leaders. Thus "slandering an officer," "creating dissension," and "undermining the union" are frequently listed as conduct

TERMS **Pluralism** The concept that a political community is made up of diverse groups and institutions whose leaderships compete for power and influence.

Loyal Opposition A political party that opposes the party in power but supports the nation and the constitutional principles that underlie its governance.

Checks and Balances Any governing arrangement whereby some elements are able to check (that is, to stop) the actions of other elements. For example, the U.S. Supreme Court can overrule the President; the President can veto a bill passed by Congress, etc.

violating the member's obligations and are punishable by fine, other penalty, or even expulsion. There are due process guarantees that protect members from arbitrary or capricious punishment for breach of obligations, but the thrust of the union effort is to control the behavior of each member and to prohibit political divisions within the organization. The constitution of the International Brotherhood of Electrical Workers spells out the point (and problem) most clearly. It provides that the following activities are punishable by the association:

> Attending or participating in any gathering or meeting whatsoever, held outside meetings of a L. U. [local union], at which the affairs of the L. U. are discussed, or at which conclusions are arrived at regarding the business and affairs of a L.U. or regarding L.U. officers or a candidate or candidates for L.U. office.
>
> Mailing, handing out, or posting cards, handbills, letters, marked ballots or political literature of any kind, or displaying streamers, banners, signs or anything else of a political nature, or being a party in any way to such being done in an effort to induce members to vote for or against any candidate or candidates for L.U. office, or candidates to conventions.

The essence of such regulations is to turn the quest for organizational unity into a requirement of *uniformity* among the members. Such an approach is contrary to that used in public government in the United States, but it is justified for private associations (such as unions) on the grounds that they have a single purpose and must be strong enough to achieve it.

Unions also translate their internal governmental philosophy into a political structure in fairly uniform ways. Consequently, their political structures have many of the same features. (See Figure 8-1.) The ultimate source of authority in the union is the membership. Its rights and obligations are delineated in a **constitution,** which is subject to change through the participation of the membership or its representatives. If the organization is small enough, the membership can meet and vote on proposals in the fashion of classical democracies. In such a case, which is frequently found in

TERMS   **Constitution**   Any fundamental law or set of principles which establishes the framework for further governance. Thus, the U.S. Constitution creates the framework for American government. In a similar fashion a union's constitution puts forth the rules for its governance.

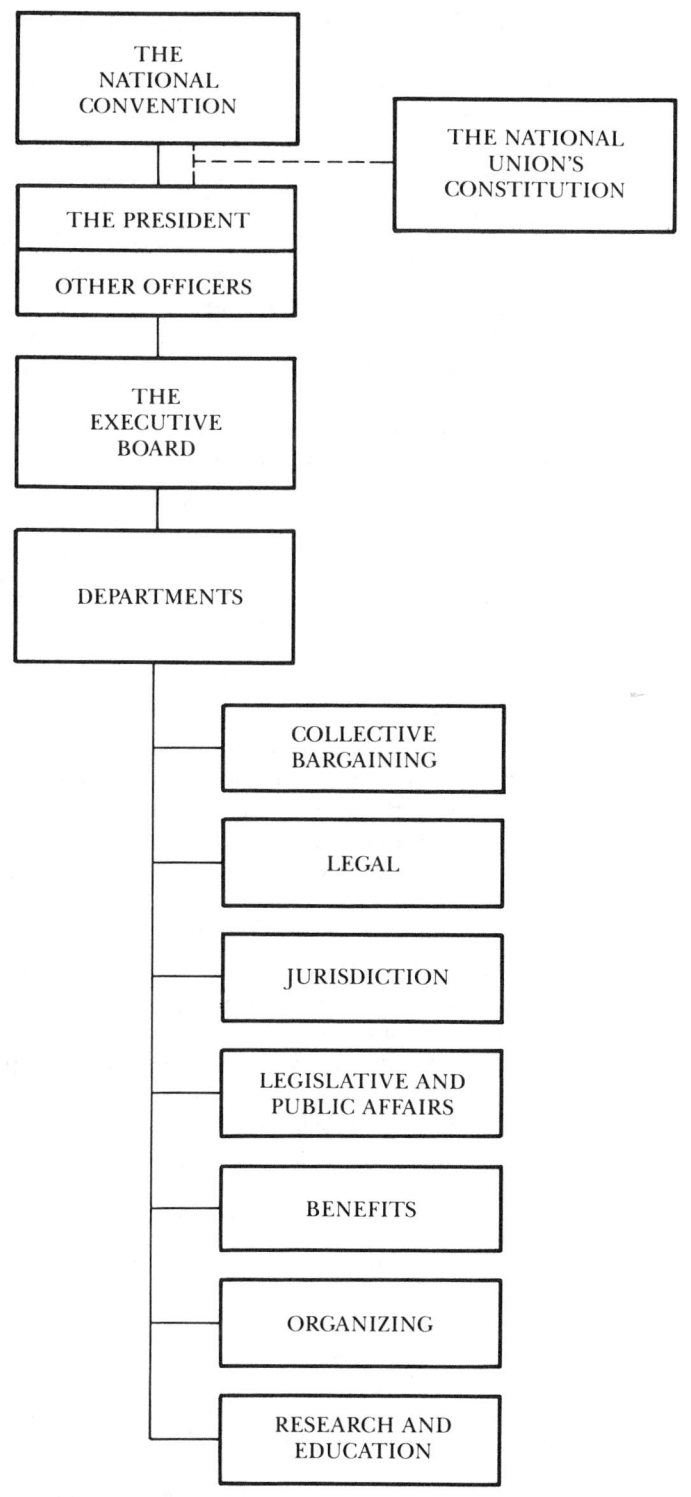

Figure 8-1. *The Structure of a National Union*

locals, the officers mainly preside, rather than rule. However, a union organizational structure often has three levels: the local, a regional level consolidating the activities of many locals in a given geographic area, and an international level which is the union as a whole (it combines all the regional and subregional local levels). With few if any exceptions, governance at the regional and international levels involves far less direct democracy. Instead, the principle of **representation** is used.

The convention is the governmental body having the greatest formal authority in most unions. It is elected directly or indirectly by the membership, although **apportionment** schemes vary. Election may be on a **per capita** basis within locals, which serve as electoral districts in this sense. Representation may also be apportioned according to the size of the locals. For instance, the Amercian Federation of State, County and Municipal Employees (AFSCME), which is the largest union restricted to public employees, has apportioned delegates to its international convention in the following fashion: one delegate per 100 members in a local up to 400 members, one delegate for each additional 1,000 members or fraction of that number, with the proviso that every local has to have at least one delegate.

The convention is usually a union's highest legislative body. It passes rules, declares policies, and gives direction to union officials. In some cases, the convention can also adopt amendments to the union's constitution. When the convention is in session, the union's leaders preside over its meetings, serving in the capacity of moderators. There are two major differences between conventions and governmental legislative bodies in general. First, the convention may meet infrequently. In about 35 percent of all national unions in the United States conventions are held only once every four or five years. During the interim, legislative authority is typically vested in the union's officers, who are supposed to act in accordance with the guidance passed on from the convention. Second, conventions are large relative to the membership and consequently take on the air of a "town meeting" more than a professionalized

---

TERMS   **Representation** Any system of governance which has all of its citizens (or members) elect agents to represent their interests in another (possibly legislative) forum.

Apportionment The formal allocation of the number of representatives that a political subdivision (such as a state) or an organizational unit (such as a local union) may elect to represent them in another political forum.

Per Capita Latin phrase meaning "by heads." In a per capita election each member would have one vote.

legislature such as the U. S. Congress. They are not in session very long. They are as much a governmental as a social event, since they also serve to bring delegates elected from the various locals into contact with one another.

THE LOCAL UNION   At the other end of the spectrum is the local union, which remains the basic organizational unit for the governance of labor unions. The local performs so many functions that it is in some ways an organizational microcosm of the labor movement as a whole. (See Figure 8-2.) Locals in industrial unions are generally organized on a plant basis, while craft locals tend to draw their members from a specific geographical area. In either case, the local is a highly political organization because it is the level of the union with which the members identify most. It is most salient to them, and their voices carry more weight within it than at any other level of the union structure. The election of officers at the local level is often hotly contested, and the turnover of leaders at this level is generally greater than at the regional or international levels.

The local is critically important to the member because it is the unit that engages in contract enforcement. It also engages in collective bargaining (though much of this function now rests with the national or international union); enforces the international union's rules and regulations pertaining to the conduct of members and their obligations; administers and implements the general policies and programs of the international union, and provides a variety of services to its members including opportunitites for further education, and channels for involvement in politics and community affairs.

The typical local has a number of officers and some have paid staff. The officers are often designated as president, secretary-treasurer, and members of an executive board. Locals are also likely to have a number of committees to carry out specific functions. Some locals, especially the larger ones, employ a business agent. This functionary is responsible for the administration of union affairs, including such activities as keeping records, maintaining files and membership lists, overseeing the operation of hiring halls in the construction industry, arranging for meetings and participating in the setting of their agendas, and engaging in many facets of the collective bargaining process itself. The influence of business agents varies widely. Much depends on the size of the local, the personality of the business agent, and the desires of the elected

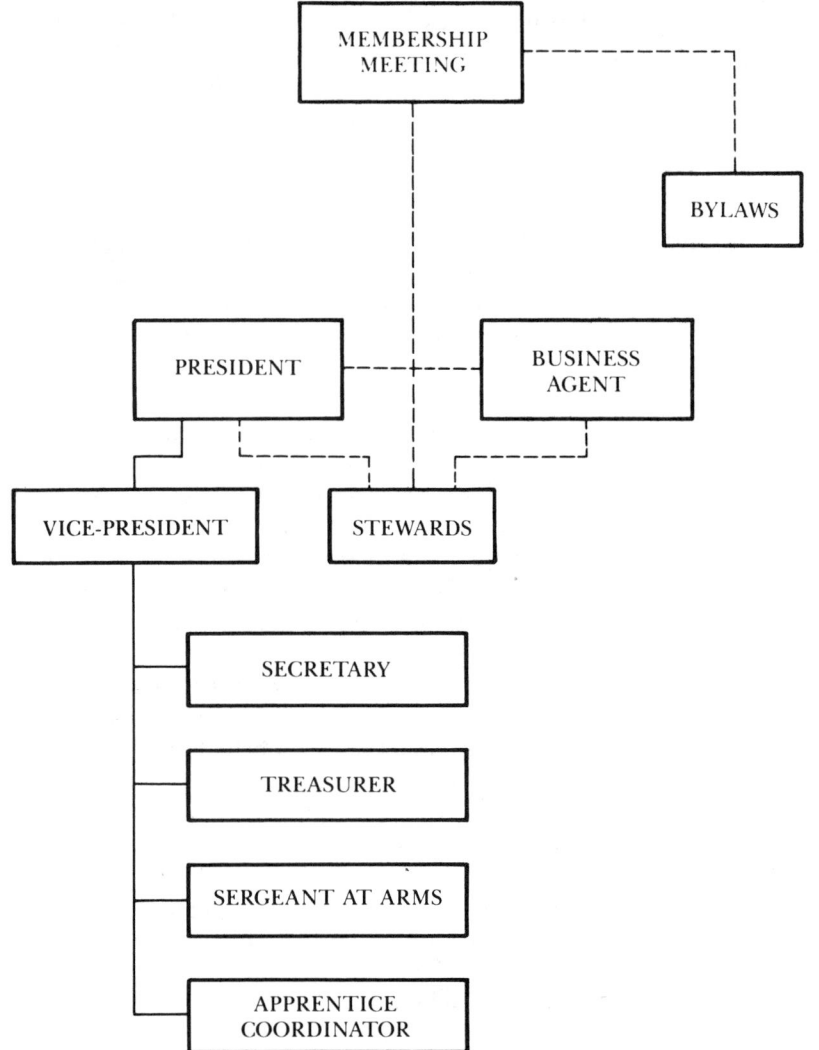

Figure 8-2.   The Structure of a Local Union

leaders and members. Some locals have come to rely very heavily on their business agents, who more or less "run" the local on a day-to-day basis. Business agents in large locals may also have a considerable number of staff at their disposal. Many elected union officials at the local level continue to hold their regular jobs, depending, again, largely on the size of the local.

The extent to which a local union is autonomous within the international union varies from organization to organization. A local union can be disbanded, suspended, or placed under direct administrative **trusteeship** by the international of which it is a part, if it violates the international's constitution, policies, or some aspect of public law. Locals may also be forbidden from striking without the permission of the international. Moreover, the international often controls strike funds and other benefits, which can serve as a lever over the behavior of locals.

One of the outstanding features of locals is the extent to which they vary. Some 70,000 local unions are believed to exist in the United States. Ford Local 600 of United Auto Workers is the largest; it has about 60,000 members. Local 32B of the Service Employees International Union, representing building service employees in New York City, has about 40,000 members. But there are some locals with no more than seven or eight members. Only about 2 percent of all locals are unaffiliated with an international union. These are referred to as independent locals. Like unions generally, they are regulated by law; but they are not subject to the authority of international unions or the AFL-CIO.

Regional and district governmental levels exist in some **national** unions. For example, the Teamsters has four "conferences" to cover the nation. The International Association of Machinists has approximately 175 "lodges" at the district level. AFSCME uses "district councils." The general purpose of such regional levels is to coordinate the provision of services to locals in the geographic areas as well as to exercise a greater degree of control by the national union over its locals. These regional arrangements are typically headed by a district director with a staff. In some cases, the regional level employs the business agents on behalf of the smaller locals, who otherwise would be unable to afford such paid professional assistance. In AFSCME, the council level is considered by some to be the backbone of the union. AFSCME seeks to staff each of these councils with a director appointed by the president of the national, several additional representatives of the national, and a variety of staff specialists in education, research, and public relations.

TERMS   **Trusteeship**   The legal designation of one person or organization to manage the affairs of another.

National   A union composed of a variety of widely dispersed affiliated local unions. The Bureau of Labor Statistics defines a national union as one with agreements with different employers in more than one state. The terms "national union" and "international union" tend to be used interchangeably; the only difference being (in the American context) that "international" unions have locals in Canada.

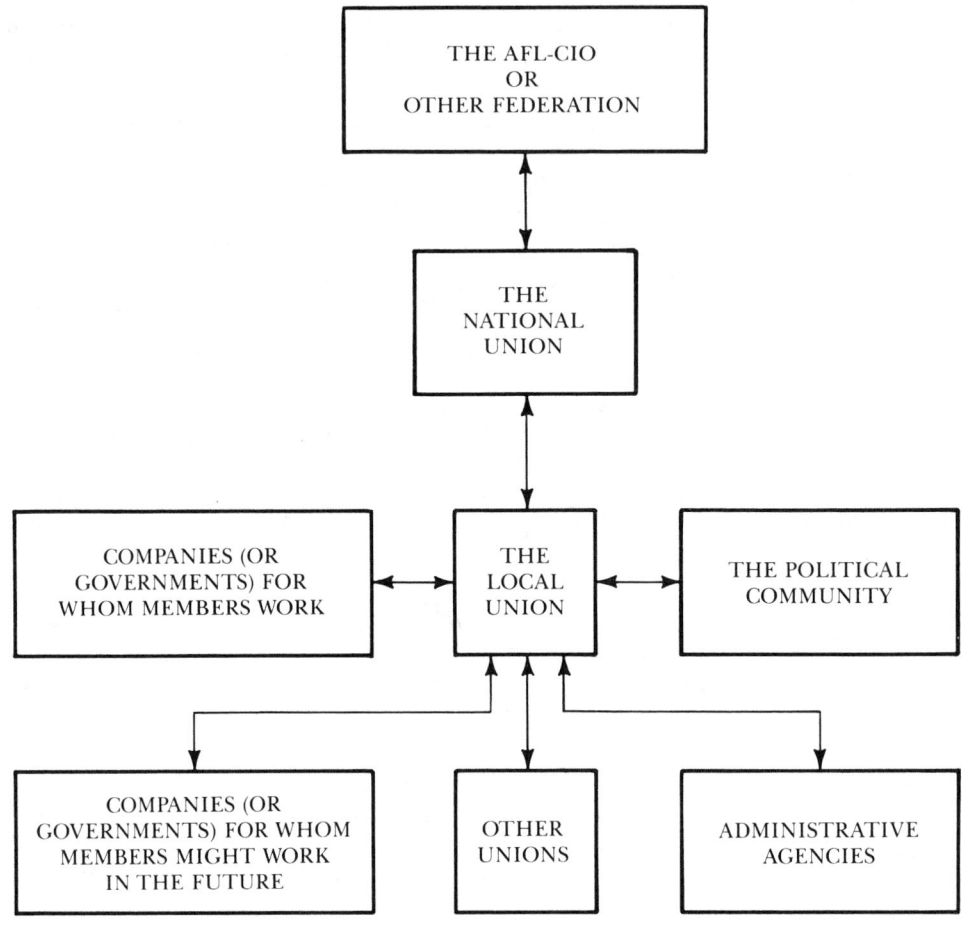

Figure 8-3.   The Local Union's Relationships

THE GRAND
FEDERATION: THE
AFL-CIO About 65 percent of all the national unions in the United States are affiliated with the American Federation of Labor-Congress of Industrial Organizations (AFL-CIO). But their membership accounts for about 80 percent of all the union members in the nation. Thus, at the center of the present day structure of American unions stands the AFL-CIO. Indeed, the only sizeable unions not affiliated with it are the Teamsters, the United Mine Workers, the United Electrical Workers, and the Longshoremen and Warehousemen, each of which was at one time a part of either the American Federation of Labor, the Congress of Industrial Organizations, or the current AFL-CIO federation. They are not presently affiliated with the AFL-CIO for reasons mainly having to do with personalities and union politics—and there is almost always

talk about one of these unions or another joining with the AFL-CIO. Because the development of the AFL-CIO was discussed in Chapter 1, this chapter need be concerned only with its present day structure.

The AFL-CIO is sometimes called a "union of unions." That is an apt term because it is a federation, not a labor union in the normal sense. For example, the AFL-CIO does not engage in collective bargaining or call strikes; nor does it negotiate with employers. Indeed the AFL-CIO does not even have individuals as members. Rather, its "membership" is comprised of national unions and directly affiliated locals. These organizations greatly prize their sovereignty. They have great control over their own affairs, they represent their individual members, and it is they who engage in collective bargaining. Thus, the major purposes of the AFL-CIO are to coordinate matters among its affiliate unions, to pool labor's strength into a potent political force, and to provide a variety of services to its members. Coordination is achieved through AFL-CIO state and local *central bodies*. The AFL-CIO has also developed a **jurisdictional disputes** resolution plan, as mentioned in Chapter 4.

The AFL-CIO has considerable resources at its disposal to present labor's voice, when unified, in politics. It is engaged in extensive lobbying at the national and state levels of government. It promotes its views on all matters of labor policy, as well as such national policy areas as education, public housing, foreign affairs, and civil rights. Many political activities are also carried out by the organization's state and local central bodies. Despite declining union membership as a percent of the workforce, the AFL-CIO remains a potent political force. In part, this is true because the organization devotes substantial resources to the research and development of legislative proposals.

The AFL-CIO also provides a wide variety of services to its constituent member unions. Aside from providing them with charters, it helps its members organize bargaining units, provides legal and technical assistance to them, and maintains a staff of organizers that can facilitate the process of gaining and maintaining exclusive recognition.

Structurally, the AFL-CIO is comprised of the following major units, as shown in the accompanying organizational chart. (See Figure 8-4.) It is headed by a national convention that is held every two years. Representation at the convention is according to

TERMS   **Jurisdictional Dispute**   A disagreement between two unions over which should control a particular job or activity.

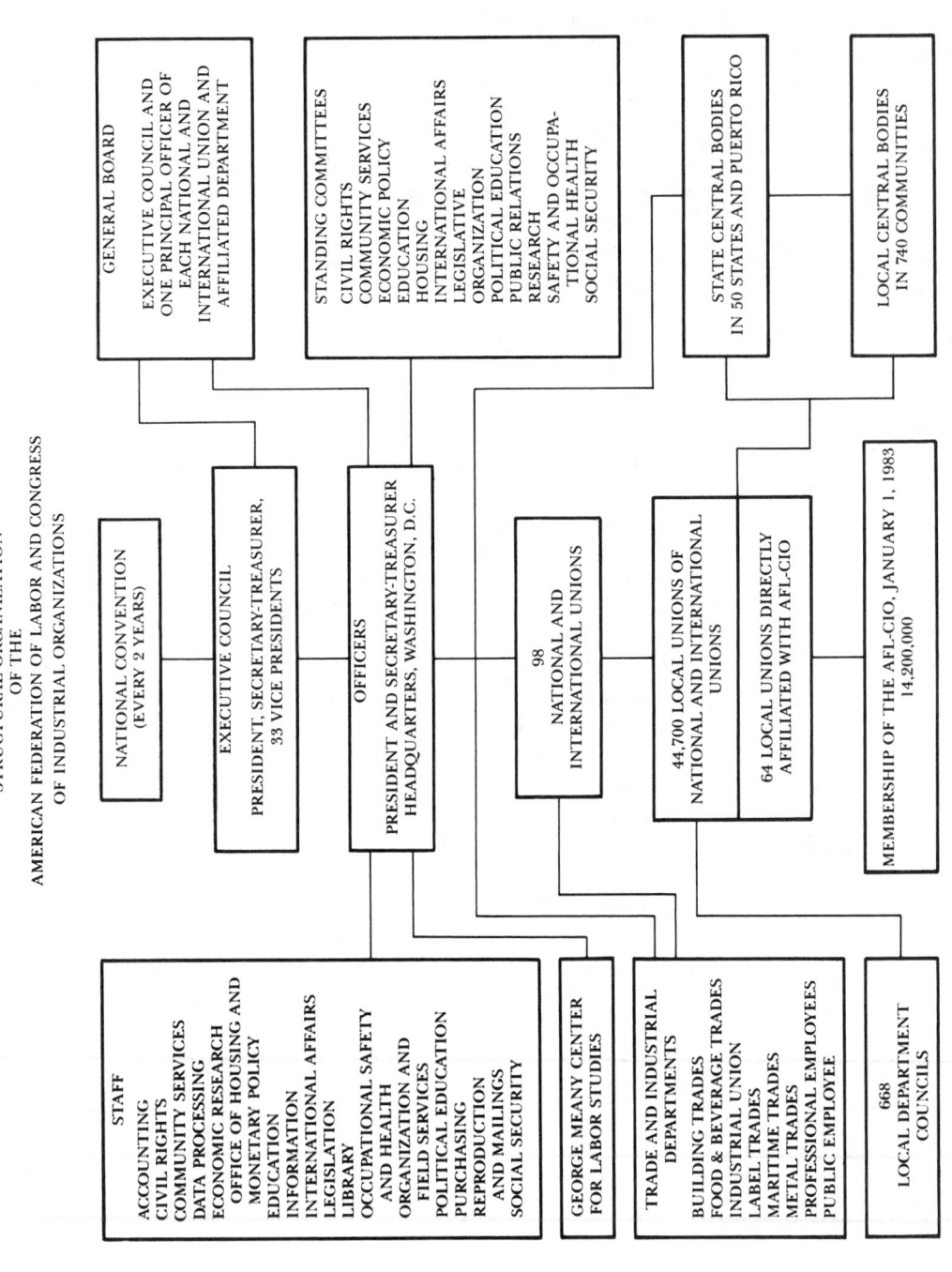

STRUCTURAL ORGANIZATION
OF THE
AMERICAN FEDERATION OF LABOR AND CONGRESS
OF INDUSTRIAL ORGANIZATIONS

GENERAL BOARD

EXECUTIVE COUNCIL AND
ONE PRINCIPAL OFFICER OF
EACH NATIONAL AND
INTERNATIONAL UNION AND
AFFILIATED DEPARTMENT

STANDING COMMITTEES

CIVIL RIGHTS
COMMUNITY SERVICES
ECONOMIC POLICY
EDUCATION
HOUSING
INTERNATIONAL AFFAIRS
LEGISLATIVE
ORGANIZATION
POLITICAL EDUCATION
PUBLIC RELATIONS
RESEARCH
SAFETY AND OCCUPA-
TIONAL HEALTH
SOCIAL SECURITY

STATE CENTRAL BODIES
IN 50 STATES AND PUERTO RICO

LOCAL CENTRAL BODIES
IN 740 COMMUNITIES

NATIONAL CONVENTION
(EVERY 2 YEARS)

EXECUTIVE COUNCIL

PRESIDENT, SECRETARY-TREASURER,
33 VICE PRESIDENTS

OFFICERS

PRESIDENT AND SECRETARY-TREASURER
HEADQUARTERS, WASHINGTON, D.C.

98
NATIONAL AND
INTERNATIONAL UNIONS

44,700 LOCAL UNIONS OF
NATIONAL AND INTERNATIONAL
UNIONS

64 LOCAL UNIONS DIRECTLY
AFFILIATED WITH AFL-CIO

MEMBERSHIP OF THE AFL-CIO, JANUARY 1, 1983
14,200,000

STAFF

ACCOUNTING
CIVIL RIGHTS
COMMUNITY SERVICES
DATA PROCESSING
ECONOMIC RESEARCH
OFFICE OF HOUSING AND
MONETARY POLICY
EDUCATION
INFORMATION
INTERNATIONAL AFFAIRS
LEGISLATION
LIBRARY
OCCUPATIONAL SAFETY
AND HEALTH
ORGANIZATION AND
FIELD SERVICES
POLITICAL EDUCATION
PURCHASING
REPRODUCTION
AND MAILINGS
SOCIAL SECURITY

GEORGE MEANY CENTER
FOR LABOR STUDIES

TRADE AND INDUSTRIAL
DEPARTMENTS

BUILDING TRADES
FOOD & BEVERAGE TRADES
INDUSTRIAL UNION
LABEL TRADES
MARITIME TRADES
METAL TRADES
PROFESSIONAL EMPLOYEES
PUBLIC EMPLOYEE

668
LOCAL DEPARTMENT
COUNCILS

Figure 8-4. **Structural Organization of the AFL-CIO**

the payments made by its affiliates. These reflect the size of these national and international unions. (In 1980, AFL-CIO affiliates paid nineteen cents per member per month to the AFL-CIO.) The convention elects AFL-CIO officials, considers constitutional amendments, hears committee reports, and considers a wide variety of matters of union and public policy. It is not unusual for national political officials and aspirants for elective office, including the President, to address the AFL-CIO convention.

Between conventions, the AFL-CIO is presided over, or run, by the president and secretary-treasurer, both of whom are elected by the convention. They are assisted by an executive council of thirty-three vice-presidents, who are also elected by the convention. The vice-presidents are also presidents of the organization's affiliated unions. The executive council is assisted by a general board. This includes all the members of the council, plus a representative of each affiliate member and a representative of each of the AFL-CIO's departments. The board provides policy advice to the council.

The remaining elements of the AFL-CIO structure of governance that bear mentioning are the standing committees and the trade and industrial departments. The former are primarily engaged in developing policy advice and implementing the AFL-CIO's policies across industries and trades. The latter are more specifically oriented to issues of concern to particular trades or industries and are often involved in resolving jurisdictional matters.

In passing, it should be noted that the AFL-CIO is not the nation's only labor federation. For instance, there is also an Assembly of Government Employees and a National Federation of Independent Unions. In general, these federations seek to provide the same kinds of services (coordination, lobbying, etc.) to their members, who for one reason or another find affiliation with the AFL-CIO undesirable.

UNION STAFF   It is evident that the American labor movement has reached large proportions, demanding large organizations. But large organizations cannot be run by conventions once every few years. Nor can a few elected officers manage them. Such organizations need **staff**—and the staff are in fact an integral part of the governing structure

---

TERMS   **Staff** Specialists who assist line managers in carrying out their duties. Generally, staff units do not have the power of decision, command, or control of operations. Rather, they make recommendations (which may or may not be adopted) to the line personnel.

of the AFL-CIO, its affiliates, and other unions. We have already broached this subject with reference to business agents, some of whom are quite powerful actors in the management and governance of unions. But as the organizational chart of the AFL-CIO indicates, the staff of a federation or its affiliate members can be quite varied.

The need for all manner of clerical staff is obvious. But the contemporary union or federation also needs lawyers, economists, accountants, actuaries or other specialists in insurance and pension matters, personnelists, computer technicians, and other professionals. Because the staff are experts in their respective areas, their influence can be considerable. They may also seek to exert influence over unions by unionizing themselves! That's right. The staff of some unions are unionized, engage in collective bargaining with their employer (the union) and may even strike against it.

As unions become more sophisticated in their approaches to collective bargaining and more involved in the administration of services and benefits (such as insurance programs and pension funds), the staff tends to increase in proportion to union membership. One union in which dramatic increases of this nature have occurred is AFSCME. In 1952, it had one staffer per 1,500 members; by 1970, the ratio had become one staffer per 764 members. Figures for other unions vary widely. It is important to note that the apportionment of staff also varies considerably. The Teamsters, for instance, employ about 90 percent of their staff at the local level, while AFSCME employs most of its staff at the district council level.

GOVERNMENTAL PROCESS: DEMOCRACY VERSUS OLIGARCHY

In theory and form, the governance of unions is democratic. However, in practice many observers have noted that political competition within unions seems decidedly lacking and that there is a tendency for unions to fall victim to Michels' "iron law of oligarchy." Many observers see that power in unions tends to be centralized in the hands of the elected leaders, who operate rather freely when the convention is not in session. These are the officers who control the budget and the information and communications networks of the unions. They may also have considerable authority and leverage over the behavior of local unions and individual union members. And they certainly play the major role in directing the national political activities of unions. In theory, the elected and appointed union officials direct the professional staff; in practice, their control is sometimes likely to be imperfect, though their influence is always present.

Is it not likely, then, as many would argue, that union leaders will tend to be self-perpetuating? Won't they have so many advantages over would-be dissident challengers that for most intents and purposes elections within the unions, at least at the national level, will be unfair because of the great advantages that incumbents have? Will not the union leaders use the resources at their command to develop political machines within their organizations? Moreover, isn't there a good rationale for stability in the leadership of unions? If it is good that such leaders be powerful, then why limit their power? If the union leadership has the same goals as the union members, then limiting the power of the leadership becomes not only undemocratic but also irrational.

But is it really irrational and undemocratic to place checks on the governance of unions? Any attempt to answer such a question depends upon a consideration of the extent to which unions do tend to be oligarchic as opposed to democratic in their governance. Unfortunately, despite a great deal of research on the matter, evidence remains incomplete and even somewhat anecdotal. However, it is known that there is generally a gap between the democratic structure of unions in form and the existence of democracy in substance. In other words, the reality of union democracy is more surface than real. There are a variety of indicators of this:

1. *The Tenure of Labor Leaders.* Union constitutions very seldom place limits on the number of terms of office a union president can serve. While the maximum length for a single term is usually five years, there have been many cases of the spectacular longevity of labor leaders. For example, Dan Tobin led the Teamsters from 1907 to 1952—a period literally covering the transition from the horse and buggy age to the era of superhighways. John L. Lewis was president of the United Mine Workers for almost 40 years. George Meany's tenure at the head of AFL-CIO, though shorter, was also legendary.

2. *The Salaries of Incumbent Labor Leaders.* Again, the word spectacular comes to mind. There are many examples of union leaders whose income is so high that it appears implausible that they can remain in touch with the average union member. Nevertheless, many union leaders, especially at the local level, earn little more than the typical member.

3. *The Centralization of Authority.* Since union democracy clearly works best at the local level where members generally have a greater voice and more avenues for participation, shift in authority upward in the union structure necessarily militates against democracy. However, the transfer of decisionmaking

authority to the national or regional level is also a product of a changing economy and the need to engage in a more sophisticated kind of collective bargaining.

4. *The Rejection of Contracts by Members.* Many unions must submit negotiated contracts to their members for ratification. Currently the members are rejecting these in about 10 percent of the cases. Since rejection requires a majority and is considered an extreme rebuke to the leadership, the rejection rate is an indication that the leadership has failed effectively to represent the will of the membership.

5. *The Growing Staff Component.* An increasing staff implies an increasing institutionalism. The staff's interests are not identical to those of the members, yet the staff plays a critical role in union finances and communications. Because staff will generally seek to perpetuate their own positions, this may sometimes cause them to place their interests above those of the members.

6. *Slight Participation at Meetings.* Apathy, disinterest, and nonparticipation are often signs of oligarchy. In these instances members decide, for one reason or another, that their participation is unnecessary or pointless.

7. ***Political Machines*** *within Unions.* Some unions have leaders who are very similar to the urban "machine politicians" of yore. Their major purpose becomes to insure their incumbency and to keep the machine going. Consequently, they not only seek to generate support by providing the members with good representation, but they also seek to stifle dissent through **cooptation** and repression. Examples of unions sometimes likened to political machines have been the Teamsters, the United Mine Workers, the New York City Sanitation Men's Association and the New York City Transport Workers Union.

Those who consider democracy within unions to be inadequate point to these, and perhaps other, factors as indicators of oligarchy. Yet, the indicators are difficult to interpret. Long

---

TERMS   **Political Machine** An informal system of governance in which power is concentrated into the hands of a central figure, the "boss," who may or may not have a formal position of power. The "boss" manages a hierarchy that is usually created and maintained by the use of patronage and largess.

Cooptation The efforts of an organization to bring in and subsume new elements into its policymaking process in order to prevent such elements from being a threat to the organization or its mission.

incumbency can mean good representation and service to the membership. High salaries may be necessary to enable the leader to stand up to the corporate chieftains with whom bargaining ultimately takes place. The centralization of authority enhances the provision of services to locals and enables the union to engage in more effective political lobbying at the national level. Whether contract rejection is high or low depends upon one's perspective. The union's staff contributes to its strength. Low participation, like low voter turnout in governmental elections, can be interpreted as a sign of satisfaction with the way things are going. And politicial machines cannot exist without the support of the membership or voters.

What can one conclude from all this? At least two observations are in order. First, union leaders must inevitably reflect the desires of their members *to some extent* if they hope to be successful. This extent is probably greater at the local level than at the regional or national level of unions. Indeed, even those who find the extent of democracy within unions unsatisfactory may conclude that at the local level the attitudes of the members of a union have a tremendous impact on the union officer—an impact that will probably affect his or her attitudes and actions. This seems to be borne out by some of the public statements of labor leaders, even those who some would label "oligarchs." For instance Victor Gotbaum, Executive Director of District Council 37 of AFSCME—a man who some have accused of waging urban guerrilla warfare on New York City—maintains that the labor leader is always under the gun, "a sitting duck for sharpshooters within his own union." He believes that in part the longevity of leaders is due to a simple fact: "union leaders either fall by the wayside with remarkable rapidity or become heroes in the eyes of the people they represent." Heroes are rewarded with reelection.

A second conclusion pertaining to union democracy is that even if "substantive democracy" is imperfect, "procedural democracy" must be assured. It is for this reason that statutes have been enacted to protect the rights of union members vis-à-vis their unions and to attempt to assure that unions are democratically governed in form.

GOVERNMENT REGULATION OF UNION GOVERNANCE

In the 1950s Congress conducted investigations and held hearings on alleged widespread corruption and racketeering in the labor movement. The response of rank and file unionists and public opinion was so overwhelmingly in favor of legislating reform of union practices that Congress didn't even wait for the main investigatory committee, the **McClellan Committee,** to issue its final report. Rather it enacted the Labor-Management Reporting and Disclosure (Landrum-Griffin) Act in 1959. This act was premised on the beliefs that internal union democracy could be established by government regulation and that democracy within unions was the best way to combat the corrupt practices of some union leaders. In one sense, the act was proof of Samuel Gompers' earlier prediction that if goverment were to become involved in collective bargaining, it would eventually seek to regulate the internal affairs of unions.

The Landrum-Griffin Act not only requires unions to report on aspects of their financial matters, it contains several sets of provisions of importance to union democracy. Section 101(a)(1) of the act legislates a degree of equality of participation for union members in union political affairs; it has been called a **bill of rights** for union members. It holds that every member shall have equal rights and privileges to nominate candidates, to vote in elections, to attend meetings, and to participate in deliberations subject to reasonable rules and regulations in the union's constitution and bylaws. These protections apply only to members of the union, not to other employees who are also represented within bargaining units. The provisions do not convey any actual substantive rights; they simply seek to guarantee that whatever rights the union extends to its members shall be extended to *all* its members on an equal basis.

Bill of Rights of Members of Labor Organizations

Sec. 101. (a)(1) Equal Rights.—Every member of a labor organization shall have equal rights and privileges within such organization to nominate candidates, to vote in elections or referendums of the labor organization, to attend membership meetings

---

TERMS   **McClellan Committee**   Formally the Senate Select Committee on Improper Activities in the Labor or Management Field. Its chair was Senator John L. McClellan (1896–1977) of Arkansas.

Bill of Rights   *The* "bill of rights" was the first ten amendments to the U.S. Constitution. Nowadays the term is also used for any important listing of rights or privileges.

and to participate in the deliberations and voting upon the business of such meetings, subject to reasonable rules and regulations in such organization's constitution and bylaws.

(2) *Freedom of Speech and Assembly.*—Every member of any labor organization shall have the right to meet and assemble freely with other members; and to express any views, arguments, or opinions; and to express at meetings of the labor organization his views, upon candidates in an election of the labor organization or upon any business properly before the meeting, subject to the organization's established and reasonable rules pertaining to the conduct of meetings: *Provided,* That nothing herein shall be construed to impair the right of a labor organization to adopt and enforce reasonable rules as to the responsibility of every member toward the organization as an institution and to his refraining from conduct that would interfere with its performance of its legal and contractual obligations.

(3) *Dues, Initiation Fees, and Assessments.*—Except in the case of a federation of national or international labor organizations, the rates of dues and initiation fees payable by members of any labor organization in effect on the date of enactment of this Act shall not be increased, and no general or special assessment shall be levied upon such members, except—

(A) in the case of a local organization, (i) by majority vote by secret ballot of the members in good standing voting at a general or special membership meeting, after reasonable notice of the intention to vote upon such question, or (ii) by majority vote of the members in good standing voting in a membership referendum conducted by secret ballot; or

(B) in the case of a labor organization, other than a local labor organization or a federation of national or international labor organizations, (i) by majority vote of the delegates voting at a regular convention, or at a special convention of such labor organization held upon not less than thirty days' written notice to the principal office of each local or constituent labor organization entitled to such notice, or (ii) by majority vote of the members in good standing of such labor organization voting in a membership referendum conducted by secret ballot, or (iii) by majority vote of the members of the executive board or similar governing body of such labor organization, pursuant to express authority contained in the constitution and bylaws of such labor organization: *Provided,* That such action on the part of the executive board or similar governing body shall be effective only until the next regular convention of such labor organization.

(4) *Protection of the Right to Sue.*—No labor organization shall limit the right of any member thereof to institute an action in any court, or in a proceeding before any administrative agency, irrespective of whether or not the labor organization or its officers are named as defendants or respondents in such action or proceeding, or the right of any member of a labor organization to appear as a witness in any judicial, administrative, or legislative proceeding, or to petition any legislature or to communicate with any legislator: *Provided,* That any such member may be required to exhaust reasonable hearing procedures (but not to exceed a four-month lapse of time) within such organization, before instituting legal or administrative proceedings against such organizations or any officer thereof: *And provided further,* That no interested employer or employer association shall directly or indirectly finance, encourage, or participate in, except as a party, any such action, proceeding, appearance, or petition.

(5) *Safeguards Against Improper Disciplinary Action.*—No member of any labor organization may be fined, suspended, expelled, or otherwise disciplined except for nonpayment of dues by such organization or by any officer thereof unless such member has been (A) served with written specific charges; (B) given a reasonable time to prepare his defense; (C) afforded a full and fair hearing.

(b) Any provision of the constitution and bylaws of any labor organization which is inconsistent with the provisions of this section shall be of no force or effect.

Source: Landrum-Griffin Act.

Other sections of the act deal with substantive rights. Section 101(a)(2) conveys to all union members virtually an absolute right to freedom of speech in union meetings, elections, and union affairs generally. A union member cannot be punished by the union even if he or she makes false and slanderous charges against the union leadership or other members. Moreover, presiding union officials can even be in violation of this section if they fail to keep proper order at a union meeting or otherwise prevent a member from speaking in that forum. There are only two general exceptions to this "absolute" right to free speech. One is that union members are not free to support another union by urging members to join it. This and similar kinds of behavior fall under the rubric of **dual unionism** and can be punished by the union on the grounds that it has a right to require loyalty from its members. The other exception is that a member can be punished for advocating a breach of a contract, such as calling for a wildcat strike.

FAIR ELECTIONS   Equality and political rights to freedom of speech are extremely important in creating a framework for democracy within unions. But yet another step was required: elections had to be held and regulated to assure their fairness. Title IV of the Landrum-Griffin Act seeks to achieve this. It requires that a local union *elect* its officers for terms not exceeding three years, and that the elections be by secret ballot. In addition, the union must provide its members written notification of the election not less than fifteen days before it is scheduled to occur. The union is also required to distribute the campaign literature of any candidate to all union members, at the

TERMS   **Dual Unionism**   A situation where two rival unions claim the right to organize workers in a particular industry or locality.

candidate's request and expense. This provision seeks to assure that the incumbent candidates will not reap advantage from control of the union's internal administrative organization. For the same reason, the union is formally prohibited from discriminating in favor of one candidate or another.

As important as these rights are, they would be insufficient to establish union democracy if the union were free to exclude anyone that it considered a threat to its governing establishment. So the Act also seeks to deal with this problem. While it does not regulate the union's internal procedures for admitting individuals to membership, it does extend the same rights of political participation in union affairs to nonmembers who have sought membership but been denied it on arbitrary grounds. In other words, if an applicant for membership meets the normal occupational skills and other legitimate requirements for membership, but is denied it, he or she must be treated as a member for purposes of political participation. This clearly reduces a union's incentive to try to operate on a "closed" basis. Moreover, under Title VII of the Civil Rights Act of 1964 unions are prohibited from discriminating on the basis of race, color, religion, sex, or national origin. Coupled with the Landrum-Griffin Act, this serves to extend participation in union governance to virtually all employees covered within its realm of exclusive recognition.

Democracy also demands that those who particpate in the process of governing be provided with or be able to obtain the information necessary to enable them to make informed choices. The Landrum-Griffin Act requires that every employee be able to obtain a copy of the collective bargaining agreement and that they likewise be informed of the provisions for internal democracy found in the Act itself.

Although fair elections and equal rights to participation are viewed by the act as the best way of preventing oligarchy and any corruption that may be attendant to it, the Act did not go so far as to prevent elected union leaders from seeking to establish political machines within their organizations. In *Finnegan v. Leu* (1982), the Supreme Court upheld the right of a successful challenger for the leadership of a union to dismiss all the business agents who had supported the incumbent in the election. The Court reasoned that democracy itself would be served by enabling elected union leaders to carry out their programs and policies without resistance from business agents who were in opposition to them. The Court also maintained that the removal of a business agent on these grounds, which was allowed under the union's constitution, was not an act of discipline that interfered with the agent's rights of freedom of speech.

On the other hand, although only tangentially related to elections, the Act does seek to prevent union leaders from developing unfair or corrupt advantages over would-be challengers by abusing the authority to raise money through membership dues. It requires that dues be raised only if a majority of voting members agree to the increase in a secret ballot election of which there is adequate notice. Such elections can take place at the national or local levels.

DISCIPLINARY PROCEDURES

The Landrum-Griffin Act further seeks to protect union members by placing limitations on unions' ability to discipline them. Unions are prohibited from disciplining any member for the exercise of his or her rights under the Act. This means that the member cannot be punished for exercising any of the rights outlined in the "bill of rights" section of the statute. Nor can a member be disciplined for filing a charge against the union with the National Labor Relations Board. Discipline is possible, however, if a member crosses a lawful picket line. Members who violate production quotas or limits can also be subject to discipline. The law regarding the disciplining of supervisors who are union members is rather complicated. Suffice it to say that in general a supervisor cannot be disciplined by the union for doing supervisory work; but he or she is subject to discipline if engaged in the work of the bargaining unit during a strike.

In any event, with the exception of discipline for failure to pay dues, the union member is entitled to some procedural safeguards in disciplinary matters. Section 101(a)(5) of the Landrum-Griffin Act provides that: "No member of any labor organization may be fined, suspended, expelled, or otherwise disciplined except for nonpayment of dues by such organization or by any officer thereof unless such member has been (A) served with written specific charges; (B) given a reasonable time to prepare his defense; (C) afforded to a full and fair hearing." The **hearing** itself must afford some of the rudiments of due process, including the right to confront and **cross-examine** accusers and hostile witnesses and to present evidence, and the entire procedure must be adjudicated in a fair forum. In practice, the forum can be virtually any kind of trial board the union sees fit to use as long as it does not include

TERMS **Hearing** A trial-like proceeding that takes place in a noncourt setting.

Cross-Examine To question the opposition witnesses during a trial or hearing.

individuals who are known to have prejudged the matter or who have been openly hostile to the defendant. For the most part rules of evidence in such hearings are flexible and do not imitate those used in courts of law. Defendants in disciplinary cases may be represented by counsel, depending upon the union's regulations. Even if a union member is disciplined under these procedures, he or she cannot be fined an unreasonable amount. However, it has been left up to the state courts to determine what is reasonable in this context.

If an individual does not want to be subjected to union discipline, he or she has a way of avoiding it. Under the Supreme Court's ruling in *National Labor Relations Board v. General Motors Corporation* (1963) no individual can actually be required to join a union, even under the union security device of the union shop. At most an individual can be required to be a "financial core member"; that is, someone who pays the initiation fees and monthly dues, but does not actually join. Such employees are entitled to fair representation in collective bargaining and grievances by the union, but they have no right to political participation in its affairs. By the same token, however, the union has no disciplinary authority over them.

TRUSTEESHIPS   What if for one reason or another a local union fails to abide by the constitution, bylaws, or regulations of the national or international union to which it belongs? Traditionally, the national would send a representative to direct the operations of the local. This is a logical step; but from the perspective of internal democracy, it can be abused. This representative or trustee may be authorized to take over the local's treasury and engage in collective bargaining and sign contracts for it. This can clearly short-circuit union democracy at the local level since the members have no voice in determining how their local will be run if it is placed under trusteeship. Moreover, in the past, some locals were held for decades in virtual captivity under this device. In this fashion, labor leaders could avoid democratic procedures and build up a power base by "milking" or otherwise victimizing some locals. Remember, prior to 1947 the "closed shop" was legal, in which case an employee who wanted to retain his or her job would have to be a union member—even in a local under trusteeship making no pretense of actually representing his or her interests.

There were enough serious abuses of the trustee device to prompt Congress to regulate it through the Landrum-Griffin act.

Today, any union engaging in the trusteeship of one of its locals must

1. Provide a report on certain facets of the trusteeship situation;

2. Assure that the trusteeship is in accordance with its constitution and bylaws; and

3. Engage in the practice only for the purpose of correcting corruption or financial malpractice, fulfilling collective bargaining agreements, restoring democratic procedures, or achieving other legitimate objectives of labor unions.

For the most part, a newly created trusteeship that follows proper procedures under the union's constitution is immune from suit for eighteen months. After that, however, the U. S. Secretary of Labor or any member of the local union under trusteeship can bring a suit against it. Even if the trusteeship is legal, however, elections within it for delegates to the union's national convention must be by secret ballot. Nor can funds, other than normal assessments, be transferred from the local to the national level.

CIVIL RIGHTS LEGISLATION

As noted above, the Civil Rights Act of 1964 is also of some importance to union structure and democracy. Unions cannot discriminate on any of the prohibited bases, but they can treat some members differently than others, and this can cause some problems in terms of equal rights for their members. The basis for differential treatment can be a **bona fide occupational qualification** (BFOQ). Seniority can be considered a BFOQ—but it cannot be intended to create or perpetuate discrimination against anyone because of his or her race, color, religion, sex, or national origin. Nevertheless, collective bargaining agreements making seniority a basis for preference in terms of overtime, layoffs, work scheduling,

TERMS   **Bona Fide Occupational Qualification** (BFOQ)   A *necessary* occupational qualification. Title VII of the Civil Rights Act of 1964 allows employers to discriminate against job applicants on the basis of religion, sex, or national origin if they lack a BFOQ. However, what constitutes a BFOQ has been interpreted very narrowly by the Equal Employment Opportunity Commission and the federal courts. There are no generally recognized BFOQs with respect to race or color. Overall, a BFOQ is a job requirement that would be discriminatory and illegal were it not for its necessity for the performance of a particular job.

promotion, and other matters may have an **adverse impact** on less senior members of the bargaining unit, who are often women and minorities. Thus, women and minorities may continue to fall victim to the "last hired, first fired" syndrome that has long limited their equality in the workplace.

This situation is compounded from the perspectives of union democracy if the more senior members in the union are those who play the greatest role in its governance and contract negotiation. In fact, some have considered unionization hostile to racial and gender equality in the workplace. Of course many unions have sought to negotiate agreements that both protect seniority and promote equal opportunity. In any case, as women and members of minority groups continue to benefit from equal employment and affirmative action policies, the seniority problem will work itself out. Nevertheless, where members of a bargaining unit are divided by both seniority and social attributes, the representation of the least senior members by the union may be inadequate.

CONSTITUTIONAL
RIGHTS

To a large extent, regulations pertaining to the rights of union members in the public sector and the structure of unions representing public employees parallel those in the private sector. Sometimes the language of a statute for public employees is different from the Landrum-Griffin Act. While these statutes are too numerous to be covered here, by and large the essentials are similar, if not identical. Sometimes the laws are even more direct in requiring democracy and noncorruption.

However, there is one major difference between the public and private sectors. Public employees have **constitutional rights** that must be protected by the government, even when the government is their employer. This raises some peculiar problems from time to time. For example, the public employee's right of free speech may be greater than that afforded private employees in some contexts, but lesser in others. For instance, in 1981 at the height of the PATCO strike, a low-level Federal Aviation Agency supervisor spoke at a union meeting and said: "I'm so happy that

TERMS   **Adverse Impact**   A differential rate of selection (for hire, promotion, etc.) that works to the disadvantage of an applicant subgroup, particularly subgroups classified by race, sex, and other characteristics on the basis of which discrimination is prohibited by law.

Constitutional Rights   Rights guaranteed to all citizens by the U.S. Constitution or rights guaranteed to all union members by the union's constitution.

you're together—stay together, please—because if you do, you win." He was fired the next day, and so far his dismissal has been upheld by the **Merit Systems Protection Board.** Thus, while any private citizen would have the constitutional right to advocate a strike (even against the government) and while any union member speaking in a union meeting would have an almost "absolute" right to free speech, including the right to advocate a strike, this federal employee was dismissed on the grounds that his remarks were not constitutionally protected since he was not speaking directly to the public!

In another case, some nonunion members of a bargaining unit spoke to a school board at a public meeting, indicating that they and several other teachers were opposed to the negotiation of an "agency shop" union security device. The school board was engaged in negotiations with the exclusively recognized union at the time. Subsequently, the union charged the school board with an unfair labor practice since it heard directly from members of the bargaining unit, rather than through the unit's *exclusive* representative. Both the state employment relations commission and the state supreme court upheld the union's charge that this was an unfair labor practice. In other words, a state supreme court was willing to condone the silencing of the teachers at a *public* meeting because it thought that state collective bargaining legislation should override their rights to freedom of speech under the federal Constitution! Eventually, the U. S. Supreme Court in *City of Madison, Joint School District No. 8 v. Wisconsin Employment Relations Commission* (1976) overturned the state court and upheld the right of the teachers to freedom of speech in a public forum. However, if the case were purely in the private sector there is little doubt that the employer would have violated the principle of exclusive recognition because the private employee has no *constitutional* right to freedom of speech vis-à-vis his or her private employer.

It would be impossible to examine all the subtle differences between the public and private sectors when it comes to union structure, union members' rights, and the regulation of both by governmental directive. Yet the central point remains that the public sector is somewhat different as a result of constitutional law and the government's role as agent of the people in making public policy.

TERMS   **Merit Systems Protection Board**   An independent federal government agency created by the Civil Service Reform Act of 1978 and designed to safeguard both the merit system and individual employees against abuses and unfair personnel actions.

REVIEW QUESTIONS

1. Looking at organizations with which you are familiar, do you think Michels' "iron law of oligarchy" is as pervasive as he claimed?

2. Unions are organizations intended to

   a. Project a united and strong front vis-à-vis management;

   b. Represent workers individually and collectively; and

   c. Help workers in general by providing ongoing institutions which can represent and promote their interests.

   What aspects of federal law regulating union structure promote each of these aims?

3. Do you think the union members' "bill of rights" is adequate? How might it be strengthened?

4. Unions are private associations. Since federal law conveys to them certain rights such as collective bargaining, it can also regulate their internal affairs. This is partly why Samuel Gompers favored "voluntarism." On balance, do you think federal regulation of union internal affairs is desirable or undesirable?

5. Can you suggest indicators of oligarchy within unions other than those listed in the chapter?

6. If you are familiar with a private work organization, can you find any employment practices that might be unconstitutional if they occurred in public employment?

FOR ADDITIONAL READING

Brill, Steven. *The Teamsters*. New York: Simon and Schuster, 1978.

Edelstein, David J. and Malcolm Warner. *Comparative Union Democracy: Organization and Opposition in British and American Unions*, Revised Edition. New Brunswick, NJ: Transaction Books, 1979.

Estey, Marten. *The Unions: Structure, Development, and Management*, Third Edition. New York: Harcourt, Brace & Jovanovich, 1981.

Herling, John. *The Right to Challenge: People and Power in the Steel-workers Union.* New York: Harper & Row, 1972.

Leslie, Douglas L. *Labor Law.* St. Paul, MN: West, 1979.

McLaughlin, Doris B. and Anita L. W. Schoomaker. *The Landrum-Griffin Act and Union Democracy.* Ann Arbor, MI: University of Michigan Press, 1978.

Miller, Robert W., Frederick A. Zeller and Glenn W. Miller. *The Practice of Local Union Leadership.* Columbus, OH: Ohio State University Press, 1965.

Sayles, Leonard R. and George Strauss. *The Local Union.* New York: Harcourt, Brace & World, 1967.

Stieber, Jack. *Governing the UAW.* New York: John Wiley, 1962.

9   The Future

Prologue
Beware of the Brontosaurus Effect

It has been almost two centuries since the Philadelphia Cord-wainers joined together in the first true American labor union. During those centuries, the labor movement and its economic, political, legal, and social environments have undergone remarkable—indeed revolutionary—change. Once considered an "illegal conspiracy," the labor movement is now a pillar of the political establishment. Although viewed in the past as a force inimical to **productivity,** today many employers recognize that collective bargaining may be an important key to greater productivity in the workplace. Once virtually banned by common law and later prevented from exercising economic force by it, today unions and their concerted activities enjoy a great deal of statutory protection. In fact, labor relations has been transformed from a process that was essentially outside of the law, to one that is now comprehensively and strictly regulated by law. Once based on small groups of craft workers, today unions are national in scope and include not only craft, but industrial, white collar, and professional workers as well. Change itself has been one of the few constants in the history

---

TERMS   **Productivity**   A measured relationship between the quantity (and quality) of results produced and the quantity of resources required for production. Productivity is, in essence, a measure of the work efficiency of an individual, a work unit, or a whole organization.

of the labor movement. Consequently, it behooves us to conclude this book by turning our attention to its future prospects.

John Naisbitt, in his best-seller, *Megatrends,* compares contemporary American labor unions to the brontosaurus, a dinosaur that grew so huge that it could only survive in water because it could not support its weight on land. Its continuous growth clearly became **dysfunctional** and did not help its chances for survival. Naisbitt sees the same tendency among unions. He notes that "there were thirty-five mergers of labor unions between 1971 and 1981." But bigger may not be better and Naisbitt warns of "the sunset effect." That is, "the sun gets largest just before it goes under!"

There are at least two reasons why the sheer size of unions might be a dysfunctional force. First, the larger the union structure, the more oligarchical it is likely to become, and the less well it is likely to represent its constituent members. The leadership of a huge union is more likely to become divorced from the membership. From the Cordwainers to the present day, the major reason for unionization is to collectively represent workers. A union that is too big to do this well is like a dinosaur whose brain cannot effectively coordinate its body. And a union that is too large for its own good can be a powerfully destructive force. It can become entrenched in favor of maintaining the **status quo**—a status quo that might well be witnessing declining productivity. Specifically, unions may seek to use their political power to protect their members from foreign competition through **tariffs.** Some unions have used their economic power to resist the adoption of new and more productive technology. Others have negotiated work loads and production rates that can at times act as barriers to increases in productivity.

Secondly, very large unions are particularly prone to negotiating incredibly detailed and elaborate contracts that can get in the way of productivity. Some contracts run into hundreds of pages and the **work rules** they create can all but eliminate essential

TERMS **Dysfunctional** Not performing up to expected standards. A dysfunction is a failure of some kind.

Status Quo The existing state of things at a particular time.

Tariff An import tax or the rate at which imported goods are taxed.

Work Rules Formal regulations prescribing both on-the-job behavior and working conditions. They are usually incorporated into a collective bargaining agreement at the insistence of the union in order to restrict management's ability to unilaterally set production standards or reassign employees.

managerial flexibility. For example, George Steinbrenner, the owner of the New York Yankees baseball team whose hirings and firings of Billy Martin have made them both national celebrities, recently complained about another of his business endeavors, Amship, a shipbuilding concern in Lorain, Ohio: "The work rules were horrendous. A carpenter couldn't fix a light bulb—it had to be an electrician. Everyone was worried about their own little bailiwick." According to Steinbrenner, the "work rules were so archaic and the wage rates were so high" in Lorain, that the company was able to save 30 percent of its labor costs by shifting work to its Tampa, Florida, shipyard. A union's unwillingness to see the job classification system revised was a major factor in the permanent closing of the Lorain shipyard. Was the union like the dinosaur? Did the union simply develop too big an appetite to survive?

PRODUCTIVITY   Of all the forces that are likely to have an impact on the future of the labor movement, the quest for greater productivity in the workplace must surely rank at the top. In simple terms, productivity is the output of goods or services per unit of labor input, such as a **manhour.** In other words, the purpose of productivity is to obtain a greater yield out of allocated resources. This can be achieved through greater **efficiency** and **effectiveness.** And, the labor movement has a great deal to do with achieving both.

Today in the United States much of the pressure for increased productivity comes from international competition. For a brief period in history, the United States enjoyed advantages and conditions that enabled it to become the world's leading economic power and richest nation. With the exception of Pearl Harbor, its territory was left unscathed by World War II, which destroyed the

TERMS   **Manhour**   The amount of work that can be accomplished in a normal hour of work by an individual.

Efficiency   The promotion of methods that will produce the largest store of results for a given objective at the least cost; the reduction of material and personnel costs while maximizing precision, speed, and simplicity in administration.

Effectiveness   Traditionally, the extent to which an organization accomplishes some predetermined goal or objective; more recently, the overall performance of an organization from the viewpoint of some strategic constituency.

economies of all possible competitors. The United States also reaped great advantage from abundant and cheap energy, readily available natural resources, and a large and talented population. As a result of these and other factors, the United States became an exceedingly productive economy. For example, in the two decades following World War II, productivity increased at more than 3 percent per year. In other words, the same amount of input yielded 3 percent more output each year. This was the result of greater efficiency and effectiveness. In 1960, the sale of products manufactured in the United States accounted for about a quarter of the entire world market in manufactured goods. Some 95 percent of all the automobiles, steel, and consumer electrical goods sold in the United States in 1960 were manufactured by domestic companies. These are now thought of as "the good old days"—before significant foreign competition.

In the wake of the energy crisis of 1973 and the recession and rampant inflation that followed it, productivity declined. By 1980 the United States' share of the world market in manufactured goods had dropped to 17 percent. The average American was far more likely to buy autos (21 percent) and electronic equipment (more than 50 percent) from foreign companies. A wide range of imports from foreign manufacturers were now threatening American industry.

There are a great number of complicated reasons for the world's economic condition and the relative decline of the United States. Among them are the age of many American industrial plants; the tendency of American managers to place too strong an emphasis on short-term profitability at the expense of long-term productivity; the declining advantage of the United States in terms of energy and other natural resources; and the changing demographics of the American workforce. Then there is the question of the role of the labor movement in American productivity. On this there are two main perspectives: (1) to view unions as an inherent obstacle to productivity and seek to prevent or get rid of them, or (2) to view unions as partners in the search for greater productivity.

VIEWING UNIONS AS OBSTACLES

What does a rational employer do to avoid being trampled by a large and powerful union? One approach is to move from its territory. This is a primary cause of the continuing shift of jobs from the industrialized and unionized North to the South. Another approach is to avoid unionization in the first place. Employers have become increasingly sophisticated in the art of union avoidance and union busting. **Pinkertons** and police are no longer used to break union organizing drives. Today sophisticated management campaigns account for unions now *losing* about 60 percent of NLRB elections. Compare this to 1950 when unions were *winners* in 75 percent of the contests.

What are some of the techniques employers use to avoid unionization? One is to consult studies such as Shervin Freed's *Measuring Union Climate.* This book analyzes NLRB certification and decertification elections from a number of perspectives including geographic location, size of the voting unit, existence of a "right to work" law, type of enterprise (manufacturing, retail, etc.), the percentage of the employees in the industry already unionized, and the union involved. By consulting its pages, an employer who wants to locate or relocate a plant, can make an informed judgment as to the prospects that it will become unionized. To an extent, employers can also make judgments about the possibilities of certification and decertification. This is not to say that every or any particular employer would locate or relocate a business operation solely on the prospects of it becoming unionized. However, when all other things are more or less equal, being able to predict something about the future of labor relations can be a powerful motivator in choosing a location.

Employers have also become more sophisticated in mobilizing their efforts to keep unions out of existing facilities. Some larger companies even have departments whose sole concern is forestalling unionization. The first news or suspicion of a union organizing drive triggers a strategic contingency plan. Employers have become quite sophisticated at picking up the informal signals that unionization may be underfoot. For example, articles and books on "how to avoid unions" advise looking for the following telltale signs of organizing activity:

1. Are normally friendly employees suddenly unusually quiet?

2. Are normally unfriendly employees suddenly too friendly to managers?

3. Are certain employees suddenly receiving a great deal of attention from fellow workers?

TERMS   **Pinkertons** Employees of the Pinkerton Detective Agency who were frequently hired to harass and otherwise oppose strikes in the late nineteenth and early twentieth centuries.

4. Are small groups of employees gathering together during breaks or going to the rest rooms together?

5. Is there a sudden spate of questions about personnel practices and policies?

6. Are employees or strangers handing out leaflets or union authorization cards near a plant or office?

Once an employer picks up these and other signs of organizing activity, an anti-organization drive may be started which incorporates the following tactics:

1. Those supervisors who are not covered by collective bargaining legislation are mobilized to combat union propaganda and activity. They are often told that unionization will mean that they will lose much of their authority to shop stewards. Supervisors who seem sympathetic to unionization may be transferred or fired.

2. Anti-union propaganda is displayed on bulletin boards and disseminated in newsletters. Such messages warn employees about the high cost of union dues, that unionization will not lead to higher wages and better working conditions, that current benefits may be curtailed as a result of collective bargaining, that strikes are an inevitable and very harmful consequence of unionization, that strikers can be legally replaced, that union leaders are more concerned with their own welfare than that of their members, and that the employer has been fair in view of how similar employees in the area (or with competitors) are treated.

3. Encouraging employees to vote, since a certification election is decided by a majority of the ballots cast rather than a majority of the employees in the bargaining unit. In other words, abstention may make it easier for the union to win.

4. A general media campaign indicating that unionization can mean "trouble" for the community.

When such approaches are used in a sophisticated fashion, they are not only legal, but they may be quite convincing as well. The negative image that unions, and especially their leadership, have among many workers creates a predisposition on the part of a substantial proportion of employees to oppose unionization. Moreover, many people are inherently conservative and reluctant to deal with the "uncertainties" of collective bargaining.

President Eisenhower on Union Busting

Today in America unions have a secure place in our industrial life. Only a handful of unreconstructed reactionaries harbor the ugly thought of breaking unions. Only a fool would try to deprive working men and women of the right to join the union of their choice.

Source: Speech (as presidential candidate) to the convention of the American Federation of Labor, September 17, 1952.

When plant location and anti-union drives are combined, today's employer has a very good chance of preventing unionization. But what can the many employers who already have unions do to reduce the union's power or even "bust" it entirely? One powerful strategy is to shift work from a unionized to a nonunion plant, or to one where the union is weaker. As long as the employer has good "business reasons" for doing so (lower wage rates is one such reason), and is not openly engaged in union busting, this is likely to be held legal.

Another tactic is to mobilize workers for a decertification election. Legally, the employer must be neutral in such an election, but there are still steps it can take to increase the likelihood that employees will petition for it and prevail when the ballots are counted. One of the classic tactics is to hire permanent replacements during a strike (which may have been provoked by the employer) with the understanding that they will initiate a **decertification petition** in the future. Employers might also suggest to employees that decertification would be a good idea—but this must be done surreptitiously or in the vaguest of terms. Such

---

TERMS   **Decertification Petition**   A formal request to the NLRB (or other appropriate administrative agency) that a decertification election be held. If the union loses, it will no longer have the right to represent workers in the bargaining unit where the election is held.

prompting of a decertification election, though illegal, is difficult to combat since the NLRB tends to judge the fairness of an employer's actions based on the totality of the employer's conduct. Such a standard may allow the employer to engage in isolated instances of questionable conduct.

Another approach to reducing union power is to try to negotiate contracts that create divisions, often based on seniority, within the bargaining unit. For example, in early 1984 it was reported that General Motors was seeking to negotiate a contract with the United Auto Workers that would allow it to hire new workers at lower pay and benefits than those covered by past union contracts.

Where unions are seen as obstacles to productivity, employers may seek to avoid them, reduce their power, or bust them entirely. But such tactics are a short-run approach. There are few who would deny that in the long run increased productivity depends upon workers' participation, in some fashion, in determining the methods and conditions under which work is performed.

VIEWING UNIONS AS PARTNERS

It has become increasingly recognized that traditional American management practices, based on the notion that management must control workers in almost every detail, present a serious barrier to greater productivity. Nowhere was this approach more influentially developed than in the writings of Frederick W. Taylor, the founder of the scientific management movement. According to Taylor, in the past management allowed workers too much discretion over the way work was performed. Even skilled workers often used "rule of thumb" practices that were unscientific in their use of resources. Moreover, traditional practices could be used to limit productivity as workers often feared that greater efficiency would result in fewer jobs. So Taylor advocated enhancing productivity by assigning management a far greater role in specifying precisely how job tasks were to be done. Consequently, **Taylorism** relied heavily upon **time and motion studies** to determine how the highest degree of efficiency could be achieved.

TERMS   **Taylorism**   While this term refers to the scientific management teachings of Frederick W. Taylor, it is also used as a general description for the mechanistic and authoritarian style of management so common in American industry.

Time and Motion Studies   Measures of the time required, under standard conditions, to complete a task requiring human effort. These studies then analyze the work (sometimes motion by motion) to find and eliminate inefficient work methods and replace them with more efficient ones.

Few would dispute Taylor's sincere efforts to achieve greater productivity for the benefit of both management and labor. Nor would many deny that one of the effects of his approach was the dehumanization of workers. In the past, the worker determined a great deal about the methods of performing work. Under scientific management the worker would be told in precise detail how to behave. This meant he or she would be told when to raise one hand or the other, when to bring both hands to rest, when to pick up this or that, when to take a rest pause, and so on. In reading Taylor's *Principles of Scientific Management* (1911) one cannot help but come away with the impression that he saw workers as more or less animals, with limited powers of speech and thought.

As the influence of scientific management spread, the "efficiency engineer" became the hero of the workplace and the most productive organization became the best one in a moral sense. That is, greater efficiency was viewed as a moral virtue. Under these conditions management, with its enlarged responsibility for control in the workplace and its contributions to the moral worth of society through greater efficiency, quickly became aggrandized and revered. Thus, the maintenance of managerial authority, which would enable management to perform its functions, was seen as critical to the future good of the society. Under these conditions, the workers would have few rights, indeed.

Taylorism went considerably beyond the realm of production management. It also became a cornerstone of contemporary personnel theory and practice. Taylor's workers were portrayed as simpleminded; some of his most noted examples were immigrants with limited English abilities. Under Taylor's crude concept of motivational psychology, the typical worker could be controlled by the manipulation of pay periods and the use of **piece work** compensation systems. Since the worker was viewed as essentially one-dimensional, with pay being the only thing that mattered, personnel administration would join with management in constructing an elaborate system for controlling workers and presumably enhancing efficiency. So personnel departments took on responsibilities not only for compensation administration (which included job evaluations, pay, fringe benefits, and incentive programs), but for a host of other organizational functions as well. Among these were selection, including the administration of performance tests, physical examinations, written tests, interviews,

---

TERMS   **Piece Work**   An incentive wage program in which a predetermined amount is paid to an employee for each unit (piece) of output.

background checks and so forth. Perhaps most importantly, personnelists engaged in job design. Jobs can be designed with a greater or lesser amount of responsibility, to be highly repetitive or varied, to be interesting or dull, or to require the exercise of independent judgment (or the elimination of it).

In very large part due to the influence of Taylorism, job design had two major tendencies. One was to create highly specialized and repetitive jobs requiring little discretion and allowing for little independent judgment on the part of the worker. The other was to rely upon an impersonal approach to work by designing jobs according to abstract principles rather than the abilities, traits, characteristics, or personalities of those individuals who actually held them. Eventually, these approaches resulted in elaborate job classification systems that limited mobility and change within large organizations.

One of the great problems of scientific management was that it tended to treat the worker as but another factor of production having no individual personality. By the 1930s, it began to be recognized that work premised upon Taylorism would not be satisfying to the worker or yielding of the highest productivity. Initially, this was put forth by the **Hawthorne Studies** where researchers discovered that productivity increased when they consulted workers on proposed work changes and showed some personal interest in them. An evolving "human relations" approach to management also argued that it was desirable for workers to develop a sense of participation and social belonging in the workplace as a matter of political and social stability for the society as a whole. Taylor's model workers, it was argued, had too few social and political attachments. Consequently, they felt isolated or suffered from **alienation.** As traditional means of social

TERMS   **Hawthorne Studies**   Conducted at the Hawthorne Works of the Western Electric Company near Chicago, these are probably the most influential management studies ever reported. Beginning in the late 1920s, a research team led by Elton Mayo (1880–1949) of the Harvard Business School started a decade-long series of experiments aimed at determining the relationship between work environment and productivity. The experimenters, because they were initially unable to explain the results of their findings, literally stumbled upon what today seems so obvious—that factories and other work situations are first of all social situations.

Alienation   A concept originally from Marxism which held that industrial workers would experience feelings of disassociation because they lacked control of their work (and thus be ripe for revolution). The word has lost its Marxist taint and now refers to any feelings of estrangement from one's work, family, society, etc.

control—the family, religious organizations, or stable communities—gave way to the pressures for industrial mobility, the only remaining vehicles for regulating the behavior of individuals and assuring it was not antisocial were political and economic. Political control was contrary to American notions of democracy. But economic control allowed for the free exercise of authority by managers in the workplace. Thus, from the human relations perspective, the nature of personnel management, as reflected by Taylorism, was in need of very fundamental change.

By depriving workers of rights and autonomy in the workplace, Taylorism virtually made unions necessary to protect the workers not just economically, but also from the perspective of assuring decent treatment as human beings. Indeed, it was only through collective action that workers have been able to limit the authority of management and to have an impact on personnel practices. For example, collective bargaining contracts frequently place limits on management's authority to assign work, to promote workers without regard to seniority, to lay them off, and to discipline them. The widespread use of grievance arbitration (as discussed in Chapter 7) is testimony to the extent to which unionization has been able to curtail the unbridled authority of management. Where "hiring halls" are used, unions have even been able to cut into the realm of personnel by selecting and assigning workers to jobs.

But the placement of management and labor in an *adversarial* position is now considered to be dysfunctional in several respects. Adversaries often try to gain strength through growth. Eventually, the adversary relationship may grow to be one of union dinosaur versus industrial dinosaur. Now if unionization and productivity are declining simultaneously, and if unionization is considered to be a barrier to further productivity gains and personnel management practices seem wanting, should not the entire system of relationships in the workplace be rethought?

Today there are many who would argue that the time has come for the United States to become serious about participative management. **Theory X** management, the authoritarian model, has proven itself to be dysfunctional; according to many analysts, including Naisbitt, it "has cost America top honors in world productivity growth." **Theory Y** has managers view workers from a more humanistic perspective; it seeks to reduce managerial authority and promote worker consultation on a whole range of working conditions and practices. Now some organization theorists such as William Ouchi argue that America is ready for Theory Z management.

Theory Z seeks to apply aspects of Japanese management in the context of American culture, stresses a guarantee of long-term employment, and emphasizes joint decisionmaking and a more wholistic concern for the worker's well-being. In some respects, Theory Z's emphasis on participative decisionmaking is viewed as a substitute for "community" in an age when other groups may not provide workers with a full range of social contacts.

But does greater participation really work? The answer is more yes than no. Increased participation rarely leads to an actual decline in productivity. The usual result is the same or increased productivity. Today, almost half of all American companies with 500 or more employees have some kind of employee participation program. While such programs take many forms, they all can be subsumed under the rubric of "quality of worklife" concerns.

QUALITY OF
WORKLIFE

Quality of worklife concerns emphasize the desirability of redesigning jobs to introduce the kind of variety, autonomy, and **feedback** that will lead to enhanced **job satisfaction** and motivation. One of the better known mechanisms for job redesign along these lines is the establishment of self-managing, semi-autonomous work teams that have the authority to decide on such issues as schedules, the distribution of tasks, the nature of supervision, and even production goals. The work team also takes on a greater share of responsibility for **quality control.** In more advanced cases, such as one at the General Foods dog food plant in Topeka, Kansas, the production teams have even participated in a range of personnel activities, including hiring, firing, and wage-setting. The Topeka

TERMS   **Feedback**   Information about the effect or results of the behavior of a person or system that is communicated back to that person or system so that human behavior or organizational performance might be modified—presumably improved.

Job Satisfaction   The totality of an employee's feelings about the various aspects of his or her work; an emotional appraisal of whether one's job lives up to one's values.

Quality Control   The totality of concern for, including the inspection of, the goods and services that are produced by an organization.

case also involved a marked reduction in status differentiation among managers and workers in terms of parking, decor in lounges, need to punch a time clock, and the right to make personal phone calls on company time.

The "quality circle" is a related approach. Here workers performing similar tasks meet in small groups to consider work-related problems and search for ways of resolving them. It is assumed that the individual worker knows best how the work is performed, is most aware of problems, and is best able to introduce improvements. While the quality circle approach can overlap the production team arrangement, its thrust is somewhat different as it encourages communication with management on matters related to productivity in particular. Hundreds of major American companies now place substantial reliance on quality circles. The Honeywell Corporation may be the best known; it has over 1,000 active quality circles.

These and other increasingly important new concerns about the quality of life on the job will require new attitudes on the part of labor leaders as well as on the part of corporate management. Old line labor leaders—those schooled in combative, adversary relationships with management who have displayed little interest in more than "bread and butter" issues—face a very substantial challenge. But suspicion remains. According to Howard D. Samuel, head of AFL-CIO's Industrial Union Department, worker participation represents "mostly a surface effort which barely masks a corporate effort to dump collective bargaining obligations." The problem here is not so much that unions are not committed to democracy in the workplace, which in fact they seem overwhelmingly to be, but rather that quality of worklife issues are "integrative" as opposed to "distributive" matters. Distributive issues are essentially adversarial in nature. What one side gains, the other loses. Integrative issues, on the other hand, do not produce a pattern of winners and losers. They offer the potential for both sides to be winners, as when labor and management cooperate to find mutually satisfactory ways of increasing productivity.

A major challenge facing unions is to develop leadership and organizational processes that will enable them to take advantage of the growing interest in worker participation. These leaders should view the greater autonomy of workers as a positive development. Unions can continue to play a major role even when workers take over some of the functions formerly performed by managers. Grievances may be reduced and work rules must become far more flexible, but equity, health, safety, and the basic issues of compensation retain their critical importance. The trick for unions is to recognize the benefits of self-managing work teams and quality circles, while making sure that the basic bargaining unit retains effective representation by the union on larger-level issues. At present, there appears to be increasing interest in strengthening and modernizing union structures and governance in ways that mesh well with worker participation. Some believe that there is already a "new direction" for labor. The efforts of the United Auto Workers, the Communications Workers, the Electrical Workers, the United Steelworkers, and other major unions to substitute cooperation for conflict, to increase workers' participation, and to improve the quality of worklife bear witness to this.

TRENDS TO WATCH   There is a wide variety of mechanisms for greater worker participation and vesting the worker with a greater interest in productivity. One example is a more formalized arrangement than quality circles for management consultation with employee representatives. Sometimes this approach involves the establishment of employee committees, representing more workers than the typical quality circle. Meetings between management and employee representatives may be less frequent as well.

In Europe, it has long been common for workers to have formal representation on the boards of directors of large corporations. In recent years, the United States has gained significant experience with employee ownership of firms. Sometimes, these are failing companies that are bought by the employees in an effort to keep them going. Today there are about 5,000 employee-owned firms which employ several million people. While not all of these firms are successful, they tend to be more profitable than conventional firms. At present, it is unclear whether there is a useful role for unions in such companies. Unionization in this context is especially problematic since, as owners, employees may choose to work longer hours for lower pay as a means of protecting their investment in the firm.

Profit sharing is becoming an increasingly acceptable means of providing the rank and file worker with a greater stake in productivity. For example, managers at General Motors, who once viewed profit sharing as "socialism," currently consider it a way of avoiding paying annual increases in bad years and of "giving workers a financial stake in the company's fortunes." No doubt there are many other variants of the same theme, and that theme is increasingly clear. In the words of John Simmons, a professor of labor-management relations at the University of Massachusetts, it is "to put the head of the employee back on the body" by turning the old managerial culture based on Taylorism "upside down."

The trends we are discussing will obviously take a good deal of time to work themselves out. Given the choice between the spectre of dinosaurs clashing and crashing on the one hand, and greater worker participation on the other, the society is likely to opt for the latter. But it will take time! Talk of participation implies changing the operating premises of the modern corporation. In the immediate future, while these longer-range trends are working themselves out, here is what the observer and participant in labor relations can look forward to seeing:

1. Labor law reforms through the incremental process of adjudication by the NLRB and the courts. The prospects for comprehensive statutory reform appear dim in view of the defeat of such a move in 1978. It appears that at the political level, labor and managers are deadlocked; each has enough political clout to prevent major changes to which it is opposed.

2. More intensive efforts by corporations to avoid unionization, a greater use of Chapter 11 bankruptcy proceedings to break union contracts, and increasing sophistication in the fine art of union avoidance.

3. More intensive efforts by unions to expand. This may entail more mergers and it will certainly include greater attention by unions to the process of organizing. Unions will have to target their organizing drives more carefully. They will have to update their constitutions, leadership, and approach to relationships in the workplace.

4. Greater attention to long-range issues. The relative decline of the United States in the world economy, declining productivity, the export of jobs to countries where labor costs are cheaper, and the decline of the relative size of the unionized sector of the American workforce all point to chronic problems. Collective bargaining has an impact on these matters, but traditional negotiations to frame a contract that will be in force for only a few years may miss the wider trends and problems.

5. Greater professionalization and competence in labor relations. All of the above predictions for the immediate future will require a more professional approach. The new generation of labor leaders and labor relations specialists on management's side will have to be more attuned to recognizing that

integrative issues are taking on far greater importance. Ways of resolving them in the interest of workers, management, *and* the public will have to be found. This is a tough job that cannot be accomplished by those imbued with old-style adversarial predispositions. Yet even the distributive issues, involving compensation for the most part, will have to be resolved with greater professionalism. Bargaining is by nature incremental, but without some vision of the future it will lack direction. The job of the labor relations professional on both sides is to adopt a vision based on a sound assessment of economic, social, and political trends. And then work toward it.

REVIEW QUESTIONS

1. What is productivity and why is it so important to a nation's economy?

2. What pressures does international trade now put on the United States labor movement?

3. In what ways do you think the de-industrialization of the economy, changes in managerial philosophy, and declines in unionization are connected?

4. How could greater worker participation be implemented in your workplace or educational institution? What might be some of the problems? What consequences would you expect?

5. To what extent are quality circles compatible with the principle of exclusive recognition?

6. To some extent there are several "futures" from which to choose. In terms of labor relations, which would you select? How would you try to make sure that future came about?

FOR ADDITIONAL READING

Berkley, George E. *The Administrative Revolution.* Englewood Cliffs, NJ: Prentice-Hall, 1973.

Davis, Louis E., and Albert B. Cherns, eds. *The Quality of Working Life.* New York: The Free Press, 1975, Volumes I and II.

Ferman, Louis A., ed., *The Future of American Unionism.* Beverly Hills: Sage, 1984.

Freed, Shervin. *Measuring Union Climate.* Atlanta: Conway Publications, 1981.

Gagala, Ken. *Union Organizing and Staying Organized.* Reston, VA: Reston Publishing Company/Prentice-Hall, 1983.

Kakar, Subhir. *Frederick Taylor: A Study in Personality and Innovation.* Cambridge, MA: The M.I.T. Press, 1970.

Kilgour, James. *Preventive Labor Relations.* New York: AMACON, 1981.

Martin, Shan. *Managing Without Managers.* Beverly Hills, CA: Sage, 1983.

Naisbitt, John. *Megatrends.* New York: Warner Books, 1982.

Ouchi, William. *Theory Z: How American Business Can Meet the Japanese Challenge.* Reading, MA: Addison-Wesley, 1981.

Taylor, Frederick W. *The Principles of Scientific Management.* New York: Harper & Bros., 1911.

Index